Contents

From the Editor ǁ 1

Presidential Forum *Creative Collaboration: Alternatives to the Adversarial Academy*

Creative Collaboration: Introduction
LINDA HUTCHEON ǁ 4

Working Together: Collaborative Research and Writing in Higher Education
ANDREA LUNSFORD, LISA EDE, AND CORINNE ARRAEZ ǁ 7

A Collective Experience: Academics Working and Learning Together
NELLIE Y. McKAY AND FRANCES SMITH FOSTER ǁ 16

Stories and Songs across Cultures: Perspectives from Africa and the Americas
J. EDWARD CHAMBERLIN AND LEVI NAMASEB ǁ 24

Jobs

What Search Committees Want
WALTER BROUGHTON AND WILLIAM CONLOGUE ǁ 39

I Profess: Another View of Professionalization
JENNIFER WICKE ǁ 52

The Academic Job Crisis and the Small-Schools Movement
HOLLY FRITZ AND DAVID SHERMAN ǁ 58

Why I Teach in an Independent School
BRENT WHITTED ǁ 71

Teaching the Urban Underprepared Student
CELESTINE WOO ǁ 78

Settling for a Great Job
JENNIFER M. STOLPA ǁ 85

Pagers, Nikes, and Wordsworth: Teaching College English in a Shopping Mall
MARTIN SCOTT ǁ 92

The American Dream as a Life Narrative
MARGARET MORGANROTH GULLETTE ‖ 99

Reports from the Field

Languages and Language Learning in the Face of World English
JOHN EDWARDS ‖ 109

Degrees of Success, Degrees of Failure: The Changing Dynamics of the English PhD and Small-College Careers
ED FOLSOM ‖ 121

Redefining the Mission of the English Department at the University of Louisville: Two Years Later
DEBRA JOURNET ‖ 130

My Life as an Infomercial: On Time, Teaching, and Technology
PAT MILLER ‖ 137

Are We There Yet? The Long and Winding Road to Undergraduate Curricular Reform
HAROLD WEBER ‖ 142

Design and Consent: Notes on Curriculum Revision
MARILYN FRANCUS ‖ 149

And That I Should Teach Tolerance
BETTINA TATE PEDERSEN ‖ 161

Letters ‖ 167

MLA Committee and Survey Reports

Successful College and University Foreign Language Programs, 1995–99: Part 1
DAVID GOLDBERG AND ELIZABETH B. WELLES ‖ 171

The 1999 MLA Survey of Staffing in English and Foreign Language Departments
DAVID LAURENCE ‖ 211

Final Report
MLA AD HOC COMMITTEE ON TEACHING ‖ 225

From the Editor

The essays in *Profession 2001* demonstrate what most MLA members have always known, that life as a teacher of language, writing, or literature varies substantially depending on where one works. And I'm not thinking about the Carnegie differences we often focus on, between research and comprehensive universities or between two- and four-year colleges. More important than the highest degree an institution or department grants are the effectiveness of its courses and programs and the quality of the human interactions it encourages. The articles in this issue of *Profession* tell us a lot about what is happening in different kinds of institutions to different generations of teachers and scholars.

Because conflict is increasingly common in higher education, Linda Hutcheon focused the Presidential Forum at the 2000 MLA convention on the topic "Creative Collaboration: Alternatives to the Adversarial Academy." Andrea Lunsford, Lisa Ede, and Corinne Arráez review studies of collaborative research and writing and ask whether guidelines for tenure should be revised so that departments can recognize and reward collaborative work. Nellie Y. McKay and Frances Smith Foster describe how much more they have accomplished by working together on research projects than either could have achieved alone. More complex logistically is a partnership that spans continents and aims at preserving languages that might otherwise disappear, like the one that links J. Edward Chamberlin, who teaches at the University of Toronto, and Levi Namaseb, who teaches at the University of Namibia.

Employment opportunities remain a matter of great concern to almost everyone in the field, so the articles gathered under the heading "Jobs" should be useful to graduate students, new PhDs, and faculty advisers. A survey by Walter Broughton and William Conlogue identifies the achievements English departments look for when they decide whom to interview, invite to campus, and hire. Of particular interest in this article is information about the common errors job candidates make. Jennifer Wicke looks at a key aspect of professionalization—publication—and explains the importance of embedding one's writings in current scholarly conversations. Two articles, one by Holly Fritz and David Sherman and the other by Brent Whitted, outline the challenges and rewards of teaching in private and experimental public high schools. Three essays, by Celestine Woo, Jennifer M. Stolpa, and Martin Scott, focus on teaching in two-year colleges, where values, practices, and human interactions differ substantially from one institution to another. Margaret Morganroth Gullette looks at the past and future role of tenure and the generational conflicts that debates over job security are causing.

The essays collected under the heading "Reports from the Field" raise a variety of issues. John Edwards looks at the impact of world English on the study and use of other languages in the United States. Ed Folsom traces the long-term effects on a PhD-granting program of the national values of an "itinerant" university administrator. Debra Journet, whose *Profession 1999* article described an unusual agreement between the English department at the University of Louisville and the university administration, reports on the outcome of that agreement. (*Profession* readers may recall that the department gained six new tenure-track positions and two senior tenured appointments in exchange for a commitment that all professorial faculty members would teach first-year composition at least once a year.) Three articles focus on curricular developments. Pat Miller assesses the advantages and disadvantages of adding a Web component to a news writing course and urges faculty involvement in institutional decisions regarding the use of technology in the classroom. Harold Weber and Marilyn Francus describe different but equally effective ways of encouraging faculty agreement on the reform of the English major. Bettina Tate Pedersen writes in response to the call in the Report of the Task Force against Campus Bigotry for publications about teaching tolerance.

The last section of *Profession 2001* brings together staff surveys and a committee report. The first survey, "Successful College and University Foreign Language Programs, 1995–99: Part 1," by David Goldberg and Elizabeth B. Welles, describes enrollment trends and curricular, pedagogical, and administrative practices in foreign language programs. Goldberg and Welles also examine the connections between these practices and stable and growing undergraduate enrollments and majors. "The 1999 MLA Survey of Staffing in English and Foreign Language Departments," by David Laurence, analyzes the findings from the MLA's study of the staffing of undergraduate English and foreign language courses. A list of institutional responses to the survey has been available at the MLA Web site since

December 2000. The final report of the MLA Ad Hoc Committee on Teaching, which proposes a variety of ways of strengthening teaching in the field, was written by Helen R. Houston, Elizabeth L. Keller, Lawrence D. Kritzman, Frank Madden (chair), John L. Mahoney, Scott McGinnis, Susannah Brietz Monta, Sondra Perl, and Janet Swaffar.

I conclude with thanks to the members of the *Profession* Advisory Committee: Idelber Avelar, Lydie Moudileno, Linda Ray Pratt, and Mary Beth Rose. Their thoughtful readings of the many submissions we received shaped *Profession 2001*. I wish also to thank my colleagues on staff—David Laurence and Elizabeth Welles—for their comments on new submissions and recommendations of *ADE Bulletin* and *ADFL Bulletin* essays for reprinting. The responsibility for the final selection of articles, however, is mine.

For *Profession 2002*, we welcome articles about professional matters that are on your mind. We are also interested in articles that consider quality-of-life issues in departments in various types of institutions; articles on curricular developments in language and literature majors; articles on the changing shape of MA- and PhD-granting programs; discussions of academic unionization; and reports from new PhDs who are working either in the academy or in the business, government, or not-for-profit sectors. In addition, we seek essays about cooperative courses and programs organized jointly by English and foreign language departments, responses to the Report of the Task Force against Campus Bigotry, and information about the study and teaching of the humanities in a global context.

Phyllis Franklin

Creative Collaboration: Introduction

LINDA HUTCHEON

It will not be news to MLA members that the adversarial ethos that governs the media, government, and the law has also found a comfortable abode in the academy. As Deborah Tannen notes in *The Argument Culture*, public discourses of conflict, confrontation, and competition have helped create a culture of agonistic argument in which the university has become more a war zone than a place of learning, or, as Lennard Davis puts it, "more of a snake pit than an ivory tower" (B8). Elaine Showalter has not been alone in publicly lamenting the "rampant incivility" of our professional life (B4), for today the politics of coercion and censure seem to be invoked as easily by the left as by the right—though with different targets, of course. The communal and the collegial have given way to alienation and isolation, argues David Damrosch throughout *We Scholars: Changing the Culture of the University*. Opposition and confrontation have replaced negotiation and cooperation in an unproductive and debilitating downward spiral toward a mean-spirited nadir.

Do we as a profession have to put up with this? Are there no alternatives to the corrosive and indeed often ritualized discrediting of others that has become part of scholarly argumentation, as Jane Tompkins asks in "Fighting Words: Unlearning to Write the Critical Essay"? Do we not think with, as much as against, the work of others? Can rigorous critical thinking be rescued from its current definition in terms of only attack and critique? The papers that follow are responses to a challenge to explore—and enact—the possibility of positive alternatives to this adversarial vision of the

---

The author is University Professor of English and Comparative Literature at the University of Toronto and a past president of the Modern Language Association.

academy; more specifically, they are responses to a request that their authors consider whether there exists an invitational intellectual rhetoric or a structure of working together that could offer new models for us, for it seems to me that we are in great need of new ways of thinking and acting.

The solo scholar model may have its roots in now-questioned ideologies (both the capitalist notion of ownership and the Romantic concept of genius), but its dominance is firmly entrenched in the academy and its reward system. None of the authors of these papers is naive about this dominance or about the reality of competition in our world. But accepting without question an adversarial model renders all sense of a community of scholars impossible—at the level of our research as well as our communal life. But beyond even the pressures of competition, something else has been happening to our critical discourse. In Tannen's words, it often betrays an "attitude of contempt toward scholars who work in a different theoretical framework" (248) or, frankly, who simply take a different position in the same framework. Why do we choose the mode of attack? Tannen's explanation is that "attacking an established scholar has particular appeal because it demonstrates originality and independence of thought without requiring true innovation. After all, the domain of inquiry and the terms of debate have already been established" (269). Arguing is easy, in short; constructive engagement is harder. Despite the work of Bruce Wilshire (264–65) and others suggesting that a gender bias exists—that men are more comfortable in a culture of debate than women—I doubt that this bias can really be proved. Gerald Graff does want us to teach the debates, for sure, but maybe there are other models for teaching our discipline and doing research in it. Finding those models is the challenge addressed by these papers.

There are models out there already, of course. Following Mikhail Bakhtin, Wolfgang Iser has offered the image of the dialogue (736)—an image that each of these presentations at the 2000 convention in fact enacted, because the six speakers of our forum presented in pairs. Tannen has suggested the model of the "believing game" to replace the "doubting game" (273) and has outlined ways for us to see ourselves other than as actors in a war scenario of attack and defense—for example, as builders, guides, cooks, and conversation participants (161). In writing of the "micropolitics of research" (116), Jonathan Arac has focused on the figure of the creator "treated as a distinctive, single, isolated individual" (118), a model that replicates the Romantic ideology of which Jerome McGann wrote so cogently. Yet it has been over twenty years since Sandra Gilbert and Susan Gubar wrote their first book together, *The Madwoman in the Attic: The Woman Writer and the Nineteenth-Century Literary Imagination*, and the authors of the first paper in this forum, Andrea Lunsford and Lisa

Ede, literally wrote the book on collaborative research, *Singular Texts / Plural Authors*. Therefore, why have so few people outside rhetoric and composition circles followed in their footsteps? Are the professional costs too high? Is collaboration un-American, as Arac suggests (126), smacking somehow of communism? If so, other nations should not have been slow to get on the bandwagon. The sciences, of course, with their laboratory model, already have an ethic of mutual dependency: information, insights, interpretations are all pooled. Cathy Davidson suggests that the humanities could do with some of this same interdependency as a way to offer an alternative to the disputation and disrespect that too often characterize our intellectual exchanges (B5). The collaboratively written (and originally collaboratively delivered) papers that follow offer examples of just how that constructive and creative interdependency might be achieved.

WORKS CITED

Arac, Jonathan. "Shop Window or Laboratory: Collection, Collaboration, and the Humanities." *The Politics of Research*. Ed. E. Ann Kaplan and George Levine. New Brunswick: Rutgers UP, 1997. 116–26.

Damrosch, David. *We Scholars: Changing the Culture of the University*. Cambridge: Harvard UP, 1995.

Davidson, Cathy. "What If Scholars in the Humanities Worked Together, in a Lab?" *Chronicle of Higher Education* 28 May 1999: B4–5.

Davis, Lennard J. "The Uses of Fear and Envy in Academe." *Chronicle of Higher Education* 11 June 1999: B8.

Ede, Lisa, and Andrea A. Lunsford. *Singular Texts / Plural Authors: Perspectives on Collaborative Writing*. Carbondale: Southern Illinois UP, 1990.

Gilbert, Sandra M., and Susan Gubar. *The Madwoman in the Attic: The Woman Writer and the Nineteenth-Century Literary Imagination*. New Haven: Yale UP, 1979.

Graff, Gerald. "Other Voices, Other Rooms: Organizing and Teaching the Humanities Conflict." *New Literary History* 21 (1990): 817–39.

Iser, Wolfgang. "Twenty-Five Years of *New Literary History*: A Tribute to Ralph Cohen." *New Literary History* 25 (1994): 733–47.

McGann, Jerome J. *The Romantic Ideology: A Critical Investigation*. Chicago: U of Chicago P, 1983.

Showalter, Elaine. "Taming the Rampant Incivility in Academe." *Chronicle of Higher Education* 15 Jan. 1999: B4–5.

Tannen, Deborah. *The Argument Culture: Stopping America's War of Words*. New York: Ballantine, 1998.

Tompkins, Jane. "Fighting Words: Unlearning to Write the Critical Essay." *Georgia Review* 42 (1988): 585–90.

Wilshire, Bruce. *The Moral Collapse of the University: Professionalism, Purity, and Alienation*. Albany: State U of New York P, 1990.

Working Together: Collaborative Research and Writing in Higher Education

ANDREA LUNSFORD, LISA EDE, AND CORINNE ARRAEZ

[. . .] the first university to reward collaborative work by scholars in the humanities will not only be sponsoring interesting publications, but will also be promoting a different sort of society in [. . . English] studies. A collaborative [. . . English] department would look as different from today's historical model as collaborative feminist scholarship looks when contrasted to traditional criticism.

—Holly Laird

Today we stand at unmarked crossroads, knowing that our future depends on creatively rethinking who we are and what we do.

—Nellie Y. McKay

These epigraphs speak to issues at the heart of the 2000 MLA Presidential Forum convened by Linda Hutcheon as a call to members of the association to engage in "creative collaboration" as one powerful alternative to the adversarial academy. In many ways we, the first two authors of this essay, have been hoping for and working toward such a moment since 1983,

---

Andrea Lunsford is Professor of English at Stanford University. Lisa Ede is Professor of English and Director, Center for Writing and Learning, at Oregon State University. Corinne Arráez is Academic Technology Specialist, Program in Writing and Critical Thinking, at Stanford University. A version of this paper was presented at the 2000 MLA convention in Washington, DC.

when we applied for one of the few national grants then available to collaborative pairs or groups of scholars in the humanities. That grant application grew out of our desire to work together and out of our related dissatisfaction with the professional barriers to such work. Our colleagues' incredulous response to our collaboration ("How can you possibly write together?" "How do you ever expect to get tenure?") captured our interest and imaginations—and also influenced our lives in more material ways. When one of us went forward for early promotion, for instance, the chair told her in quite an offhand manner, "Of course, we will discount any work that is coauthored." Shortly thereafter, in "Why Write . . . Together?" we explored why, despite considerable resistance, we found writing together stimulating and rewarding, and we called attention to the need not only for scholars to write together but for students to do so as well (Lunsford and Ede). Though in recent years students in composition classes have often learned and worked together, they have seldom been allowed, much less encouraged, to write together.

During the years of research that followed, we documented a rich though largely unacknowledged tradition of collaborative writing and research, especially outside the academy. We also discovered that the collaborative practices we identified tended to be obscured if not entirely erased by powerful ideologies of individualism. Here are two striking examples of such erasures. As part of the research for *Singular Texts / Plural Authors: Perspectives on Collaborative Writing* (Ede and Lunsford), we surveyed 1,400 members of seven professional associations, including the MLA. To our surprise, a large number of respondents reported on one page of our survey that they never wrote collaboratively but on the very next page said that they often, very often, or always worked with others to produce texts. Closer to home, a colleague who has coauthored a major textbook and with whom one of us has written a number of coauthored reports also declared (in response to our survey) that he never wrote collaboratively. When queried about this apparent contradiction, he responded, "Oh, I thought you meant *real* writing." This implicit distinction between real writing—individually produced discourse that reflects a unique self—and all other writing led us to recognize one of the most important reasons that collaborative discursive practices are so readily trivialized, ignored, or erased. It also taught us that working for change in the academy, for a recognition and valuing of collaborative work as real, was going to be a lot harder than we had anticipated.

And so it has proven. Despite our research and work like it, despite a protracted and thoroughgoing critique of the author construct and of ideologies of individualism, despite the attempts of many feminists to articulate an agency not bound by those ideologies, little in the academy has changed in the ten years since we published *Singular Texts / Plural Authors*. Whether one is an undergraduate hoping to do well in a class, a graduate student struggling with the oxymoronic mandate to produce an original dissertation, an assistant professor worrying about meeting both explicit and implicit criteria for tenure and promotion, or a senior faculty member striving to gain recognition for scholarly work, everyday practices in the humanities continue to ignore, and even to punish, collaboration while authorizing work attributed to (autonomous) individuals. Autonomous authors may be dead in theory, but in practice they are alive and thriving. If we ever needed proof that critique does not equal change, this is it.

So what can those of us interested in effecting significant institutional change in the academy do now? We must, first of all, understand the truth of the old maxim: If you want to hear, you have to listen; if you want to see, you have to look. We must, in short, retrain our vision so that we can see, credit, and learn from successful collaborative endeavors already under way around us. In addition to seeing what already exists, we must learn how to see what does not yet exist, those possibilities that commonsense ideologies of individualism now make unthinkable—such as collaborative dissertations, collaborative sabbaticals, or, for that matter, a reward structure that would allow a beginning assistant professor to build a tenurable career in the humanities through collaborative research and publication. Would we look at the traditional distinction between service and research differently, we wonder, if we acknowledged the role that radical individualism plays in valuing research over service? Why does it continue to seem commonsensical that a singly authored article makes a more important contribution to the discipline than does, say, a collaboratively produced document aimed at curricular reform? Such questions take on greater urgency at a time when the humanities are under attack, when universities are turning more and more to distance education and to what time-management bureaucrats call unbundling, and when the corporatization of higher education seems a fait accompli. Such questions reinforce for us the wisdom of Nellie McKay's insight that "our future depends on creatively rethinking who we are and what we do" (5).

One way to reassert the centrality of the humanities and to respond to the reductive changes taking place in universities today is, indeed, to rethink who we are and what we do and to do so in collaborative rather than adversarial ways. To begin this work, let us turn to several powerful examples of contemporary collaboration, ranging from those that pursue traditional scholarly goals to those that go well beyond the academy. Based at the University of Alberta, the Orlando Project—whose participants come from schools in Canada, the United States, England, and Australia—is undertaking "the first full scholarly history of women's writing in the British Isles" while also "conducting an experiment in humanities computing" and providing "training and scholarly community for graduate students" (*Orlando Project*). Even a cursory look at the project Web site will indicate that this effort could not proceed without the kinds of collaboration the participants describe. The sheer number of scholars involved, the breadth of the goal, and the multiple perspectives necessary to illuminate the writing of women across such a broad span of time—all suggest the crucial role collaboration plays in bringing this project and others, such as Brown University's Women Writers Project, to fruition.

In the field of rhetoric and composition, efforts to establish a national research agenda that could bring together the interests of scientists and humanists around issues of information technology are also currently under way. Launched at a discussion meeting held during the 2000 Rhetoric Society of America Conference, the IText Working Group—whose participants come from eleven different research universities—has collaborated to produce a white paper that "defines future directions for research on the relationship between information technology and writing," a vision the participants will further elaborate at the 2001 American Educational Research Association meeting.

Other projects illustrate the degree to which humanities scholars are currently attempting collaborative research and writing that reach beyond the academy to address a broad public audience. At the 1998 MLA Presidential Forum, for example, Jay Winter described the varying kinds of collaboration needed to produce the documentary series *The Great War* for PBS and BBC. In that talk, Winter called on senior scholars in the humanities to take the lead in creating and carrying out such large-scale projects. Indeed, he argued, the survival of public history depends on such a change in our scholarly practices.

Projects like the one Winter describes almost always call for interdisciplinary collaboration. The most recent work of Shirley Brice Heath provides another strong case in point. For the last dozen years, Heath and a group of researchers have been documenting the practices of youth art groups around the United States as part of an effort to demonstrate (to public policy makers, funding agencies, and the public) the essential value of arts and humanities to young people. To make this argument, Heath wanted to go beyond the traditional audiences that a book or research report might reach. The result, a documentary film entitled *ArtShow* (screened during autumn 2000 on many PBS stations) required two years of intensive collaboration among Heath, members of the research group, the young people involved in the four groups the film focuses on, film directors and editors, digital sound and visual effects experts, and other technical artists. In addition, participants in the youth art groups that were featured often comment on the crucial role collaboration plays in their work. Like Winter's *The Great War*, Heath's project aims at the kind of collaboration necessary to bring humanities research to a broad public audience—and to affect public policy as well.

During the last decade, we have been encouraged by the development of several new humanities centers that explicitly define their mission as collaborative (see, e.g., Ohio State University's Institute for Collaborative Research and Public Humanities [*Institute*] as well as a newly funded collaborative research in the humanities center established at Stanford [*Stanford Humanities Laboratory*]). Most recently, the University of Illinois, Chicago, announced that it will develop a humanities lab, under the direction of Sander Gilman, to serve "as an incubator of sorts for collaborative projects in the humanities involving professors, graduate students, and undergraduates," and that incubator will result in such products as "books, Web sites, and museum exhibitions" and in so doing move scholarship "from an individual to a collaborative model" (Schneider).

In all these efforts, a group of humanities researchers has come together to identify an issue or problem of mutual interest or concern, drawn up plans for addressing the issue from different perspectives and areas of expertise, and begun the hard work of carrying out those plans. These projects point up the high stakes involved in achieving the collaborative goals they set—such goals as the survival of public history, the record of women's writing, the crucial connections between new technologies and humanities-informed theories of writing and reading.

Other collaborations that have inspired us are:

- the editorial collective that produced a full decade of *Sage: A Scholarly Journal of Black Women*, which provided "a forum for critical discussion of issues relating to black women, promoted feminist scholarship, and disseminated new knowledge about black women to a new audience" (2)
- the administrator, faculty, staff, and student conversations that led to the guiding vision of California State University, Monterey Bay, as "essentially collaborative" (*Vision Statement*)
- the rich and long-standing institutional partnership between Carnegie Mellon University's program in writing and rhetoric and the Pittsburgh Community Literacy Center (*Community Literacy Center*)
- the extensive collaboration between faculty members and teacher-students at the Bread Loaf School of English, a collaboration that in some instances has changed the scholarly work of the faculty members as well as the research and classroom practices of the teacher-students (Flint)

These are positive and even inspiring achievements that, if we look carefully, we can see. (Another long-standing collaboration in the academy is the Society for Critical Exchange, founded in 1975 to encourage cooperative inquiry and research in critical theory.) As scholars of rhetoric and writing we would argue, however, that if collaborative efforts in the academy are to thrive, those in the academy must not only see but also study these efforts.

Collaboration, after all, is no panacea, no surefire corrective to agonistic individualism. Collaborative practices pose significant difficulties for faculty members and students, difficulties that must be faced and interrogated rather than ignored. (The endnote to this article represents one attempt to interrogate the authors' own collaboration and the difficulties entailed in such seemingly straightforward decisions as those related to attribution and to pronoun use.)[1] Anyone who has worked on a collaborative project is aware of the frustrations that can accompany such work, leading more than one scholar to recall an earlier meaning of the term *collaboration*: during warfare, after all, collaboration was a punishable offense. The dynamics of collaborative research will be affected by any number of differences, primary among them those of gender, race, class, and disciplinarity. Beyond the difficulty of personal dynamics lie material and logistic problems—and difficulties raised by differences in methodology and style—that can also impede efforts at collaboration.

Thus, in our research, we attempted to identify not only those conditions that made for productive, satisfying, and ethical collaboration but also those that did not. In our on-site visits with collaborative writers, for instance, we identified some modes of collaboration that led, participants told us, to deep dissatisfaction and alienation. Our first impulse in identifying these modes was to establish a taxonomy that would characterize modes of collaboration as either hierarchical or dialogic, productive or unproductive, ethical or unethical. But as generative as taxonomies can be, they also inevitably oversimplify and can lead to the kind of either-or thinking long associated with the adversarial rhetoric of the academy rather than to the deeply situated and nuanced analysis required to understand behaviors as complex as collaboration. In our view, such highly situated analysis is a key feature of what Sonja Foss and Cindy Griffin identify as an "invitational rhetoric," one that attempts to practice both-and rather than either-or inquiry. In the spirit of invitational rhetoric, then, we want to stress that in advocating the value of collaborative practices for both faculty members and students, we are not proposing a totalizing argument against single authorship and the practices associated with it. If we have learned anything from the last thirty years of scholarly work in English studies, it is that the power-knowledge nexus is a place of danger as well as of opportunity and that the human ability to bracket one's own experiences and understandings from critique is substantial. These truths apply as much to collaborative work as to work undertaken individually.

Such a recognition does not mean that we should not pursue the kind of institutional change that would enact alternatives to the adversarial academy, including the alternative offered by collaborative and invitational practice. It does mean that we must recognize the difficulties inherent in collaboration even as we make a space for and encourage collaborative projects and secure the funds necessary to carry them out. It also means addressing related professional standards and practices, as suggested by the following questions:

- What do subtle but entrenched conventions, such as the use of *et al.* or the conventional distinction between the author first mentioned and the other authors, do to erase the work of those engaged in collaborative practices?
- What changes at the level of the department, college, university, and profession at large must occur in order for junior faculty members to participate in collaborative projects without jeopardizing their careers?
- What work of redefinition will further the understanding that the contributions of doctoral dissertations come not from some abstract originality but rather from their participation in complex layers of knowledge production?
- Are we willing to undertake the potentially time-consuming and contentious work required to revise tenure and promotion guidelines so that collaborative research and publication will really count?
- Perhaps most important, can we learn to take pleasure as well as pride in our scholarly work when the traditional egocentric rewards of proprietary ownership and authority must be shared?

Responding constructively to these questions will call on our ingenuity, our goodwill, and our commitment. Moreover, it will call on our ability to learn how to work collaboratively, to build coalitions across disciplinary and methodological divides, and to take seriously the imperatives of an invitational rather than an adversarial rhetoric. As one material step in this direction, we invite readers to visit and contribute to a new Web site devoted to collaborative writing and research in higher education: *Collaborate!* (www.stanford.edu/group/collaborate/). This site will, we hope, serve as a clearinghouse for information on productive models of collaboration in the humanities and on best practices for institutional change. More important, it has the potential for the kind of synergistic collaboration necessary to effect such change. Readers whose departments have developed promotion and tenure guidelines that recognize collaborative work can share these guidelines on the best-practices page of the site. Those who know of good funding sources for collaborative work or strategies for effective long-distance collaboration can contribute them to the site's collective-wisdom pages.

Web sites are necessarily works in progress, and the one we have constructed will succeed only if many colleagues contribute to it. At the very least, establishing a collaborative Web site exemplifies the kind of modest but concrete intervention that can begin to make a difference in how we think about who we are and what we do and, along the way, offer one viable alternative to the adversarial academy.

NOTE

[1] In this endnote we comment on the nature of the collaboration that resulted in the development of a Web site, the inclusion of this site in a presentation at the 2000 Presidential Forum, and, finally, the publication of this article. Invited to participate in the forum, the first two authors of this essay spent considerable time discussing ways that their presentation might intervene in practices that discourage or even prohibit collaboration in the academy. The idea of building a Web site devoted to collaborative practices in the humanities quickly emerged, followed almost immediately by the recognition that bringing such a project to fruition would require a kind of collaborative process that these two longtime collaborators had not yet experienced. Fortunately Corinne Arráez, who shares a commitment to collaborative work, agreed to lend her expertise to this project. Like many collaborative projects, it entailed a division of labor. Drawing on their twenty years of research on collaborative writing, Lunsford and Ede sketched out the major issues that the site would address and conceptualized the site's role in the MLA presentation. Arráez, meanwhile, designed and constructed the site.

We mention these details here for two reasons: to clarify the responsibilities of the three authors of this project and to raise issues about the differing ways that collaborative practices are recognized and valued in the academy. As the project moved from a relatively intimate collaboration to an oral presentation at the forum and finally to this print publication, the authors discovered that their assumptions about the collaboration they engaged in were not necessarily shared by others. For example, during the forum presentation, they sat together on the stage as a visual representation of their collaborative effort. By mutual agreement (reached after discussion of possible speaking roles) Ede and Lunsford, who had written the talk, read the prepared text, which (as this article does) acknowledged Arráez's crucial role in designing and constructing the Web site. What all three authors intended as public acknowledgment of a complex and rich collaboration struck some, however, as marginalizing Arráez's participation in the project. Several members of the audience suggested this to Arráez after the presentation.

In preparing their presentation for publication, the authors confronted additional difficulties. They wished to emphasize their three-way collaboration by listing all three participants as coauthors of the published version of this project. But how to list the names? Their first instinct was to use alphabetic order. Such a listing quickly led to textual difficulties, particularly in terms of the pronoun *we*. Early in the essay, "we" refers specifically to personal experiences that caused Lunsford and Ede to undertake research on collaborative writing. An alphabetic listing of the authors' names would confuse readers about whose experiences were being represented.

How to be true to the lived experiences of two authors without erasing the contribution of the third? After several discussions about this question, the authors agreed on the name order that appears at the start of this article. They also agreed, however, that this resolution was at best an awkward compromise, one that taught all three that issues of attribution in collaborative projects pose challenges that have yet to be addressed in the academy.

WORKS CITED

Collaborate! Collaborative Writing and Research in Higher Education. Andrea Lunsford, Lisa Ede, and Corinne Arráez. 19 Dec. 2000 <http://www.stanford.edu/group/collaborate/>.

The Community Literacy Center. English Dept. Pittsburgh: Carnegie Mellon U. 7 Sept. 2000 <http://english.cmu.edu/clc/default.html>.

Ede, Lisa, and Andrea A. Lunsford. *Singular Texts / Plural Authors: Perspectives on Collaborative Writing.* Carbondale: Southern Illinois UP, 1990.

Flint, Kate. "Crossing Cultures, Changing Practices." *Changing Practice.* Ed. Chris Benson. Spec. issue of *Bread Loaf Teachers Network Magazine.* Spring-Summer 1999: 8–9.

Foss, Sonja K., and Cindy L. Griffin. "Beyond Persuasion: A Proposal for an Invitational Rhetoric." *Communication Monographs* 62 (1995): 2–18.

Heath, Shirley Brice. *ArtShow: Youth and Community Development.* Alweis Productions, 2000.

Institute for Collaborative Research and Public Humanities. Ohio State U Coll. of Humanities. 10 Nov. 2000. 20 July 2001 <http://www.cohums.ohio-state.edu/hi>.

IText Working Group. *A Project to Define Future Directions for Research on the Relationship between Information Technology and Writing.* 12 Dec. 2000 <http://www.rpi.edu/~geislc/IText/>.

Lunsford, Andrea, and Lisa Ede. "Why Write . . . Together?" *Rhetoric Review* 1 (1983): 150–58.

McKay, Nellie. *1997 MLA Elections: Candidate Information Booklet.* New York: MLA, 1997.

The Orlando Project: An Integrated History of Women's Writing in the British Isles. English Dept. U of Alberta. 15 Dec. 2000 <http://www.ualberta.ca/ORLANDO/orlando.htm>.

Sage: A Scholarly Journal of Black Women. Ed. Patricia Bell-Scott, Beverly Guy-Sheftall, Jacqueline Jones Royster, Lucille P. Fultz, Janet Sims-Wood, Miriam DeCosta-Willis. 9.2 (1995): 1–113.

Schneider, Alison. "Peer Review." *Chronicle of Higher Education* 9 Sept. 2000: A12.

Stanford Humanities Laboratory. Stanford U. 15 July 2001 <http://www.stanford.edu/group/shl>.

Vision Statement. California State U, Monterey Bay. 20 Sept. 2000 <http://www.monterey.edu/vision/>.

Winter, Jay. "Doing Public History: Producing *The Great War* for PBS and BBC." MLA Annual Convention. Presidential Forum, Washington, DC. 27 Dec. 1998.

A Collective Experience: Academics Working and Learning Together

NELLIE Y. McKAY AND FRANCES SMITH FOSTER

Nellie: I want to thank Linda Hutcheon for bringing us together to address this very important subject. For where better to confront the problem of the adversarial academy than before a group of keepers of the keys to the study of languages and literatures, the heartbeat of the American academy? The search for creative collaborations and the nonadversarial academy is not an attempt to diminish the value of competition that motivates us to discover the best in ourselves. What dismays many of us, however, is the degree to which we perceive competition fostering adversarial attitudes among us. What does that say about how we're doing our business of producing knowledge and training graduate students to succeed us? Thus, we see a need for some investigation of this issue.

While saying that, I acknowledge how fortunate I am to be able to speak from a historical place in which the values of many of my close peers and colleagues in the profession at large always propelled me toward connecting with others and not away from them. Even as we prepared for this forum (in a very brief telephone conversation), my partner, Frances Foster, commented that, in terms of how we live our lives, the dimensions of academic collaboration are much larger than I thought or conceptualized for our presentation.

Nellie Y. McKay is Evjue-Bascom Professor of English at the University of Wisconsin, Madison. Frances Smith Foster is Charles Howard Candler Professor of English and Women's Studies at Emory University. A version of this paper was presented at the 2000 MLA convention in Washington, DC.

Frances: In collaborating with Nellie on how we would do our portion of this presentation, I realized that we might come off as the most conservative pair on the panel. Not because of what we do or why we do it but because of the ways that we go about it. For a brief moment my competitive nature was roused, and I wondered how we could add a bit of flash! But I recalled—or rationalized—that Linda Hutcheon had urged us to try to enact our collaborative methodologies and let style and substance reinforce each other.

The conversation began with a polite disagreement. "Nellie," I said, "I don't really know anything about collaboration. I've nothing novel to say." "Nonsense, Frances Foster," she replied. "We can talk about our project." "Which one?" I queried. "Harriet!" she said, and continued, "We've worked on two projects only, and on the *NAAAL* (*Norton Anthology of African American Literature*) we didn't work as closely together as we did on Harriet." I thought for half a second and countered, "I don't think so, Nellie. I think we've been collaborating for a long time. Remember the time you convinced me to go to Milwaukee, where you were being honored as the Delta Sigma Theta author of the year, then added the *free* show-and-tell at the African American Community Center and the visit to the neighborhood library and the signing of Norton anthologies at the local black bookstore? That was your gig, remember? We worked—all day—for food and not much of that! Actually, Nellie, I think we've been collaborating for years, because collaboration doesn't mean only coauthoring or coediting. It means also being part of an intellectual community; it means consulting and counseling on teaching, it means doing service—sharing the podium at conferences and seminars as we did in Zimbabwe and Portugal, or reading proposals as we did for the Harvard Divinity School Women in Religion Board, which repaid us for our time and labor by inviting us to dinner with the dean and donors to the program, thereby adding fund-raising to our list of contributions. Think of all the years we've exchanged syllabi, consulted on which text would be most appropriate for what course, commiserated, ranted, raved, vented, then planned how to solve the problem presented to us by yet another one or seven of our students, or justified why we ought to give up yet another hour of trying to sleep and write another letter of recommendation, tenure evaluation, or manuscript review for yet another colleague or someone who really needed a candid collegial comment." And so we agreed that we had to present as we work, with cooperative independence, based on fundamental respect for the abilities and attitudes each of us has, and since we both had no time to start on this project earlier and therefore no time to get together to practice—well, here we are!

Nellie: As for having time to get things done, I'll add only that last December I made an entire off-the-top-of-my-head presentation at the MLA convention on why I had no time to write the paper I was supposed to write for that panel. And I was very serious. Having no time is a situation that African American women in the academy all face! The work that we do for our institutions, along with the students we are training and the multiple areas of professional service we also do, is stupendous. We have no time, and always we are tired. However, we continue, because the work is important.

In Frances's rebuttal of my limited definition of collaboration, it struck me that both she and I could, without thinking too deeply, come up with different lists of several other women colleagues, and a man here and there, with whom we have similarly shared both the heat and the burdens of the day as well as the laughs, the gossip, good meals, family tragedies, and the joys in our successes. Not to suggest that the activities that Frances drew into her net here are unknown to other faculty members. However, I suspect that today the makeup of many current higher education faculties is quite different from what it was twenty-five or thirty years ago, that certain activities not only have increased but also are now more visible than before. For, although far from achieving enough, the struggle for diversity in higher education achieved marked successes. The thirty-year influx of women and minority racial and cultural group faculty members and students into institutions previously closed to them has significantly altered how people in these institutions carry out their work. But before the changes occurred, the new groups had to discover coping strategies to ensure their survival. What needs to be known is that there were no models and no blueprints to guide them; they made a way where there was none.

For example, in the 1970s and early 1980s African American scholars invited into unfamiliar white colleges and universities across the country, with few other black faculty members around, knew that they needed an academic community with which to identify. For those of us in literature, the MLA, through its annual conventions, played a crucial role in providing a professional space where we could meet at each year's end. During the rest of the year, in those precomputer, prefax days, we cemented relationships through telephone calls and snail mail, with much frustration over snail-mail delays. Most of us then were from that generation of black scholars who composed the first such critical mass inside the white academy. Many of us were from the first generation of our families to receive college degrees, and an even larger percentage of us were the first among our relatives to earn PhDs. As beneficiaries of the barnstorming tactics of young black college students who, in the wake of the civil rights movement, demanded representation of the black experience in their educational programs, we brought black literature into our institutions and into the MLA as well. The MLA gave space, formal (as in the opportunity to offer convention sessions of our own making and not only to attend those of others) and informal (as in the semiboisterous, spontaneous gatherings of black folks that went on well into the night in hotel bar areas). In these gatherings we learned from one another and kept abreast of new developments in the field. Through our MLA contacts we learned to be professionals. African American women scholars coming into the profession simultaneously with the emergence of black women writers in large numbers on the national scene in the 1970s and 1980s created a conjunction of voices in a duet that engaged racism and sexism in the academy. The collaboration among black women literary scholars that Frances speaks of emerged in the 1970s and 1980s as a survival strategy and developed into long-term, significant personal and work relationships.

Frances: Nellie, I don't know how long we've been collaborating, but Harriet goes back to March 1983, on that dark and stormy night in Madison, Wisconsin, when Barbara Christian, Barbara Smith, and I responded to your call to participate in a forum and to do workshops on black women's studies—events you put together by collaborating with the Women's Studies Program and the Department of Afro-American Studies, supported by your college's Anonymous Fund and open to the public. It was there that I understood that I wasn't working in isolation at San Diego State; I had, in fact, the option of belonging to a community joined not by geographic proximity or unanimity of expertise but by the common idea that knowledge production and distribution need not be entrepreneurial. We survived, even flourished, in a profession that was not happy about our being in it in the first place, because we believed that to complete was better than to compete. I understood myself to be commissioned to unlearn destructive and erroneous information and to learn, articulate, and promulgate knowledge that allowed people to be as healthy and productive as they wanted to be.

Nellie: Frances, I think we were flying with blindfolds on in those days. We sometimes did not know where we even wanted to go, and we certainly had no assurances that wherever that was, we'd end up there. Besides, our numbers were very small and most of us were still untenured. I had some lessons in collaboration (although I would not have thought of them as such then) from my association with the still fledgling Women's Studies Program at Madison. There I saw strong and powerful women disagree vehemently with one another in program meetings but close ranks for the good of the whole. In the absence of women of color among my colleagues, several white women in that group reached out to me with support and lasting friendships.

I think of my scholarly collaborative work as mostly in concrete materials like the *NAAAL*, on which I worked with Skip Gates and nine additional editors; the *Casebook on* Beloved, which I coedited with Bill Andrews; the *Approaches to Teaching the Novels of Toni Morrison*, which I coedited with Kathryn Earle; and the newly minted McKay-Foster edition of the Norton Critical Edition of *Incidents in the Life of a Slave Girl* by Harriet Jacobs. I am certainly very proud of these texts that others can see, touch, feel, and learn from. But I can also understand that there are other kinds of collaboration equally important and that much of that work grows out of and in conjunction with my relationships with others. These relationships are products of networks created with colleagues and friends: a we woven through the fabric of individual lives and activities that developed into something of major significance in our lives because we called on one another for, and responded to one another with, advice, help, and comfort. With selfless willingness we walked the last mile with the other, even when we had no energy left to do it, because we knew that the other would be there in our moments of need. But I blather on, and Frances says that I tend to digress into idealism.

Frances: Nellie and I sometimes tend to digress into idealism, but in the no time we had to address what to do for this MLA forum, we managed to get back to the task. So now we will focus on Harriet, that is, the Norton Critical Edition of Harriet Jacobs's *Incidents in the Life of a Slave Girl*. It is not even "the book" to us. We call this latest project Harriet, for as we worked on it, we felt ourselves collaborating with Harriet Jacobs, with other scholars who have worked and will work in this area, and with those who will (we hope) read this volume to understand better what Jacobs's life and letters might mean to their (and our) own. We knew that our friends and colleagues Jean Fagin Yellin and Nell Irvin Painter were also editing *Incidents*, and we carefully outlined our work as complementary to theirs, emphasizing our particular strengths and interests so that there would be minimal overlap. We decided that our version would include nineteenth- and twentieth-century responses to Jacobs and her work as well as other writings by and about the author. We would choose the best and most representative scholarly articles we could find, but we would look especially hard for works by scholars and critics of philosophy, history, religion, and other disciplines who claimed the text as significant to their disciplinary and interdisciplinary lives. We consciously included younger and older scholars in the conversation, a conversation we hoped to continue with our version of what this text, this author, this enterprise was, is, and can be about.

Nellie: For me, the opportunity to work on this edition of Jacobs's text was an offer I could not refuse. The chance to work with Frances, with her nineteenth-century American literature expertise, made the prospect even more compelling. Jacobs holds a special place in my history as a scholar of African American literature and African American women writers in particular. I "met" Harriet in Madison, Wisconsin, when, in 1979 or 1980, my new colleague Susan Friedman gave me a copy of *Incidents*. Until then I did not know that a slave woman had written a full-length account of a portion of her life. Seen in the light of my subsequent friendship with Susan, I see that particular gift from my new white colleague as a symbol of what was ahead for us. The first time I taught *Incidents* to a large class of undergraduates, Harriet and I were a complete flop, even though the students knew nothing about the controversy surrounding the text's authorship. The magnet for them was Douglass's *Narrative*, and they just never took Jacobs seriously. But I did not give up, and after a few other attempts to interest students in the book, she began to catch on. So I've always felt that in Madison, where we met, Harriet and I shared peculiar struggles to find her a place among the African American writers I assign to my undergraduate classes. I approached the task of creating the Norton Critical Edition of her narrative with the sense of our having been together through a conflict that we won.

Frances: We divvied up the tasks. We also hired a couple of our graduate students to read our drafts and to contribute their opinions of what needed elaboration or clarification. I like library work, so I got to find and select nineteenth-century resources and to compile bibliographies of relevant materials—editions, articles about, articles relevant to, and so on. Nellie has more patience than I do with bad scholarly writing and obtuse ways of saying simple things, so she got to vet the twentieth-century criticism. Later we exchanged our results, edited, argued, and compromised on what should go in and what should not. We queried our friends and searched our archives for proper illustrations and hounded our editor at W. W. Norton until she agreed to include illustrations of Jacobs's grave; of the plantation house at which Jacobs worked and from which she escaped to the crawl space in her grandmother's house; and of the present-day historical marker in Edenton, North Carolina, that says (in effect), "Harriet Jacobs lived here." Two weeks ago we learned that the collaboration was not perfect—certain illustrations were lost during the publishing process and didn't get into the book. Still the result, I hope, is what my colleague in German philosophy has informed me is called a "symphilosophized text," one in which no one can actually tell who authored or chose exactly what and one that is greater than the sum of its parts.

Nellie: Working with Frances on this project was a very positive experience for me. As a generalist and twentieth-century African Americanist, I can hold my own fairly well in most things connected to my work life. Frances helped me fill in gaps in my nineteenth-century knowledge that another generalist, a twentieth-century scholar, or even a less experienced nineteenth-century scholar might not have been able to fill. There is a great deal to be said for collaborative scholarship that brings together experienced scholars from different literary periods. This project will also help me offer better training to graduate students in nineteenth-century African American women's writing. Over the past three years more students than before have chosen to work in the area. One of them helped me with the edition and was delighted to have the firsthand experience of doing the research and helping read the proofs for a real book publication. She too adopted Harriet, also occasionally confusing others who overheard us referring to Jacobs as familiarly as if she were someone we knew and loved. The knowledge that Lynn Jennings gained will serve her well in her own work. I exposed other graduate students to the project during its development, though in a less continuous way. They were quite impressed by the process of such a production.

Although Frances and I were committed to making our book the best that we could make it, so it would be a major contribution to existing Jacobs scholarship, we also wanted to give full credit to the work of the scholars who came before us and made Harriet Jacobs the significant literary figure she is today. We owe them all for what they did. We are especially indebted to the pioneering work of Jean Fagin Yellin. For many years Yellin fought against those who denied Jacobs authorship of her text, and Yellin's Harvard University edition of the narrative set the bar very high for all who followed. Without her work our achievement would have been considerably harder. Frances, is there anything else you'd like to say?

Frances: Collaboration is not new in the academy, and it can take many forms. Increasingly familiar to the humanities is the science lab model, where a first author and multiple technicians provide the necessary data and get credit in proportion to the perceived significance of their contribution or the prestige of their professional positions. I knew one couple who actually sat together and composed their book line by line. I have coauthored articles with a professor of political science and with a few graduate students who also knew things I did not. I've served as a consultant for scholars who needed my expertise to complete their projects, and I've completed projects begun by others. Each collaboration is different, influenced by personality, expertise, power position, and purpose. But no collaboration is that far removed from what I am convinced we do always in the humanities. I believe that the idea of individual, independent work is a myth. All of us benefit from, exploit, or are given the gift of the ideas and thoughts and suggestions and encouragements of our teachers, students, colleagues, family, friends, and, yes, even neighbors who've never heard of our topic but who respond with questions and comments that push us toward a better articulation of the questions and the answers. I learned that nice word *symphilosophy* in conversation with a colleague during one of those university committee meetings that "take us away from our *real* work." And in a second meeting that same week, another colleague, who works in Middle Eastern studies, said that we needed to redefine *labor* and understand that in a university collaboration is what we're supposed to do. It's time we dropped the guise of intellectual independence and understood that there's too much work and too few laborers with too little time not to share the responsibilities and the results. Healthy competition makes us all do more than we thought we could and do it faster and better. Adversarial competition wastes time and talent—and makes enemies. It's time to give credit where credit is due.

Nellie: I'd like to thank my fellow participants who made this session work for us. I'm also especially grateful to my many friends and colleagues who have collaborated with me over the past twenty-five years in one way or another and whose efforts enrich my personal and work experiences despite the things that often get us down. As Frances points out, there has always been collaboration among scholars; it's just that we do not always recognize it. The task is for us to call it by its right name and to encourage others to do the same. Finally, I want to thank our graduate students, those who have recently entered the profession and those still struggling to get there. We thank them especially for keeping us connected to the pulse of the next generation, from whom we have much to learn. Some of them are already developing networks through which to support one another in graduate school and beyond. We applaud those efforts. The future of creative collaboration in the academy is in their hands.

Stories and Songs across Cultures: Perspectives from Africa and the Americas

J. EDWARD CHAMBERLIN AND LEVI NAMASEB

So. Tsî i ge koma ge hâhe Khoe-ōreb xa.

S, o i ge nēsisa khoeb xa hais !gâb ai mâhe tsî ge sâhe hâ i. Tsîb ǁnāti sâmâ hîab ge nēsisa khoe-oreba nē khoeba ge mû, ǀGarudanab ti gere ≠gai-heba. So, tsî go nēsisa khoebab go mû, o a ǀkhuri. Tsî go ǀkhuri, ǀkhuri tsî ǀgūb go o . . . !ôb ǀkha a ǀnami. Tsî go ǀnamib ta hîab ge nēsisa khoeba !gam!gâ tsî ge xoasen. So, ob ge !ôba !kharu tsî khoeb mâ!gao hais ≠amai hā "ǁam" ti go mâ. Ob ge nēsisa khoeba kōb go o ra mû: "Nee, khoe-ōreb !ôb ge nēba!" O go nēsisa hais ǀguisa naba tsî a ǁhai.

"ǁGapi, ǁgapi, ǁgapi, ǁgapi, ǁgapi, ǁgapi" ti ǁhai tsî go khoe-ōreba sāb go !khaisab go mûo, naba tsî khoeba go sauru. Tsî go saurub go !khaisab ge mûheo ai!â a ǁhai tsî go nēsisa !homma ≠oa !homma ǁgôa, !homma ≠oa !homma ǁgôa, !homma ≠oa !homma ǁgôa ti a hî. Ob ge khoe-ōreba nēsisa !khoedāheb geo mâ tsî ra kō. Tsîb ge mâ tsî kō tsî "Ae, ǀGarudanatse! Ti ǀkhomtse !khoe ti! !Homma ≠oa !homma ǁgôa, !homma ≠oa !homma ǁgôa. Tae-i ǀgui-e si khoena nî mîbahe, ǀhuru-ū bis ǀguisa ta goro hî !khais xa?" ti i ge ǁnapa khoe-ōreb xa mîhe tsî ǁnāpa go toa.

That was Levi Namaseb speaking in Khoekhoe, and I am Ted Chamberlin. First a parable. There was a meeting between an Indian community in the northwest of British Columbia and a group of government foresters about jurisdiction over the woodlands. The foresters claimed the land for

---

J. Edward Chamberlin is Professor of English and Comparative Literature at the University of Toronto. Levi Namaseb is Lecturer in Linguistics and African Literature at the University of Namibia. A version of this paper was presented at the 2000 MLA convention in Washington, DC.

the government. The Indians were astonished by the claim; they couldn't understand what these relative newcomers were talking about. Finally one of the elders put what was bothering them in the form of a question. "If this is your land," he asked, "where are your stories?" He spoke in English; but then he moved into Gitksan—the Tsimshian language of his people—and told a story himself.

All of a sudden, in a classic contradiction, everyone understood—even though the government foresters couldn't understand a word, and neither could some of his Gitksan colleagues. They understood not what he was talking about—though they had a pretty good idea—but something ultimately more important and more sophisticated: how stories give shape and substance to the world and how they give it meaning and value; how they bring us close to the real world by keeping us at a distance from it; how they hold people together and at the same time keep them apart; how they are both true and not true.

And they all understood the importance of the Gitksan language, even—or especially—those who did not speak it. Language is the stuff of stories and songs, and a language makes them incomprehensible to those who do not speak it. It is these moments of incomprehensibility—*defamiliarization* is a less unnerving but also less accurate term—that tell us something about literature. Language is the signature of individual and collective identity, and it makes those who do not speak it—who do not speak Gitksan, say, or /Nu, the language of the ≠Khomani people of the southern Kalahari that you will hear in a moment—less certain of their identity than those who do.

Like most of us, I have always worked with others, most obviously with librarians and editors who helped me with the process of discovery and invention that is at the heart of literary studies. I have written books with others—two of them, in fact, with Sander Gilman, the distinguished former president of the MLA—and coedited journals with scholars such as our current president, Linda Hutcheon. But my collaboration with Levi Namaseb of the University of Namibia and (as of this year) the University of Toronto has been different in many ways. It has given me new insight into the nature of our profession and the elements of our craft and into the importance of those moments of incomprehensibility and uncertainty that, I believe, are at the center of our experience of all literatures. The story you have just heard was in Khoekhoe, his mother tongue.

Levi Namaseb and I first met four years ago in Durban, where he was working with Edgard Sienaert at the Centre for Oral Studies at the University of Natal. I had come to speak about an international project I was directing on oral and written traditions. I stayed to listen.

I have worked for over three decades with aboriginal communities in the Americas and Australia on interrelations among language, land, and livelihood that converge in territorial claims and in challenges to the political sovereignty of so-called settler societies. I thought I knew a lot about language and literature, oral as well as written. But Sienaert (see Jousse) is one of the very few contemporary scholars who has seriously challenged the deeply misinformed typologies of orality and literacy promoted by Walter Ong and accepted by a lot of contemporary literary theorists. His work offered a new way of approaching everything from the entangled issues of authority regarding Indian treaties—whether, when, and how the oral or the written version has precedence—and the equally vexed problems of authenticity surrounding local and literary language in poetic texts. Levi Namaseb, for his part, is one of the most gifted linguists of southern Africa; a dedicated scholar of narrative, lyric, and dramatic traditions of performance; and a traditional storyteller of his Khoekhoe people So I was among colleagues who knew much about language and literature and about those connections to land and livelihood that the Gitksan elder had highlighted.

I had heard about a land claim by the ≠Khomani, a group of San (Bushmen) in the southern Kalahari. They were once a relatively large group—large for a hunter-gatherer society, at least—living in the surprisingly rich desert and semiarid lands that make up the west central highlands of what is now South Africa, north of Cape Town. Over the last couple of centuries they almost disappeared, in a holocaust whose numbers may not match those of the Nazi regime or the slave trade, or the murderous campaigns against aboriginal people in Australia and the Americas, but whose horrors rival them all. A few were left, scattered around the Northern Cape; and with the encouragement of the new postapartheid government of South Africa, the African National Congress, they were putting forward a claim to their original homeland in the desert. Their language was said to be extinct; but Levi spoke a close cousin to it, Khoekhoe, and he also spoke Afrikaans, in which I knew they told some of their stories.

So Levi and I went there, on a hunch—a hunch that their situation would take us closer to fundamental questions about who tells tales, to whom, in what places, on what occasions, in what language, and what (if any) difference it all makes. Though we give these questions much more complicated names, they are the same ones we pose in literary studies.

I am a great believer in hunches and, of course, in someone to back them, which the University of Toronto kindly did with substantial resources and an understanding that this enterprise was high-risk, for in an old-fashioned sense I had no idea what we were doing, though from thirty years' experience I had a pretty good idea how to do it. That sounds both intellectually foolish and ethically dangerous, but I think it is a precondition for basic theoretical research. It is the folks who have a clear agenda who in my experience cause the most damage.

The first thing we found astonished us, and we came across it by accident. I am a great believer in accidents too, at least in the good kind, and in putting yourself in places where they can happen to you. The success of any land claim depends on a detailed demonstration of use and occupancy of territory; and stories, as the Gitksan elder said, are central to this demonstration. Being able to identify places and events in an indigenous language is very helpful—in fact, it will usually do the trick—but the language of the ≠Khomani had been pronounced dead by the senior linguists of southern Africa in the 1970s. This fact led one of the lawyers to say nostalgically to the leader of the group, Petrus Vaalbooi, "It's too bad nobody still speaks the language." "Mum does," Petrus replied.

Elsie Vaalbooi was the mother of the mother tongue. She was also ninety-seven, living up by the Namibian border. She thought that she was the only one left alive who spoke the language—Petrus, her son, certainly didn't, nor did his children—and that it would soon die with her. But in a gesture of faith she spoke into a tape recorder, sending a message to anyone who could hear. Fortunately her faith was not misplaced, and so far we have found about twenty more speakers—Levi and colleagues at the South African San Institute took the lead in this search—following rumors about people who spoke funny, looked funny, knew the old ways, or could find their way in the desert. There may be a couple dozen more scattered around the Northern Cape.

Many of them were living alone or with no other speakers around. But there were three sisters and their cousin—/Una, Kais, /Abakas, and Griet —who spoke the language, and together they had a remarkable range of tales to tell. We were with them on their first return from Babylonian exile to their homeland in the Kalahari desert since they were driven out, first in the 1930s and later in the 1950s. We watched them stand on the red sand and take back the land, mapping out a precise geography of the imagination in stories and songs.

Some languages survive all sorts of violence. Some do not. Others just slip away, less counted than spotted owls. As I speak today, only /Una and Kais are still alive. Griet died of cancer, /Abakas of heart failure following a lifetime of living with the tuberculosis that is endemic in their community. The situation of their language is perilous but certainly not unique. Though most of us remain unaware, we are surrounded by languages on the verge of extinction. Hundreds of native North American languages have died out over the past fifty years, their communities broken up by dislocation and dispossession and disease; many other languages are currently in jeopardy. Meanwhile, our university language departments and our modern language associations have flourished. Maybe we forget that these ancient languages are modern too.

In the southern Kalahari, Levi Namaseb has done something about this. He has put in place a program to teach the youngsters /Nu, the language of their ancestors. And he has developed an orthography for a language extraordinarily rich in sounds, with its five clicks and eight tones. It is a remarkable achievement; but, in another unnerving contradiction, keeping a language alive depends on keeping awkward questions open.

For example, is it really so important to preserve /Nu? Why not just write it down and put it away in a library? Given the age of the few remaining speakers and the generation gaps in the community, why not let Afrikaans or English take over or let Khoekhoe hold on? One of the great stories of Western culture has to do with the proliferation of languages in the Tower of Babel and the promise of a day when these rivalries will be erased and common ground across cultures will be based on a common language. Most societies have a version of this story, calling themselves "the people," as the Dene and the Inuit do up in my part of the world, and giving their languages a universal name, such as "to speak," which is exactly what /Nu means.

My response to this question of what to do about an endangered language such as /Nu will not ensure its future or preserve its remarkable tradition of literary expression. Nor will Levi's response, though he is a crucial part of its current revival. At the end of the day, only the answers given by the people themselves will determine what happens to their language. That is where collaboration such as ours must move into the community. There it becomes even more compelling, and even more complicated. But ultimately it is where we must be most deeply involved.

Beyond the community, however, beyond the ≠Khomani and the Kalahari, the question is important to all of us as literary scholars. If we don't ask it, discuss it, debate it, and sometimes disagree about the answer, we cannot hope to understand the importance of language in our own stories and songs. I have had the privilege of asking it together with Levi for the past three years. We plan to continue for a long while yet.

Now let my friend and colleague, Levi Namaseb, speak again.

This time I give you both a story and its translation.

Khoe-ōrekha ge koma ge hâ i

Tsî kha ge ǀgamse ǀgui ge !gau hâ i. Tsî ge !gau hâ i khoe-ōrekha ge ǀgamse ǀguipa gere !au – nē ra mîhe sîsenǁares khami ǁnaosab tsî

‖nurisab tsîkha. So, o kha ge !nūse !au ǀgūse !au, !homgu !nâ !au !goagu !nâ !au, xawe kha ge khoe-e hō tama ge hâ i. Xawe kha ge ǀûsen tamase gere !au khoena, ǀnîsi xawe kha khoero-e nî ǀhao-ū ti hâ ≠âis ǀkha. Tsîkha ge ra !au ǀkhomadi ≠amai, ≠gādi !nâ, !homgu ai tsî !āgu !nâ xawe kha ge ûitsama khoe-i di dao-i karo-e mû tama ge hâ i. ‖Nāti khaa ge gere !au tsî hā gere ‖goe !â ǀnâb ǀkha tsî ‖khawa nautse gere dītsâ. ‖Nāti kha hâ hîab ge ‖naosaba ge ǀaesen tsîb ge ‖nurisaba ǀguri ge !au. ‖Nātib ǀguri ra !au xaweb ge ‖îb tsîna ‖khāb as kōseb ra dītsâ xawe khoe-e hōǀhau tama ge hâ i. !Nonaǁlî tsēs aib ge ‖nurisaba furuse ge oaǀkhī ǀnaib gere oaǀkhī ‖aeb xa. Ob ge kaikhoeba !noeǀalom rase ra dî: "Kha, xū-ets ho?" "Hî-î, xū-e ta hō tama!"

‖Naosab ge ‖khawa !gamsen tsî ge ‖goe. Khoen ge huga kairan gere o gere doexūhe ‖aegu aob ge axaba nēti ge dî: "‖Naos, sats ge aitsama a ≠an sakhom ge ǀguipa gere !au ǀgausa. Sakhom ge hoa !âpegu ai khoena gere ôa xawe khom ge khoe-e hō tama ge hâ i. ǀKhomagu ai, !homdi ai, ≠gādi !nâ tsî !āgu !nâ. Hîats ge satsa go ǀaesen. O ta ge tita ǀguri ra !au xawe ta ge khoe-e hō tama hâ."

Axab ge ≠kharirose !nōro tsî nēti ra aoǁgui: "O ‖naos ‖nātits nēsisa sats tsîna ≠uru īsiba ra hō-oase ‖gausen tama hâo, ta ga . . . satsa '!gâb' ti a mîo tae ga hî?"

Kaikhoeb ge aibe ≠khari ‖aero-e !nō tsî nēti ge aoǁguitsâ: "Ama-ets ge ra mî nau !nâsa. Xawe kōriro te re ǀnîsi xawe ǀgam tsērora ǀnîsi xawe ta nî khâi xuige."

"Tae ǀgam tsē-e? Hî-î, ‖gan-i ra ‖gaia!nâ xawe. Hâ-â" ti mî tsîb kom ‖nurisaba ‖îb ‖naoba ge xoraxorao.

The Two Ogres

There were only two ogres left in that region, the uncle and his nephew. They hunted together, in the same process as our theme today: collaboration. They did not give up and were looking for humans all over the region. They hunted far and near, on top of the mountains, in the plains, on the hills, and along the riversides, but they found no trace of any human presence. They continued in the same way every day—going in the morning, returning empty-handed, sleeping with hunger, and trying again the next day. So it went on. One day the uncle fell sick and stayed at home, and the nephew hunted alone. The nephew tried his best, going all over, looking for humans, but could not find any trace of them. The third day the nephew came back earlier than before. The uncle asked with little excitement, "Did you find something?"

"No, I didn't."

The uncle subsided. As it was those times when elders used to be left behind to die when young people went on to migrate, the younger one started asking his uncle, "Uncle! You know that we used to hunt together. We went all over the mountains, hills, plains, and rivers but could not find anything. Then you fell sick, and I am hunting alone all over but don't find anything." He paused for a while and suggested, "Now, Uncle, you do not show any signs of improvement. Will there be a problem if I . . . eat you?"

After a pause the uncle suggested, "Your suggestion is fine, but can't you observe me for a few more days? Maybe I will improve soon."
"What few more days? No, the flesh is getting worse the more I wait!"
So the nephew cooked and ate his uncle.

Ted Chamberlin and I met in June 1997, in Natal at an international conference on oral literatures. He invited me to join forces with him in an effort to record and revive a dying Khoesan language of the Northern Cape.

We met the ≠Khomani San, and his invitation was echoed by the San themselves. They wrote a formal letter to me in Afrikaans (now the first language of the younger generation) in which they made a plea to have their language saved from rapid extinction by its being written down and taught to the youth. A humble request, which was very difficult to refuse or sidestep. I did a preliminary survey of the language, which I completed in June 1998.

My interest in the languages of the aboriginal hunters and gatherers of my part of the world goes back a long way. When I would read in the written histories that some of the rock paintings in the region are over 1,500 years old, and when I would visit such sites, I always wondered what the language was like around this area when these paintings were being made. Urged by this curiosity and by Ted, I started to get as deeply involved as possible. Much of the time he was in Toronto and I was in Namibia or in the field, and I remember his e-mail messages to me, saying "Keep the momentum!" For months on end, it was a remote-control collaboration.

The language is classified as belonging to the Southern Khoesan language family with the name ≠Khomani, also called /Nu. It was recorded by the University of Witswatersrand for phonetics and classificatory purposes under that category, but no efforts were made to develop it as a written language. All languages of the Southern Khoesan group are today widely believed to have become extinct. /Nu does not have mutual intelligibility with Khoekhoe (my mother tongue), which belongs to the Central Khoesan language family, though there are some mutual lexical borrowings through language contact. Northern Khoesan has the most surviving languages, but most of them are still unwritten.

My preliminary observations show that /Nu is rich in vowels (some twenty vocalic phonemes or vowel alternations), consonants (nineteen phonemes), five basic clicks (with seven effluxes from the possible twenty-one different effluxes [Ladefoged and Maddieson 278]), and eight tone melodies. That these observations are orthographic—phonemic rather than phonetic—typically produces more interesting issues than the numbers here cited. As I developed the orthography, Ted urged me to continue looking at the words; then he said, "Go to the folktales."

Using as a basis the International Phonetic Alphabet system, I developed an orthography for /Nu. The surviving elders could not manage to hide their excitement when they first saw their language in written form and heard their folktales read by me. It was the first time their language had been spoken by a foreign speaker. With their almost impossible dream realized in such a short period of time, ≠Khomani youth volunteered to learn the language and its orthography. We had always known that this cooperation would be the key to the ultimate success of the work. The first workshop took place mid-May 2000 and the second in November 2000; elders volunteered to attend to our immediate problems just outside the school. The next workshop was planned for June 2001.

The elders who speak the language are few in number. Furthermore, from about twenty-one fluent speakers who we know are living, seven can still tell folktales but only four are real performers of this ancient oral art. With the orthography in place, however, we were in a position to record the performers and in the future to use these recordings to teach others the complex art of storytelling in their aboriginal language and culture.

We went with some of the elders to their homeland in the Gemsbok National Park (now called Kgalagati National Park), and on one trip the sight of an ostrich reminded one of them, Anna Kassie, of a story about the Ostrich and the Tortoise. The story was confirmed by her colleague |Una Rooi. They explained that the Ostrich does not have marrow in its bones as a result of a race with the Tortoise. They promised to narrate this event to me once we arrived back at the camp where they had settled, a recently acquired farm with a modern farmhouse, part of the land claim settlement that also confirmed their right to a very large tract of land adjacent to the park. In the warm-up session before the storytelling and recording we sensed an argument about the true version of the tale. Hannie Koerant, who speaks the same language as Anna Kassie but grew up in a remote but linguistically related region, was adamant that the race between the Ostrich and the Tortoise was won by the Ostrich, not by the Tortoise as Anna Kassie and |Una Rooi claimed. We were able to save both versions of the tale by dividing the narrators and recording each version at a separate location without the influence of the other.

I now tell you this folktale, which I recorded. Reproducing it in print, of course, is something that was impossible to do until this year, when I was able to develop an orthography for the language. /Nu is but one of the many languages that were spoken by people who roamed the mountains when the rock paintings were made in what is now South Africa and Namibia.

The first narrator is Hannie Koerant, from Olifantshoek; and she told the story on 17 November 2000 in Andriesville, where the sisters /Una and Kais now live.

Tjoe a nǀâ ǃqoe ha ǃai. Ha ǃQoe a hui ha ǀ'e ǁkhisi. A tjoe a ǃai ha ǁǁina nǃû ha ǀqûke. A ha khau u ha se ≠khaka ǃqoe.

Tjoe ha ku: "ǃQoe, ǀa ge, ǃQoe?"

ǃQoe ha ka: "N ke a ng. Ng xa ǁ'aike. Ng ke ǀ'i so ǁkhisi. Ng ǁǁu ke ka ǃu. Ng ka ǃu ≠ûi."

Tjoe ǁǁ'e ha n khau u ha nǃana. Ha ka tjoe a: "ǃQoe ǀa ge?"

"Ha-a! Ng xa ǁ'aike. Ng ka ǃunu ≠ûi, n ≠ûi. Ng ǁǁu ke ke a ǃai. Ng xa djûi. Ng se ǀ'e ǁkhisi."

Ha xa se a ǃQoe. Tjoe a xa se a ǃQoe.

Ha ku nǀâ: "Sie si ǃai!"

ǃQoe a ku ke: "Hi ǁǁ'ôa si ǃai! Nǀâ si ǀ'i ke ≠asi ǃai."

A ha n ǃai, a Tjoe nǁǁâ djo ǁǁkhoe n ǃQoe. A ha ǁǁ'e ǀqûnu ha ǃi ke nǃû.

A ha khau u ha se ka Tjoe a: " ǀA ge a?"

ǃQoe a ka: "N ke a ng. Ng xa djûi. Ng ka ǃhu ǁkx'era n ǃai."

A ha ǁǁ'î ǀqû, ha ǀqû, ha ǀqû, ke a ha ǀqû, ha se Tjoe ≠khaka ǃQoe.

ǃQoe a ǀ'i so ǁkhisi. A ha ka ǃu xa ≠gûi. Ha ǁǁu ≠ao ha ǃai. Ha xa djûi *want* ha ka ǃu ≠ûi. Ha Tjoe ǃu ke a ka ǀ'â.

" ǀA ge ǃQoe?"

"N ke a ng. Ng ǀ'i ke a ǁkhisi. Ng xa djûi."

A xa . . . Ke a xa ǁǁ'î n ǀqû n ǃina nǃû.

" ǁGa ge a a?"

"Ng ke a ǀ'i ke a ǁkhisi. Ng a ka ǃu xa a n se n ǁǁ'use ǀ'iso ǁkhisi."

The Ostrich and the Tortoise ran, but the Tortoise entered into the grass. The Ostrich ran alone and went behind the dune and danced. She was looking for the Tortoise and said, "Tortoise, where are you, Tortoise?"

The Tortoise said, "Here I am. I am tired and I am now entering the grass. I don't have legs. My legs are short."

The Ostrich went dancing again and returned, asking, "Where are you, Tortoise?"

"No, I am tired. I am going onto the grass because my legs are short. I can't keep up your pace. I am taking a rest. I am going in the grass."

The Ostrich came back again and met the Tortoise and said to the Tortoise again, "Let us run!"

The Tortoise said, "No, I can't run, but let us run in the open veld."

They ran, and soon the Tortoise was outrun. The Ostrich, knowing that it won, went between two dunes and started to dance and later returned looking for the Tortoise.

"Where are you?"

The Tortoise answered, "Here I am. I cannot keep up the pace. I cannot run."

The Ostrich went to dance again, and the Tortoise went into the grass. It has short legs. It does not want to run. It cannot keep up the pace, as its legs are short. The legs of the Ostrich are tall.

"Where are you, Tortoise?"

"Here I am. I am going into the grass. I am tired."

The Ostrich went behind the dune and danced.

"Where are you?"

"I am in the grass. My legs can't hold, therefore I sit motionless in the grass."

Three different groups of narrators were asked to explain their versions of this tale. They were Hannie Koerant, who claims that the Ostrich won the race; Anna Kassie, who believes that the Ostrich lost the race; and the Khoekhoe speakers in the village of Riemvasmaak, who share Anna's opinion. Hannie Koerant stuck to her guns and went for a more literal (biological) argument: "How can the tortoise win with such short legs compared to the tall legs of the ostrich?" Anna Kassie had an ethnological explanation. She just nodded, satisfied with the explanation that "they" belong to the "!Ao≠e," meaning "people of the mountains."

The Khoekhoe in Riemvasmaak smiled at the difference. One of them, Dre, remarked, "They still have the old version of the tale that was without 'cheating' [trickery]. We brought the cheating part into the story. Perhaps they don't know how to cheat."

The second narrator is Anna Kassie, from Upington, and she told the story on 17 November 2000, also in Andriesville. Note that she stammers. We repeat whatever she says, as the grammar of the language is still not analyzed. In any case, she also uses repetition as a literary tool.

>!Qoe ke kaua ha kn ≠hoa hm ǁamǁam, ǁamǁam, ǁam nǀâ Tjoe. A Tjoe ǁkheu ha ku n !Qoe: "Nǀâ ke a ha nǀâ si ku nǀn *wen* a."
>
>A !Qoe *klaar* ≠hoa. Ka k!û. Ha ǁ'îng ka k!a. Hn ga k!a Hn ga k!a, Hn ga k!a, Hn ga k!a. Nǁ e ke !Qoe ≠o a ku: "King ke nǁa u ǀi, nǁ e ǀi nǁâ ǁkhau."
>
>Tjoe ǁ'a ne ki ku ha ≠khake ha ǁ'a ǀ'ana. Tjoe ku ha ≠hoa: "ǀA ge a a?"
>
>"N ke a ng!"
>
>"Ki dja?"
>
>"*Skuins voor!*"
>
>"!O ke. !O koa ǁkhaua. !O koa ǁkhaua. !O koa ǁkhaua. Tjoe ku a ku tjua."
>
>"ǀA ge a a?"
>
>"N ke a ng."
>
>"Ki ke a xa nǁâ?"
>
>"Na ǁkha a."
>
>Tjoe ǁkhau. Tjoe ke a ǁkhau. Tjoe ke a ǁkhau. Tjoe ke a ǁkhau. Tjoe ku a ku tjua:
>
>"ǀA ge a a?"
>
>"N ke a ng!"
>
>!Qoe ǀ'i ǁ'ana nǀî ǀkhisi. Ha ǁkhau. Ha ǁkhau. Ha ǁkhau. Ha ǁkhau.
>
>"ǀA ge a a?"
>
>"N ke a ng ǀ'ana."
>
>!Qoe ku ǀ'i so ǀkhisi.
>
>Ha ǁkhau. Ha ǁkhau. Ha ǁkhau. Ha nǁâ ǁ'a. ǀO ka ǁkhau. ǀO ka ǁ'a. Ha ha ǁ'a !ge ǁu ha ka so nǁâ ka ǀkhuruke, nǁâ ǁaike. Ke a gao kc a ha

nou . . . ha ǁu ke so nǁâ a ha n ǁai ǁ'o ke. Ha nǁâi ǁkhau Ha n ǁâi ǁkhau. Ha nǁâi ǁkhau, a ǁ'a !'ana. Nǁâ ga ǁ'a. ≠Gamkî.

Ha ku: "Ng ke a ǀe e *bekersi*. Ng ke a ǀe e *bekersi*!" !Qoe ha ku. !Qoe, ke n . . . *laaste* !qoe.

≠Hoa ke *nou tjoa* . . . ≠Hoa ke *nou* ǁ'ing.

The Tortoise was in conversation with the Ostrich. They conversed and conversed. The Ostrich challenged the Tortoise, saying, "Look here, I will beat you if we race."

The Tortoise answered and said, "No, I will beat you."

The two made an appointment and went apart. They ran and ran and ran. The male Tortoises were sitting all along the track but invisible. Farther on the Ostrich started looking around and spoke to the Tortoise, "Where are you?"

"Here I am!"

"Where?"

"Sideways in front!"

The man ran and ran.

The Ostrich ran farther and asked again, "Where are you?"

"Here I am."

"Where are you located?"

"I am in front of you!"

The Ostrich ran and ran and ran.

The Ostrich later said, "Where are you?"

"Here I am."

The Tortoise was hiding in the grass.

He ran and ran and ran.

"Where are you?"

"I am here in front!"

The Tortoise was in the grass.

He ran and ran and ran.

The man ran at his highest speed and kept such a pace that the marrow in his bones dried up and there was no energy to run any farther. But he tried to run to stay ahead. He fell down.

He (the Tortoise) said, "I have taken the cup. I have taken the cup!" It was the last tortoise. The story is now tied up. (Perhaps to be "untied" later.)

One aspect about storytelling is that the oral form always differs from the written one. The story I narrated at the beginning of this presentation in my mother tongue, Khoekhoe, was fluent, for I was controlled not by the sequence of words on paper but by my memory, imagination, and the type of audience I had. The relations between oral and written performance and among the teller, the tale, and the audience are things Ted and I will be looking at in the near future with reference to the traditions of the ≠Khomani.

Ted referred to /Nu as a modern as well as an ancient language, one therefore belonging with all the others celebrated in the Modern Language Association. During one of the teaching workshops, several of the youngsters asked whether we could translate the following very popular Christian songs from Afrikaans into /Nu. We did so, with their help, and they sang them with much vigor. The melodies are recent, of course, and do not have any relation with the traditional way of singing ≠Khomani lyrics; but the children, like their parents and grandparents and all their ancestors going back millennia, adapt to and adopt new technologies—in this case, some religious songs.

Here are three songs they translated. First the original Afrikaans is given, then the English version, then the /Nu.

> 1. Die Here is lief vir jou
> Hy sterf op Golgota
> Die sonstraal skyn deur jou venster
> Die Here is lief vir jou.
>
> The Lord loves you.
> He dies on Golgotha
> The sunshine enters your window
> The Lord loves you.
>
> !Hirike ǁ'â a.
> Ku ǀ'a a Golgota.
> ǁ'Uike ǀ'e a nǁn hunike.
> !Hirike ǁ'â a.

(Note: the third line was changed by the ≠Khomani children to "sun," as there is no word for sunshine in /Nu.)

> 2. Kinders van die Here
> Praat van die Here Halleluja.
> Halleluja
> Halleluja.
>
> Children of the Lord.
> Speak about the Lord, Hallelujah.
> Hallelujah
> Hallelujah.
>
> Tsuǁoa ǀoeke.
> ≠Hoa n Tsuǁoa Halleluja.
> Halleluja
> Halleluja.
>
> 3. Die Here is wonderbaar vir my
> Die Here is wonderbaar vir my
> Kom ons soek Hom.
> Kom ons prys Hom.
> Die Here is wonderbaar vir my.

God is wonderful (to me)
God is wonderful (to me)
Let us seek Him.
Let us praise Him.
God is wonderful (to me).

!Hirike !kho-a nǀâ ng
!Hirike !kho-a nǀâ ng
Sie si tjui ku
A kang koe ke.
!Hirike !kho-a nǀâ ng.

These texts are the product of four years' work by Levi learning the language and developing an orthography and of forty years learning his own tradition of storytelling. It is an extraordinary achievement, deeply bound up with traditions of scholarship that go back thousands of years and are refreshingly free of the postcolonial cant that equates adaptation and change with complicity and capitulation. Levi's reading represents the very best of both storytelling and scholarship, made possible by the very best of storytelling and scholarship from the ≠Khomani elders, whose capacity for believing two contradictory things at the same time is part of their imaginative achievement and reminds us of something important about our own.

It also raises a set of questions about the relations between oral and written texts and between European-African agricultural and aboriginal hunter-gatherer traditions; about the role that the language of a story or song, secular or sacred, plays in whether we believe it or not; about whether at the end of it all we believe the singer or the song, the teller or the tale; and about how to balance engagement and detachment, sympathy and judgment, the intensity and mystery of performance with the relative casualness and clarity of commentary.

You will recall my opening parable. Here's another. A few years ago, the Gitksan went to court to assert their claim to their aboriginal territory in the northwest of British Columbia. They told the history of their people with reluctance but with all the ritual required, for the stories and songs that represent their past—*ada'ox*, they call them—are about belief and therefore need ceremony. It was a particular moment in that case that started me on my journey to the Kalahari and to my work with Levi Namaseb. One of the Gitksan elders, Antgulilibix (Mary Johnson), was telling her *ada'ox* to the court. At a certain point she said that she now had to sing a song. The judge was appalled; the request seemed to him to flout the decorum of his court. He tried to explain how uncomfortable he felt having someone sing in his court; he said it made him feel "judicially embarrassed." He tried to make the plaintiffs understand that hearing a song was unlikely to get him any nearer the truth that he was seeking. He asked the lawyer for the Gitksan whether it might not be sufficient to have the words written down and avoid the performance. Finally, he agreed to let Mary Johnson sing her song; but just as she was about to start, he fired his final salvo. "It's not going to do any good to sing it to me," he said. "I have a tin ear."

It was a stupid thing to say, for he wasn't the least bit interested in the song or its music. He would have been right at home among many contemporary literary critics, who seem to want to hear only about the subject, and the subject position, of a text. But it was also a smart thing to say, for he did have a tin ear; he couldn't have heard the music even if he had been interested in it. Most of us go through life assuming that we can make not only music but also meaning out of Mary Johnson's song. For the Mary Johnsons of the world, it is a sinister assumption that understanding sophisticated oral traditions comes naturally to the sympathetic ear. It doesn't. Just as we learn how to read, so we learn how to listen; and such learning does not come naturally. Something more than sincerity is required. It is what Northrop Frye used to call an educated imagination.

Belligerent conservatives ask better questions than sympathetic liberals do. That's why I'm interested in Judge Allan McEachern and his tin ear and his tendentious "Why not just write it down?" One answer is emerging from our work in the Kalahari, but it is also evident close to home. Across all cultures, the protocols of speaking and listening are at least as stern as those of writing and reading. Certain things must be said and done in the right order and by the right people on the right occasions with the right people present for a funeral oration to give comfort or for a celebratory song to give praise or for a history to be true.

An extreme instance of this dedication to the decorums of language and liturgy occurred several years ago among the Gitksan, when an elder was asked to speak and sing his *ada'ox*, known only to him. Because of various circumstances in the community—some people had moved away for a time, others had become uninterested—nobody had heard it for years. The elder was old, ill, and not likely to live much longer. He needed to tell the tales so that they would not be forgotten and so that a central part of the history of the people would not be lost.

He refused. He said that the kinfolk who tradition prescribed should listen to the story were all dead and that although he could put on the appropriate regalia and go to the designated spot at just the right time, it wouldn't work. It would be just words.

All kinds of arguments were put to him to get him to change his mind. But he wouldn't be persuaded. His refusal had nothing to do with denying authority or offending the ancestors. It had to do with making meaning. To perform his *ada'ox* without the right people there to listen would be meaningless, he insisted.

So he died without speaking. And with him went a whole cycle of stories and songs that had been handed down and held secure for thousands of years. A great library, holding knowledge that existed nowhere else in the world.

We—Levi and I—do not know the answers to the questions that we have raised in our presentation. We do know that our collaboration has brought us closer to an understanding of how important they are and how intimately related they are to questions we circle around every day when we read and listen to stories and songs—which is to say, when we study literature.

WORKS CITED

Frye, Northrop. *The Educated Imagination*. Bloomington: Indiana UP, 1964.
Jousse, Marcel. *The Anthropology of Geste and Rhythm*. Ed. Edgard Sienaert. Trans. in collaboration with Joan Conolly. Durban: Centre for Oral Studies, U of Natal, 1997.
Ladefoged, P., and I. Maddieson. *The Sounds of the World's Languages*. Oxford: Blackwell, 1996.
Ong, Walter J. *Orality and Literacy: The Technologizing of the Word*. New York: Methuen, 1982.

What Search Committees Want

WALTER BROUGHTON AND WILLIAM CONLOGUE

Preprofessionalism among graduate students in English has been a hotly debated topic for some time. Prominent onlookers argue that it—especially early publication and conference presentation—keeps students from "developing long-term intellectual projects and thus propagates intellectual shallowness" (Guillory 4; see Spacks). Others point out that there is nothing inherently wrong with such activity, as long as it does not amount to "inferior professionalization" (Nelson 162). Understandably, graduate students are caught in the middle, wondering what to do and when to do it.

Something is obviously wrong when new PhDs believe that before they can even enter the job market they must acquire the credentials that once earned tenure. To investigate the phenomenon, the Modern Language Association last year created the Ad Hoc Committee on the Professionalization of PhDs, whose task, in part, is to "study the growing pressure on the productivity of graduate students and the practices of hiring departments, [and] assess the educational and professional value of the publishing and conference activities graduate students pursue" (*Ad Hoc Committee*). In its deliberations, the committee must address an important question: Is the drive among graduate students to amass professional accomplishments matched by the expectations of the search committees that seek to hire them?

Though graduate students have been getting much advice about how to prepare for the job market, they have received little hard information about what search committees want from candidates (Showalter; Curren, "No

---

Walter Broughton is Associate Professor of Sociology at Marywood University. William Conlogue is Associate Professor of English at Marywood University.

Openings" 59). To shed some light on the demand side of the hiring process, we offer the results of a survey that sought answers to the following questions: How do English departments conduct a typical search? What kinds of professional qualifications do committees expect from candidates? Is a publication record really more important than teaching experience? How significant are interpersonal skills? What egregious errors kill a candidacy?

Methods

We began putting the questionnaire together in April 2000. During the summer, we reviewed issues of the *Job Information List* (*JIL*) and identified a total of 671 English departments that had conducted searches in 1998–99 and 1999–2000. We ignored departments that listed only postdoctoral and other fellowships, and we excluded interdisciplinary programs, unless it was clear from the ad that the program was housed in an English department. In mid-October, we mailed our anonymous survey to these 671 departments; sent out two follow-up letters and one e-mail message in the following months; handled dozens of phone calls, letters, and e-mail messages; and resolved several minicrises before receiving the last return on 27 April 2001. In all, we received back 368 completed surveys, for a response rate of 55%.

To show the representativeness of our sample, table 1 compares our returns' percentages regarding rank and specialty with those of the positions advertised in the October 1998 and 1999 *JIL*s (given in Franklin 4–5). Note the relatively high proportion of assistant professorships reported by our respondents, a bias that also shows up in an earlier and similar survey done by the Association of Departments of English (Huber, Pinney, and Laurence 40). Our data regarding the specialties sought by search committees are consistent with the MLA's. Rhetoric and composition constitutes 25% of vacancies in our survey and 27% of definite positions in the October 1998 and 1999 *JIL*s. Our results are heavy in British literature positions (28%) compared with those of the *JIL*s (21%), though this difference may be because our sample overrepresents assistant professorships, which are more likely to be advertised and filled as British literature positions (Huber, Pinney, and Laurence 46). Our American literature percentage is identical to the *JIL*s' (11%), as is our creative writing percentage (8%). African American and other minority literatures are underrepresented in our sample (6%) compared with the *JIL*s (11%).

To catch more small departments at small institutions—they hire less frequently than do large departments—we chose to use two years of *JIL* listings rather than one. At the same time, because we consulted only the

TABLE 1
VACANCY CHARACTERISTICS IN THE OCTOBER 1998 AND 1999 *JIL*s AND AS REPORTED BY SURVEY RESPONDENTS (PERCENTAGE)

	POSITIONS ADVERTISED IN OCTOBER 1998 AND OCTOBER 1999 *JIL*s	POSITIONS REPORTED BY RESPONDENTS IN THE SURVEY OF ENGLISH SEARCH COMMITTEE CHAIRS
Advertised rank[a]		
Instructor or lecturer	5.9	4.3
Assistant professor	75.0	84.0
Associate professor	6.4	4.1
Full professor	2.5	2.2
Open rank	4.4	4.3
Other[b]	5.8	1.1
(N) = 100%	(1,733)[c]	(368)
Specialty field		
American literature	11.1	10.9
African American, Hispanic, and other minority literatures	10.9	6.0
British literature	20.8	28.1
Rhetoric and composition	26.7	25.4
Creative writing	7.8	8.3
Other	22.7	21.4
(N) = 100%	(1,784)[c]	(368)

[a]From "Positions Listed, by Rank"
[b]Department chair and senior visiting professorships, for example
[c]Excludes fellowships and program director vacancies

JIL, our results underrepresent searches in community colleges and four-year institutions, since both are less likely than doctoral programs to advertise vacancies with the MLA.[1]

When reviewing the results of surveys such as ours, it is important to remember that the population of departments recruiting at any given time is quite different from the universe of all English departments. Departments in doctoral institutions, because they are typically big, recruit more often, hire more faculty members, and command a larger share of the labor market. For example, though departments in research universities constitute only 11% of all departments in the United States (Laurence, "Data"), they constitute 26% of our sample. Moreover, in the two years we study, doctoral departments are responsible for 48% of the listings in the

October *JIL*s (Laurence, "Request"). However, their actual market share is substantially less. In the best estimate available to date, Kurt Müller and R. Douglas LeMaster project that roughly 30% of all English positions filled in any given year are in that Carnegie sector (52).[2]

A Typical Search

Assistant professor positions make up 84% of searches in our sample (table 1). Sixty-three percent of search committees accept applications from ABDs, and the vast majority of openings in our sample are tenure-track (93%). The last percentage may be high, because departments that advertised multiple openings were able to answer our questionnaire only on the basis of one search. We surmise that respondents were more likely to report on successful tenure-track searches than on unsuccessful ones.

More than half of all search committees (58%) handle fewer than 100 applications. A significant minority (16%), however, receive more than 200. The mean number of applicants is 99. In the ADE study, the mean is 91 (Huber, Pinney, and Laurence 43). The competition for jobs is obviously stiff, but these numbers should put to rest the misconception that hundreds of applications flood every department that advertises an opening (Curren, "Response" 45; Musser 11).

A significant number of committees do not interview candidates at the MLA convention (38%). Over half (54%), however, do interview eight or more people there. Doctoral institutions are the most intensive convention users; 71% of committees at these institutions interview eight or more candidates. Nearly 60% of committees do not use remote interviews—that is, telephone or compressed video. Of those that do, the average number of interviews is five. Nearly half of all search committees (47%) bring three applicants to campus for interviews, a number consistent with psychology searches (Sheehan, McDevitt, and Ross 9).

Our survey affirms that English faculty members take active roles in the screening and hiring of new colleagues. Less than 1% of respondents reported that their academic administration conducted searches with little or no faculty participation. Committees conducted 82% of the searches in our sample; in only one case did a department chair handle a search alone. A significant minority of respondents—typically those in small departments—reported that their entire department acted as the search committee (15%).

Of the committees surveyed, 12% had a serious disagreement with the institution's administration. Of those, the most frequent disagreements centered on the committee's choice of candidates, its evaluation of candidates, the job description, and the position's funding.

In the vast majority of searches, the committee's first choice was accepted by the university's administration (97%). Weak scholarship and the perception that the candidate would make a poor institutional fit were cited as the most frequent reasons for the rejection of a first choice. The numbers here are very small, however. Only ten respondents noted that their committee's first choice was rejected; the two main reasons were each cited by only four respondents.

A significant minority of all searches ended with the position unfilled (12%). Our study and the ADE study both found that positions go unfilled primarily due to an "inadequate candidate pool" (Huber, Pinney, and Laurence 43). Among all searches in our sample, 6% were unable to fill their vacancy because candidates refused the institution's offer; in 4% of cases, the position went unfilled because no suitable candidate was found.

Evaluating Candidates

Candidate evaluation begins with a review of application materials submitted in answer to an advertised vacancy. Table 2 records the importance respondents accorded twenty-one elements at this initial stage. Most of these items come from a study of hiring in psychology (Sheehan, McDevitt, and Ross 9), but we included others of interest to us. Scores ran from 1, "extremely unimportant," to 6, "extremely important." Values above 3.5 indicate that the item is important to recruiters; items below 3.5 are unimportant. In addition to the average (mean) ranking, table 2 also records standard deviations, which indicate how far from the mean a typical respondent rated an item. The greater the standard deviation, the greater the disagreement among respondents.

In evaluating candidates, the English faculty members in our sample judged the candidate's "potential for making a positive contribution to the institution as a whole" to be more important than any other consideration. It and the letter of application were ranked highest, and both enjoyed substantial agreement—standard deviations for each are less than 1.0. Letters of recommendation were ranked fourth. General teaching experience and experience teaching the advertised specialties were both ranked highly, more highly than research specialties and the potential for future research. Farther down the list the same pattern holds: evidence of teaching ability outranks evidence of research ability. Specifically, course evaluations and teaching awards were cited as more important than the number and quality of the candidate's publications. The numbers of papers presented and authoring a book were both deemed unimportant, although authoring a book has a large standard deviation, indicating that some respondents rated it much more

TABLE 2
SCREENING CRITERIA: MEANS AND STANDARD DEVIATIONS

CRITERION	MEAN	STANDARD DEVIATION
Potential for making a positive contribution to the institution as a whole	5.36	0.87
Candidate's letter of application	5.32	0.87
General teaching experience	5.17 (4.99)[a]	0.79
Letters of recommendation	5.06 (5.37)	0.97
Experience teaching courses related to the position description	4.99 (5.10)	1.01
Fit between the applicant's research interests and the department's needs	4.83 (5.11)	1.31
Potential for future research	4.73 (4.09)	1.29
Quality of the applicant's doctoral institution	4.12 (4.04)	1.11
Quality of course evaluations	4.10 (4.55)	1.32
Awards for teaching	3.87 (4.00)	1.27
Transcripts	3.75	1.39
Quality of journals in which the applicant published	3.73 (4.45)	1.37
Ability to incorporate new technologies in teaching	3.57	1.33
Number of publications	3.56 (4.42)	1.31
Academic service activities and experience (committee work, etc.)	3.42	1.20
Number of presentations	3.37	1.14
Previous experience as a student or faculty member in a college or university with a mission similar to your own	3.23	1.46
Book authorship	2.91	1.55
Experience working with student clubs and groups	2.58	1.27
Community service	2.55	1.20
Candidate's religious preference and/or commitment	1.44	1.29

[a]Psychology means, from Sheehan, McDevitt, and Ross

highly than others. Finally, service, one of the three traditional areas of faculty responsibility, was consistently declared unimportant. Evidently, this aspect of professionalization is not generally a factor in recruitment.

Table 3 records the ranking accorded twenty items likely to be important at the on-campus interview stage. At this point, interpersonal skills and performances can be—and are—judged. Our sample's recruiters rank highest the candidate's performance at the interview with the search committee; the job seeker's performance at the interview with the department

TABLE 3
ON-CAMPUS INTERVIEW CRITERIA: MEANS AND STANDARD DEVIATIONS

CRITERION	MEAN	STANDARD DEVIATION
Performance at interview with the search committee	5.51 (5.21)[a]	0.84
Potential for making a positive contribution to the institution as a whole	5.36	0.93
Candidate's ability to relate well to students like ours	5.35	0.75
General teaching experience	4.93 (4.80)	0.83
Performance during colloquium	4.92 (5.12)	1.48
Candidate's ability to get along with other faculty	4.89 (4.84)	0.91
Experience teaching courses related to the position description	4.84 (4.91)	1.02
Fit between applicant's research interests and department needs	4.73 (5.10)	1.29
Performance while teaching a class	4.70 (4.91)	1.80
Candidate's personality	4.65 (4.62)	0.96
Letters of recommendation	4.63 (4.68)	1.16
Performance at interview with department chair	4.45 (4.60)	1.32
Quality of course evaluations	4.10	1.33
Teaching awards	3.75	1.26
Quality of journals in which applicant published	3.73	1.37
Number of publications	3.58	1.27
Previous experience as a student or faculty member in a college or university with a mission similar to your own	3.42	1.54
Number of presentations	3.22	1.15
Book authorship	2.87	1.56
Candidate's religious preference and/or commitment	1.46	1.31

[a]Psychology means, from Sheehan, McDevitt, and Ross

chair, although deemed important, is ranked much lower. Performance at a colloquium and while teaching a class are very important, but note that the standard deviation of each is quite high. Indeed, the greatest disagreement in the survey is over the significance of performance while teaching a class. The ability to relate to students and to faculty members and the candidate's personality all emerge, in that order, as important during the on-campus visit. Respondents agree on the significance of these considerations; each has a standard deviation less than 1.0.

At the on-campus stage, the candidate's potential for making a contribution to the institution as a whole is once again rated very highly. Teaching and research abilities remain important, although their values are now slightly lower than at the initial screening. Likewise, letters of reference remain important, but their value drops slightly compared with that in the first stage. Once again, service is thought to be unimportant.

Screening applications appears to be a more uncertain and contentious process than is screening candidates during the on-campus visit. Our data suggest that there is less agreement among search committees about what is important in a candidate's dossier than there is in assessing the candidate in person. Note that only four items at the application stage (table 2) have a standard deviation less than 1.0. In addition, only nine criteria have a mean greater than 4. In table 3, however, six items have a standard deviation less than 1.0, and thirteen criteria have a mean greater than 4.

Once candidates come to campus, search committees clearly direct their attention to the interpersonal skills that manifest themselves in teaching and in student and collegial interactions. Are candidates' interpersonal skills then deciding factors in who gets the job? Several respondents volunteered observations that suggest that this is so. For example, a department chair with over fifteen years of experience at a baccalaureate institution comments:

> The importance of personality, etc., vs. qualifications in hiring is difficult to [determine]. The process starts by screening out unqualified candidates; then in narrowing[,] qualifications are extremely important. So when the final decision is made among the top two or three candidates, in almost every circumstance, all of them are *highly* and *relatively equally qualified*. So in the *final* decision, personality usually plays a big part. But it wouldn't if qualifications weren't so important at all the earlier stages of the process.

Several attitude items that we asked lend support to these assertions. Over one-quarter of respondents (27%) think that personality and appearance often have more influence than credentials in the selection of candidates; nonetheless, in answer to another question, 56% agree that academic qualifications are the most important consideration. Although most believe that credentials are of paramount importance in hiring a new colleague, respondents acknowledge that a mix of factors informs a committee's decision making.

Much more than English search committees, those in psychology expect job candidates to have a track record in research presentation and publication. Tables 2 and 3 record in parentheses how psychologists rank each hiring criterion. Though the two disciplines generally agree in their ratings, psychologists tend to screen applications according to teaching and research specialization and publication. Placing less emphasis on a candidate's *potential* for research, they instead focus on the candidate's number of publications and the quality of the journals in which those publications appear. During the on-campus visit, psychologists put more weight than English faculty members do on the interview with the chair and less on the interview with the committee. Psychologists look closely at a candidate's performance during a colloquium and during the teaching of a class; they also continue to value specialization in teaching and research more highly than do their colleagues in English. Psychologists more often want "pre-professionalized" candidates.

English departments in doctoral institutions, however, resemble psychology departments in the emphasis they place on specialization and scholarly accomplishment. Twenty-three percent of search committees in doctoral institutions believe that a candidate's number of publications is "extremely important" when screening applications. In contrast, only 1% of committees in baccalaureate institutions rank publication as extremely important at this stage. Interestingly, departments in doctoral institutions also attribute greater importance than other departments to the number of presentations, but *only* in screening. Presentations are considered unimportant at the interview stage, no matter what the institution's Carnegie classification. Even among doctoral institutions, presentations are less important during screening than the number of publications and the prestige of the journals in which they appear.

An institution's Carnegie classification also predicts how much its English department emphasizes teaching in its evaluation of candidates. Table 3 shows that respondents disagree about the importance of a candidate's on-campus teaching performance. Specifically, teaching a class is extremely important for 60% of respondents in baccalaureate institutions; likewise, 52% of respondents in comprehensive institutions rate it as extremely important. When one turns to doctoral institutions, however, the percentage drops precipitously: only 28% rate teaching a class as extremely important; 32% rate this criterion as *extremely unimportant*. Finally departments in doctoral institutions rank the candidate's ability to contribute to the institution as a whole less highly than do those in any other Carnegie classification. New PhDs in English are entering a segmented labor market.

Selecting the First Choice

We asked respondents to list the top three factors used to determine the committee's first choice. We divided the responses into four categories: teaching, research, service, and interpersonal skills. Nearly two-thirds (63%) cited teaching ability, performance, or experience as a deciding factor.

Forty-four percent cited research accomplishments or potential. Twenty-eight percent volunteered that the candidate's interpersonal skills were decisive. Service was hardly mentioned (6%). These results underscore what the survey as a whole reveals: the model candidate is first a good teacher.

We also asked respondents to cite errors that "negatively affected [candidates'] chances of being hired." Half of those surveyed noted at least one error. The error most frequently cited was poor or indifferent teaching. Poor presentation of research was a close second, followed by poor interpersonal skills, ignorance of the institution, and a lack of breadth of knowledge. Here are examples of the responses that this question elicited:

Poor Teaching
"One never talked about teaching."
"Focus on release time/money—questions about ways to avoid classroom teaching."
"One taught one of the most boring classes I've ever seen. Another talked about how lazy, uninformed, and so forth our students are—of course, they're not."
"One candidate appeared to consider himself superior to the teaching required at our college. (He seemed to think that nurturing basic writers would be beneath him.)"

Poor Presentation of Research
"Reluctance to engage in discussion of research area."
"Presentations which are too technical or too insubstantial."
"Did a lousy presentation. Was churlish during dinner."
"Presented a paper in an area that she was working on but [that] did not reveal range of research experience in the field."

Poor Interpersonal Skills
"Behavior perceived as insulting, dismissive."
"During one of the interview questions, she threw up her arms and said, 'Jesus.'"
"One candidate was overly argumentative, even belligerent, during the interview with the search committee."
"One campus visitor ignored many important people and failed to thank those who helped him."

Ignorance of the Hiring Institution
"Not knowing enough about the institution."
"Emphasizing research over teaching. We are a teaching institution."
"Failure to demonstrate interest in our college or a general knowledge of who we are."

Narrow Focus
"Some were unable to demonstrate an ability to move beyond a rather narrowly focused research agenda—this lack of range and flexibility hurt a few otherwise very strong candidates."

"She came with her hair in an outlandish coif and seemed incapable of assessing the world outside her dissertation topic."

"Some could not talk beyond/outside of their own dissertations. They exhibited a deathly nervousness."

These criticisms are not unique to English; the psychology survey cites similar criticisms of candidates in that field (Sheehan, McDevitt, and Ross 10). When strangers with divergent interests negotiate for high stakes, misunderstanding and injured pride can skew people's judgment. What was happening in the interview in which the candidate threw up her arms and said, "Jesus"? Did she overreact, or was the question outrageous? Why the attention to a candidate's hair? When does the defense of one's position cross the line into belligerency? Do nervous candidates sometimes overstate their positions? Or do some committee members perceive it to be arrogant when heavily credentialed applicants cite their accomplishments? Certainly, both sides run the risk—and know the costs—of making a mistake. Is this why many committee members turn to instinct? When asked if gut-level reactions are important in the hiring process, 73% of respondents agreed that they are. Without empathy and tolerance, however, misinterpretation, selective observation, and rationalization can rule the moment.

According to our findings, the typical English department search committee seeks a tenure-track assistant professor with a PhD in literature, most commonly British. These committees are entrusted with the task and experience little conflict with the academic administration. After sifting through nearly a hundred applications, a committee interviews eight or more candidates at the MLA convention and then invites its top three choices to campus. Afterward, the committee forwards its first choice to the administration, and the search ends successfully and—for the committee—happily. Over half of all respondents (57%) to our questionnaire agreed that participating in a faculty search is a highly satisfying experience.

When screening applications and on-campus candidates, English departments generally look for evidence of good teaching first and research potential second. Only in doctoral institutions does research rival teaching. Across the board, the candidate with the best interpersonal skills—all else being equal—is offered the job.

What do search committees want? Our data indicate that the vast majority seek a candidate who can effectively teach specific courses to the students the English department serves. The committees want a colleague who will work collaboratively with their department's faculty members and who will fit in well with their institution. Only a minority of committees seek a candidate with a book or publications. Committees that do, of course, work in the same departments that are preparing candidates to work in the entire spectrum of English departments. It is perhaps mainly because this minority trains everyone that so many believe that "preprofessionalism" is required to get a job.

NOTES

The authors are indebted to Linda Hutcheon for her moral support and to the Marywood Office of Academic Affairs for its financial support. We are grateful also to David Laurence, who provided supplementary data from the records of the MLA, and to Lois Santarsiero and Meghan McCrea for their indispensable clerical work.

[1] In their 1982–83 survey of English departments, Müller and LeMaster found that 14% of community colleges and 67% of those institutions granting BA or BA and MA degrees (compared with 85% of the doctoral programs) advertised vacancies in the *JIL* (54 [reconstructed from table 4]).

[2] The 48% of *JIL* listings cited above is close to the proportion of the market commanded by doctoral institutions as reported in the surveys of Müller and LeMaster, 40% (52) and of Huber, Pinney, and Laurence, 46% (45). These surveys, however, overestimate this market share, because the response rate of doctoral programs was higher than those of all other Carnegie classifications. Moreover, doctoral programs are most likely to advertise in the *JIL*. When Müller and LeMaster project the number of hires per year, however, they apply the hiring rate of each Carnegie type in their survey to the total number of all departments of that type, thereby reducing the overestimation.

WORKS CITED

Ad Hoc Committee on the Professionalization of PhDs. MLA. 11 May 2001. 15 May 2001 <http://www.mla.org/>, click on "Committees and Commissions."
Curren, Erik D. "No Openings at This Time: Job Market Collapse and Graduate Education." *Profession 94*. New York: MLA, 1994. 57–61.
———. "Response to John T. Day." *ADE Bulletin* 111 (1995): 45–46.
Franklin, Phyllis. "October 2000 Employment Trends." *MLA Newsletter* 33.1 (2001): 4–7.
Guillory, John. "Preprofessionalism: What Graduate Students Want." *ADE Bulletin* 113 (1996): 4–8.
Huber, Bettina J., Denise Pinney, and David Laurence. "Patterns of Faculty Hiring in Four-Year English Programs: Findings from a 1987–88 Survey of *Job Information List* Advertisers." *ADE Bulletin* 99 (1991): 39–48.
Laurence, David. "Re: Fwd: Data Request for David Laurence." E-mail message to Walter Broughton. 19 May 2001.
———. "Re: Request for David Laurence." E-mail message to Walter Broughton. 22 May 2001.
Müller, Kurt, and R. Douglas LeMaster. "Criteria Used in Selecting English Faculty in American Colleges and Universities." *ADE Bulletin* 77 (1984): 51–57.
Musser, Joseph. "The On-Campus Interview." *ADE Bulletin* 111 (1995): 11–13.

Nelson, Cary. "No Wine before Its Time: The Panic over Early Professionalization." *Profession 2000*. New York: MLA, 2000. 157–63.
"Positions Listed, by Rank." Table obtained from MLA 26 Apr. 2001.
Sheehan, Eugene P., Teresa M. McDevitt, and Heather C. Ross. "Looking for a Job as a Psychology Professor? Factors Affecting Applicant Success." *Teaching of Psychology* 25.1 (1998): 8–11.
Showalter, English. "The Academic Job Search." *The MLA Guide to the Job Search*. Ed. Showalter et al. New York: MLA, 1996. 16–56.
Spacks, Patricia Meyer. "The Academic Marketplace: Who Pays Its Costs?" *MLA Newsletter* 26.2 (1994): 3.

I Profess: Another View of Professionalization

JENNIFER WICKE

Denial and disavowal are prominent features of graduate programs in the humanities but perhaps especially so in English, where there is an institutionalized reluctance to admit that undertaking a PhD in the field constitutes entering a professional arena with rules, guidelines, and protocols that may remain unarticulated yet exert an all-powerful force on the discipline. Whether this river of denial stems from the fraught history of graduate English study in Britain and the United States or whether it arises from the wellspring of complex cultural forms of literary production, reception, and circulation outside the academy, where a similar disavowal insists on the nobility and purity of the literary artifact, professionalism has been an oxymoronic bedfellow of graduate study in literature. Indeed, professionalization has only recently been acknowledged as the underpinning of the profession of English at the faculty level, since for many the teaching of English in the academy still retains a whiff of lofty amateurism or a clubby kind of apprenticeship in literary appreciation. Often the very departments and faculties who administer and award PhD degrees fail to acknowledge that by doing so a profession is being shaped and reproduced. The conservative version of this antipathy is that professionalization is crude and destructive and that professionalized students are upstarts. The ostensibly progressive wing explains its dislike by analogy to an industrial speedup of otherwise leisurely graduate study. Some find early specialization a threat to graduate education

---

The author is Professor of English at the University of Virginia. A version of this paper was presented at the 2000 MLA convention in Washington, DC.

(Bérubé; Guillory). Neither form of dislike for professionalization faces the fact that for graduate students to reproduce the profession, they must be inducted into it as professionals. Medical students, for example, climb a professional ladder, but they are considered doctors even when interns and residents. Graduate students in English departments should receive the same treatment. There can be an equally serious reluctance on the part of graduate students to acknowledge professional demands when they are veiled by the rhetoric of extraneous market forces impinging on doctoral studies. Students understandably resist or shy away from specialization or professionalization when it appears to be the antithesis of intellectual inquiry and wide-ranging study. But when we profess as teachers and as scholars, we do so as professionals, members of a professional class, and those who aspire to profess deserve training in professional codes. To wit, they need professionalization.

As a group, we are rightly suspicious of the academic market as one that can indeed devalue the integrity of the knowledge we seek and are rightly critical of market incursions or corporate interventions into previously uncolonized parts of the academy. Literature and the humanities, given their very modest commercial standing even within the university, have the most to lose in such market forays, and professionalization has been regarded as the thin edge of the market wedge. Those who adopt or advocate professional strategies are seen as the advance guard of corporate assaults on the academy or as an internal fifth column, succumbing to creeping and invidious market forces. But I would argue that it is disingenuous to ignore professional and institutional structures as if these are latter-day elements or foreign imports; they assuredly are not. The failure to professionalize graduate students in the face of the self-evident professional norms and criteria that govern our academic practice is even more damaging. Recognition of the professional aspects of our field and, above all, of how negotiating the looming job market depends on the ability to regard oneself as a professional requires one to play both sides of the net. The critique of professionalism is important and urgent where the critique is not simply nostalgia for a nonprofessional time that in fact never existed. Decrying the ill effects of specialization and professionalization on graduate students, as many faculty members are wont to do, is only helpful if students are being given a chance to think of themselves as part of the profession, not as apprentices in a mysterious guild whose meritocratic forces will work their magic in due time, around eight or ten years after the students begin graduate study. I literally cannot count the times in my own academic life when colleagues have spoken of professionalism among graduate students with smirks, sneers, or foreboding; nor can I track the many laments made in person and in print about graduate students publishing (too early!) or attending conferences (in droves!). Let them critique professionalism as professionals, fully aware of the strategies and standards that are invoked by faculty members who may try to pretend these don't exist. Our failure to provide guidance in professionalism is not critique by default; it is hiding our collective heads in the sand. Graduate students too can shrink from accepting their path as a professional one, but they ignore its strategies and demands at their peril.

Nowhere is this danger more telling than in publication, professionalism's public face. If one finds the pressures to publish unappealing or hesitates to engage the profession as a scholar and writer as well as a teacher of literature and culture, one is probably pursuing the wrong profession, at least in the twenty-first century, when the amateurist and generalist approaches have been for the most part eliminated. Even well-meaning faculty members who wish to protect their graduate students from what they see as the rather merciless rough-and-tumble of professionalism—trying to cling to an ethic of nonprofessionalization that never obtained in their own careers—are actually hindering them.

Publication is in some eyes the grimmest horseman of professionalist apocalypse. Instead publication should be viewed, along with conference attendance and other aspects of professionalization, in the context of an economy of abundance rather than of scarcity. The economy of abundance I refer to is not the job market or the national economy seen through rose-colored glasses; it is seeing the plenitude of possibilities to publish as something good for our field. Publication is neither (or not only) a means of staving off professional demise nor a magical feat far beyond graduate students whose professors hold them in thrall of something called "the publishable article." It is a way of achieving one's professional wings; of calling one's own intellectual shots; of entering an arena of debate and discussion broader than one's department; of recasting the labor of writing course papers as a step toward advancing one's writing tout court; and of reevaluating or reenvisioning the supreme effort of the dissertation. I borrow a term from mathematical set theory to attempt to explain the thaumaturgic ingredient capable of turning unprepossessing course papers, unaccepted conference paper proposals, or even discrete and inert dissertation chapters into that transmogrified thing, a published piece of work: *embeddedness*. In set theory this term refers to the way that sets lodge in other sets yet remain discrete. Embeddedness describes the sine qua non quality of publication, from a three-page review to a dissertation revisable as a book. The writing must demonstrate from the outset that it is embedded in a professional sphere where the argument or issue or theorization of the essay, conference paper, or book arises in relation to the issues, critical history, current debates, disciplinary conflicts, major figures, or major texts of that sphere.

When graduate students are presented with the directive to write essays "of publishable quality," it becomes an empty criterion in the absence of tutelage in how to publish, a gold standard that simply seems to mean good or excellent, an ineffable seal of approval from the powers that be. But most graduate courses do not prepare students for the actual genres of academic publication: twenty-page journal articles; eight-to-ten-page conference papers; one-page abstracts of proposed projects; five-page reviews; the svelte 220-page first book that has four or five, not ten to fifteen, chapters and a brief introduction. Most graduate programs do not explicitly recognize the imperatives of publication for professional entry. The lame seminar presentation, which bears no resemblance to the swift thrust and parry of a good conference paper; the patronizing mock-conference model some professors are now offering instead of advice on how and why to get into an actual conference; the lack of schooling in how to be published, which means that journals and current books must be assigned and read so that students become aware of how to frame their own approaches to texts and issues not by dint of the individual professor's example but in the light of what is going on in the field now (which can and usually does include the work and thoughts of the professor); and the mind-boggling failures in directing students toward dissertations that, if they are not ultimately publishable, are a form of professional suicide before the fact—these quite typical sins of omission and commission keep publishing behind a veil of reverent mystery, with a sign saying, "Hands off, not for you."

If you wish to write for an audience of more than one, you will find that abstracts, conference papers, chapters, and course papers are publishable (in the attenuated sense of becoming public) only when they display professional embeddedness. Embedding is a technique that can be applied to preexisting work which has lain fallow: the effect is nothing short of miraculous, when you embed an unconnected close reading or critical speculation within the larger discussion surrounding it, including other important arguments, books, essays, critics, disciplinary debates, new discoveries, contradictions, and so forth, to find that the kernel of what you had has become powerful and publishable, which means legible to a public, as a result. By embedding your argument in the professional conversations that surround that argument, its field, texts, or problematic, you make your writing part of academic discourse. You are situating your work in relation to that of others, underscoring the foundations you build on, making explicit where you part company with a standard argument or seminal critic or theoretical stance. Even nontheoretical writing needs to declare its methodology: this declaration is what separates the unpublishably naive effort from the published version. The reality of all academic writing, however pyrotechnic, magisterial, or gloriously penetrating it may be, is that no one—no one—writes out of or with reference to nothing. The subtlety of the embedding, the intellectual and even stylistic deftness with which it is accomplished, is the hallmark of powerful writing. Without such situating, even a vibrant thesis or essay or jeu d'esprit looks uncertain of its professional origins, denuded, and innocent of what has gone before.

The approach to the dissertation as a publication epitomizes the logic of professionalization. While large changes in the nature of university press publishing, in online publication, and in altered requirements for tenure are no doubt in the offing, they are nowhere near materializing yet. For the nonce, the refusal to engage with dissertations as publications-to-be is irresponsible and crushing from the faculty side of things and willfully self-destructive from the graduate student side. Even if a dissertation does not become a book, it is the job market calling card par excellence: without the embedding inherent in publishable writing, the project will be less than it could be and less compelling as a synecdoche for a person's work. To enter into the writing of the dissertation as if it is directed toward publication from its inception is the way to write a distinguished dissertation. No one can afford to write a nonprofessional dissertation anymore, that is, a work designed never to see the light of day, a work relegated to outmoded notions of scholarly apprenticeship and the *longue durée* of the professional career. If the topic is not embeddable—if it does not take account of its embeddedness in a dynamic set of debates; in a problematic; in relation to other disciplines or issues; or in its active intersection with major arguments, critics, or discoveries in the field—it is not only not publishable, it is not a good topic. Dissertations can make an original contribution to knowledge only if they play out in the present state of the field of knowledge, situated self-consciously amid it and even at odds with it. They cannot be forms of homage or duplication, they cannot reinvent the wheel or defy the protocols of publication as we now know it—even Frank Kermode couldn't get a 600-page book published, I'd wager. Their hermetic seal needs to be broken, so that fragments of the dissertation enter into publication early on, in the form of conference papers, essays, and so forth, to crystallize their embedded (i.e., professional) quality and break down the Golden Mountain Syndrome of the project as an arduous whole. To conceive of a dissertation as a porous conversation with a far-flung and ever-changing profession is to be freed from the vestiges of teacher-student folie à deux or intellectual ménage à trois by committee that can make writing a dissertation seem so insular, so impossible, so unutterably lonely.

There is a huge freedom available as a side effect of this notion of publication and professionalism: graduate students may enter any discursive conversation once they have paid the dues of embedding. Those dues are not slick gimmicks or the wages of premature specialization but the intellectual price of admission. The more you know, the more you can embed and the more your work is correspondingly embedded. Such tactics are not antiintellectual, superficial, or merely cosmetic. Deploying them offers a profound benefit, in that joining a conversation beyond the confines of one's graduate course work or institutional culture is liberating and empowering. Of course it is silly and even criminal to ignore the exigencies of the job market, the crisis in the humanities, the perils of a graduate career, and the real suffering and exploitation that abound in the academy. Accusing graduate students of too much professionalism or of a distorting preprofessionalism leaves them out in the cold and is to my mind the profession's worst instance of blaming the victim. Unless graduate students are lucky enough to be in a program where the profession's limitations and cruelties qua profession are deplored and fought yet where professionalization, with its myriad strategies and its projection toward futurity, is nonetheless taught and modeled, they will be left to do much of this on their own.

There is nothing so empowering as seizing authority for your own work, and paradoxically this empowerment is accomplished only when you acknowledge the larger professional horizon in which anything you ever do as a professor will be embedded. No longer will or should your writing be about impressing or pleasing a single mentor or professorial reader. While that reading may be extraordinarily helpful and enriching to your work—or else what is graduate school for?—there is nothing so motivating as being part of the professional conversation, part of the sphere of publication that in some senses constitutes the profession. Graduate students are professionals to the extent they break through to the public sphere inherent in the profession, helped by the tutelage of their programs but aided most by self-acknowledgment. Professionalism can be taught, in part, but at its core it is a speech act, a declaration about oneself that becomes true by the action of declaring so. Professionalization may be a double-edged sword, but it is also the necessary step toward what becomes a self-fulfilling prophecy: I am in the profession because I am professional: I profess.

WORKS CITED

Bérubé, Michael. "The Contradictions of the Job Market in English." *Chronicle of Higher Education* 19 Dec. 1997: B7.

Guillory, John. "Preprofessionalism: What Graduate Students Want." *Profession 1996*. New York: MLA, 1996. 91–99.

The Academic Job Crisis and the Small-Schools Movement

HOLLY FRITZ AND DAVID SHERMAN

One of our most serious failures in literary studies has been to resist treating public high school teaching and research as worthy work. Secondary education is perhaps the extradisciplinary field both most appropriate for our professional participation and the one we most carefully ignore. While our departments may, in their healthier moments, promote practical discussions about jobs outside academia, these discussions largely focus on anything besides high school teaching: editing, public relations, university administration, technical writing, Internet publishing, journalism, corporate and archival research, and so on. In other words, most of our plan B professional strategies forgo the teaching of literature and language in principle as much as they ignore the availability of decently paid, relatively secure teaching jobs in mundane fact. This disciplinary near blindness seems to occur for two major reasons: we don't think high school academic work is rewarding, and we fear that we're not appropriately trained and credentialed to do it.

There is a growing movement in public school reform that is trying to prove us wrong on both counts. The small-schools movement is a widely lauded effort to provide an alternative to the large factory-model schools that have proved deadening to many students and teachers, especially in the worst schools of poor school districts. Based on principles of teacher auton-

Holly Fritz teaches eighth-grade women's studies and ninth-grade English at the Young Women's Leadership School, an all-girls public school in East Harlem, New York City. David Sherman is a doctoral student in English at New York University.

omy, student-centered learning, and social justice, these small, community-oriented, mostly urban schools need teachers skilled in facilitating classroom projects, doing academic research, developing curricula, and articulating the ways that engaging literature is relevant to struggles for self-determination.

The small-schools movement, which generally encompasses charter and alternative school movements, is a reaction against the massive conglomeration and standardization of public schools—especially high schools—that dramatically intensified in the United States in 1959. James Conant, scientist and former Harvard professor, wrote the influential 1959 report arguing for the consolidation of small schools into "comprehensive" ones with student tracking and standardized curricula. The concentration in past decades has been staggering: the number of schools in the United States has decreased by 70% since 1945, while average school size has increased fivefold; 40,000 school districts have been reduced to 16,000 since 1959; the 1.5 million citizens on school boards in 1930 now number a few hundred thousand, even though the country's population has doubled (Klonsky 29; Meier, "Crisis" 34).[1]

Attempts to reform such trends have focused heavily on cities, where schools with the worst problems have provoked community leaders, teachers, activists, and educational researchers to create systems of remarkable public schools since the late 1960s. Those of us looking for living-wage jobs and sustained careers teaching literature and composition should learn about them. Below, we describe these schools in more detail, argue that English PhDs can be a part of this movement, and, finally, speculate on why underemployed English PhDs have resisted working in schools that can use their skills and passions.

Charter and Alternative Public High Schools

A large body of statistical evidence has emerged in past decades confirming what many have known all along: students learn effectively in small classes with creative curricula and often suffer in large schools that follow industrial or military organizational logics.[2] On the basis of this evidence, educational reformers have created hundreds of high schools of between 150 and 500 students with classes typically of under 20. Traditional public high schools typically have about 2,000 students, can have as many as 5,000, and have classes of about 35 or more.[3] Further, classes in many small schools meet for longer periods and fewer times a week than in traditional schools (i.e., one hour four times a week, two hours every other day). While traditional high schools often serve students extremely well, their large size, shorter classes, and pressures to standardize curricula and student assessment can make teaching and learning difficult.

What are the pedagogical and organizational logics of small public schools? These fall into two general categories with different characteristics, although students pay no tuition at either: charter schools and alternative schools.[4] Charter schools receive some money from the state but little or none from their city governments, making up the difference with money from foundations, corporations, or other private sources.[5] This financial severing from their local school districts gives them the most bureaucratic autonomy and institutional flexibility of any public school, a flexibility that includes the ability to hire noncertified teachers. In general, charter schools share no common or even typical mission, structure, or pedagogy and are often indistinguishable from traditional schools.

Alternative public schools are fully funded through a combination of state and city funds, like other public schools, but are small enough to have a great deal of autonomy from centralized government bureaucracies to meet the particular needs of their communities. They also tend to share an interest in critical pedagogy and issues of social justice. Paulo Freire is probably the pedagogical and political theorist who has most influenced the principles of alternative public schools. He writes in *Pedagogy of the Oppressed*:

> "Problem-posing" education, responding to the essence of consciousness—*intentionality*—rejects communiqués and embodies communication. It epitomizes the special characteristic of consciousness: being *conscious of*, not only as intent on objects but as turned in upon itself in a Jasperian "split"—consciousness as consciousness *of* consciousness.
>
> Liberating education consists in acts of cognition, not transferals of information. (66–67)

Freire's large body of theoretical work relates "problem-posing" education to critical consciousness, political practice, and the intimate details of humanization (he unabashedly writes of hope and love in terms of both education and politics). His classroom models are radically dialogic; his concept of democracy depends on people experiencing their power to name, reimagine, and change the world. For Freire, education should be the transformative praxis that combines reflection and action, theoretical speculation and social intervention.

Freire's ideas, first developed while he taught literacy to the poorest workers in Brazil in the 1960s, have been adapted to North America and studied alongside the work of John Dewey, Henry Giroux, and others. While adapted to new contexts, Freire's essential imperative is the same: that a teacher not only impart information but also teach students how to critically interpret the production of information. "In all of Freire's teachings, the concept of truth becomes vitiatingly unwound as the truth becomes linked to one's emplacement in the reigning narratives *about* truth" (McLaren 50). Alternative high schools attempt to put this approach to truth, which should sound familiar to anyone in a university humanities program, into daily classroom practice.

This ambition requires a complete reconceptualization of what kind of institution a school should be. The scope and ambition of the small-schools movement, and especially of the effort to create alternative schools, have helped it address this question in forceful, imaginative ways. William Ayers, educational reformer and professor of education, gives a version of such an answer:

> Just as bigness was a deliberate policy, smallness is an intentional answer and antidote, a gesture toward the personal, the particular, the integrated, the supportive. Small schools is a counter-metaphor, perhaps, a more hopeful emblem. In small schools every student must be known well by some caring adult, and every student must have a realistic possibility of belonging to a community of learners. [. . .]
>
> Small schools is, as well, an emblem for teaching as intellectual and ethical work, and for teachers at the center of classroom practice. Teachers, then, collectively are responsible for the content and the conduct of their work—for curriculum, pedagogy, assessment—and, more, for the school lives for a specific group of students. Teachers are not mindless bureaucrats, soulless clerks, obedient and conforming quislings. [. . .] Small schools are places for visible teachers, and perhaps they are places to build a cohort of crusading teachers as well.
>
> Small schools is, finally, an emblem for parents and communities as the center of the school's life. Parents are not annoying outsiders to be tolerated, nor phony "partners" in a patronizing nod toward fairness. In small schools parents must be gift and asset, and often decision-makers regarding broad policy and direction. (5)

Ayers implies what other reformers say explicitly: the movement to create small, autonomous public high schools is both a pedagogical mission and a political effort to democratize school systems as a whole, one of the most embattled realms of the United States public sphere. In other words, the small-schools movement is not just a classroom application of empowering pedagogies but also a political application of the democratic principle that communities should determine how their children are educated (Meier, *Power* 107–18).

How do teachers ideally teach in alternative schools? In the first place, teachers of different subjects plan their lessons collaboratively (i.e., history and English; math and science; math, art, and music; art and humanities) in an attempt to make the high school curriculum interdisciplinary instead of merely generalist. Teachers emphasize the role of students in the classroom by encouraging and structuring student-initiated inquiry, in which students themselves define the questions they pursue about a particular text or subject.

More specifically, students do cooperative, extended research and writing projects instead of worksheets and multiple-choice tests. Teachers seldom lecture; they mainly design projects and direct dialogue. This subtle and demanding approach to teaching is partially enabled by the way that many teachers in alternative schools remain with a cohort of students for several years, changing grade levels with them and mentoring them in "advisory" classes as well as instructing them in academic ones (Klonsky 25). All these characteristics of alternative education require the autonomy of a small school, which has fewer students in a class, longer classes, and less bureaucratic and hierarchical decision-making processes about school policies than does a large school.

At their best, alternative high schools provide English classes that have the critical energy and readerly creativity of the university classes many of us teach or hope to teach. What high school students lack in theoretical sophistication they often compensate for with a clearer sense of worldly relevance and self-presence. The work produced by high school students is no less intellectual than that of more advanced students, which is to say, it is no less a product of animated intellects learning to assert themselves in new ways. Most important, these classes are accessible to and mostly attended by poor, ethnically diverse students, who especially benefit from the physical safety and academic resources of an alternative school.

While descriptions of such schools may help us in literary studies to imagine potential jobs, these descriptions must also be understood as extremely general and slightly idealized. The principles and philosophy driving school reform don't always materialize, thwarted by lack of money for essential materials or by the incompetence and bad faith of teachers, administrators, politicians, and so on. These shortcomings exacerbate the difficulties of teaching students who commonly come to alternative schools after being underserved by public schools for many years, leaving them below grade level—sometimes very far below—in their basic reading, writing, and math skills. Further, an alternative school's exemption from standardized state proficiency tests is increasingly rare in the current political climate, forcing more teachers in alternative schools to teach to the test that politicians use to symbolize school accountability. Finally, we must view the impressive accomplishments of alternative schools in the light of the fact that, even in an incredibly varied public school system like that of New York City, which has over a hundred alternative public schools for all ages, only five percent of all students attend them (Wrigley).

Credentials and Qualifications

Almost all public high school teachers are required by state law to have a teaching credential from a BA, MA, or PhD program in education.[6] The exceptions to this policy occur mostly among small schools, which have autonomy in their hiring as well as in other policies. Charter schools typically have the most hiring autonomy under state laws and often hire people without teaching credentials. Alternative schools, which are a part of and accountable to local school districts, can usually hire the noncertified but can offer them less job security than certified teachers. These policies vary from state to state and district to district, but two general trends seem likely to increase the number of jobs for English PhDs in public high schools: the increasing number of small schools overall and the increasing number of alternative schools that are becoming charter schools in order to gain even more autonomy from city regulations.

In any case, Alison Smith is persuasive when she writes in *Profession 1996*:

> Obstacles that prevent PhDs from obtaining jobs in secondary education (such as stringent certification requirements) should be removed. The MLA could become an advocate for PhDs who wish to teach in high school; it could attempt to influence state boards of education to remove obstacles. Perhaps an acceptable alternative to certification would be a significant research project in the field of education. PhDs have demonstrated research skills that could be the source of new knowledge. But high schools must be willing to provide time and funds for such research. (71)

While we should vigorously promote alternative certification, and such research projects would indeed produce useful knowledge, English PhD programs would provide even better teacher training by finding ways for their graduate students to actually spend time in high school classrooms for degree credit. Obviously, pursuing a BA, MA, or PhD in teaching with courses on pedagogy and mentorships with experienced teachers is the best way for someone to train as a high school teacher. A PhD in English both over- and underqualifies us for high school jobs: we're pedagogically underqualified but overqualified in content knowledge. Yet this awkward combination actually provides some resources for us as potential high school teachers.

We are underqualified in that few of us have experience developing curricula or planning class time for high school students. A high school literature curriculum needs to develop the most basic interpretive skills, teaching readers that reading is an act of proliferating meanings instead of summarizing plots or messages. Even though we may teach college students this lesson again and again, few of us consistently have to break interpretation down to its most elemental assumptions: that a text is different from its author, who creates it with specific techniques; that language is a manipulated medium that we can analyze; that analyses are arguments and arguments are a way of participating in the world; that abstract thought enriches particular observations and vice versa; that reading has at stake something profound about our lives. Such fundamental reading lessons are bound up in equally fundamental writing lessons, which must break down the writing process to the level of word and sentence before approaching the paragraph and essay.

Such lessons rely on carefully detailed lesson plans that can structure several hours of class time every week; only a part of this time should be spent in the kind of open class discussion appropriate for college classes. The long class periods and curricular autonomy of alternative high schools allow teachers to use a wide range of other class activities: dramatic enactments, autobiographical and creative writing, group research projects, interactive student presentations, interdisciplinary exercises. English PhD programs rarely teach how to carefully plan each minute of a class, let alone how to use such specific activities in daily classes to create a unified progression throughout a school year. Nor do PhD programs accustom us to the sheer quantity of homework that high school teachers have to grade.

Our pedagogical underqualifications are emphasized even more by our overqualifications in terms of literary theory and field knowledge. Simply put, we probably know a lot more than we have the skills to teach high school students. While this gap is potentially productive and provides an occasion for pedagogical creativity, it is also likely to frustrate those of us used to the glacial pace of our incredibly specialized and focused research. High schools permit no such pace or specialization. However, a university academic teaching in a high school can benefit from remembering two humbling truths: (1) If you can't explain something, you don't entirely understand it, and (2) A high school class is as dense, complex, and overdetermined a text as one could ever hope to encounter.

While our most esoteric knowledges may not be valued in high schools, our research and writing skills can be applied to the massive body of literature about secondary education. Once again, an English PhD is both over- and underqualified to publish in this field: while we can analyze the most subtle linguistic phenomena with the most abstract interpretive concepts, we have less experience writing about pedagogical practices and embarrassingly little experience writing about public policies that shape students' daily lives. The ambition to add to a body of literary critical research could find, we hope, similar satisfaction in the ambition to add to the less rarefied bodies of research related to secondary education. And since publication is not necessary for a high school job, we might also suspect that high school teachers who publish are primarily motivated by having something interesting to say.

For all the differences between secondary and postsecondary teaching, research, and publication, the similarities are profound, no matter how much we ignore them: both fields are based on the professional relationships of teaching, mentoring, and faculty collegiality; both relate group engagements with literature to individual writing about literature;[7] both cultivate critical thought as a process that is its own product. These qualities are scarce in most of the nonacademic jobs we consider in the current job market, but they can be as pronounced in small, alternative high schools as in elite research universities.

Return of the Repressed

Why do so few underemployed English PhDs seek high school academic work? The MLA's most recent employment census of English PhDs (Laurence) found that of the 1,226 people who earned PhDs in 1996–97, only thirty-five took high school jobs (one took an elementary school job). Most of us prefer to continue adjuncting, despite the dreadful conditions that preclude most elements of a normal career. After adjuncting for a few years, we commonly seek private-sector, nonacademic work that can help us pay off our debts. Smith compares this narrative with her own experience teaching high school:

> Being an integral member of the faculty is an experience unlike that of being a non-tenure-track instructor at the university level. I participate in curriculum decisions, plan my courses, select textbooks and software, advise students, meet with parents, and participate on committees. I participate in professional conferences as both a teacher and a scholar, attend training workshops, and will have the opportunity to take a group of students abroad during the summer. All these experiences are contributing to my professional growth in ways not available to me as a university instructor. I am gaining valuable skills and training that are important for both secondary and postsecondary positions. (71)

Yet only about three percent of us take such jobs on earning our PhDs, and only a slightly larger percent take such jobs in the subsequent, jobless years. The naive question to ask is, Why haven't we noticed the availability of interesting, well-paid academic work in high schools (especially alternative schools)? The more appropriate question is, Why does a career in secondary teaching and research represent failure to someone with an English PhD, and what kind of failure does this career represent?

Paul G. Zolbrod glosses our discipline's criteria for success in *Profession 1999*:

> Conventional wisdom has it that the best work for English professors is teaching graduate students and publishing articles on theory and cultural criticism. A little lower in the hierarchy are those who teach upper-level undergraduates at liberal arts colleges like Allegheny. Lower still are those who teach beginning literature at unprestigious state colleges.

> Composition is handled by untenured newcomers to the academic ranks, by TAs who haven't yet proven their intellectual mettle, or by ABDs who possibly never will. Even lower are the community college drones who reintroduce poems and short stories that are considered high school level. Basic reading, meanwhile, is not even worth considering. Teaching that is done by an untouchable caste outside the English department. (186)

Zolbrod's moving account of leaving a tenured professorship at a liberal arts college to teach basic reading and writing at a Navajo reservation community college also reveals something about our attitudes toward high schools. His hierarchy reflects how high schools are almost entirely absent from our professional radar screens as appropriate workplaces. The faint moments of their presence, as above, are moments not of professional identification but of negative definition: we know we are not high school teachers even though we may not be sure (and we are not) what the discipline of literary studies is. Secondary education is an other against which our discipline constructs itself, and working in high schools is a painful transgression against disciplinary identity. PhDs are strongly discouraged from teaching in high schools if they ever want to teach full-time at colleges or universities, because a high school identification taints, delegitimizes, and confuses the attempt to construct a postsecondary identification. The MLA could help establish more salutary relations between secondary and postsecondary English by promoting alternative high school certification and by encouraging graduate students and PhDs to consider high school teaching as a career option.

A principal element of such disciplinary self-definition has been the suppression of the value of teaching for the valorization of research and publication. While this suppression is not limited to or caused by literary studies, it plays an especially important role in establishing our discipline's hierarchies. The devaluation of teaching oppositionally defines us against secondary education. It is no accident that the prestige of our most prestigious professors is indistinguishable from their minimal teaching responsibilities. Because teaching suggests the realm of the disciplinary other, our strategies for getting jobs in the job crisis have focused mostly on emphasizing and refining any skill besides teaching.

It is impossible to separate this repression of teaching from another common, even dominant, way that literary studies currently constructs itself: as political work. Mistaking politically themed academic writing for political work, some academics (and many graduate students) invest the discipline of literary studies with leftist, radical, democratic political desire. John Guillory analyzes this investment in *Profession 1996*:

> It is the emergence of an intensified investment of political desire in literary study—as a motive of teaching and publication—that I link to the

decline in the job market. I don't regard the market as the simple cause of that politicized agenda, but I do believe it is a condition for the politicization of certain intellectual practices. [. . .] The so-called politicization of criticism is driven by the increasing social marginality of literary study, its increasing irrelevance to the socioeconomic conditions of our society. [. . .] The greater the marginality, the greater the motive to politicize. At the same time, politicized expressions are inhibited from easily circulating outside this domain, by virtue of its marginality. The condition of social marginality accounts for the difficulty literary critics experience in gaining access to the public sphere of political discourse. Thus political expression is driven back into the spaces of the professional field itself [. . .]. (93–94)

Our politically themed academic writing expresses, redirects, and often exhausts the desire to affect anything recognizable as a contested part of the public sphere. The painful paradox should be obvious: the realm of political contestation closest to literary studies, where we could have the most influence—if that is our interest—is secondary education. Public high schools, as a distributor of the cultural, conceptual, and vocational resources necessary for social power, are the focus of incessant and intense political contestation. Teaching in a high school that defines itself in terms of social justice and being part of a progressive national educational movement are the kind of political work we sometimes pretend our postsecondary academic work to be.

Another painful paradox is that many of us preferred attending college to attending high school. Therefore, we want to work at a college or a university. Teaching at an alternative high school is not a version of a college job; it does not promote literary criticism or critical theory, defined as such; it is the kind of work that the worst trends of academia seem intent on repressing in its own marginal sphere. But the opportunity to cultivate critical and abstract thought, to teach students how to read and write thoughtfully, to mentor, and to participate in and write about consequential politics is available outside postsecondary institutions. You can visit high schools that do this work and see.

NOTES

[1]Needless to say, the most prestigious and elite private schools in the United States have generally not adopted principles of mass efficiency or strategies of consolidation but maintain their personalized smallness as their most essential quality.

[2]See, for example: Aiken; Cotton, "School Size" and "Benefits"; Hess; Lee and Smith, "Effects" and "Size"; McMullan, Sipe, and Wolf; Pittman and Houghwout; Raywid; Stockard and Mayberry.

[3] The average New York City public school classroom had about thirty-seven students in 2000 (Gavrin 74).

[4] Both charter and alternative schools should be distinguished from small private schools. Private schools in the United States fall into two rough categories: elite, expensive schools with small classes and much less expensive, religiously affiliated schools with, typically, large classes and traditional pedagogies. Small public school reform, in the form of charter and alternative schools, should also be distinguished from school vouchers, which allow parents to use the money allocated their children in public schools to pay private school tuition.

[5] There is a great deal of controversy about public schools becoming partially privatized by corporate investment in charter arrangements. A recent example of community displeasure at such a prospect occurred in March 2001, when Edison Schools, Inc., the nation's largest operator of public schools, failed in its bid to take over five failing public schools in New York City. Of the local parents who voted on the charter, 80% voted against it (Holloway).

[6] Emergency credentials for those without education degrees are usually restricted to the sciences, math, and foreign languages, the most extreme shortage areas. However, several cities also give provisional English credentials to those who have a BA or higher degree in English and who are willing to earn further credits in education while teaching.

[7] This commonality is exemplified by something like the New York City Writing Project, a city program that trains both high school and college teachers in writing instruction in the same workshops.

WORKS CITED

Aiken, Wilfred. *The Story of the Eight-Year Study*. New York: Harper, 1942.

Ayers, William. "Simple Justice: Thinking about Teaching and Learning, Equity, and the Fight for Small Schools." Ayers, Klonsky, and Lyon 1–8.

Ayers, William, Michael Klonsky, and Gabrielle Lyon, eds. *A Simple Justice: The Challenge of Small Schools*. New York: Teachers Coll. P, 2000.

Conant, James B. *The American High School Today*. New York: McGraw, 1959.

Cotton, Kathleen. "Affective and Social Benefits of Small-Scale Schooling." *ERIC Digest*. Charleston: Clearinghouse on Rural Educ. and Small Schools, 1996.

———. "School Size, School Climate, and Student Performance." *Close Up* 20. Portland: Northwest Regional Educ. Laboratory, 1996.

Freire, Paulo. *Pedagogy of the Oppressed*. Trans. Myra Bergman Ramos. New York: Continuum, 1984.

Gavrin, Meredith. "A Day in the Life of a Teacher in a Small School." *Creating New Schools: How Small Schools Are Changing American Education*. Ed. Evans Clinchy. New York: Teachers Coll. P, 2000. 73–79.

Guillory, John. "Preprofessionalism: What Graduate Students Want." *Profession 1996*. New York: MLA, 1996. 91–99.

Hess, G. Alfred, Jr. "Who Leads Small Schools?" Ayers, Klonsky, and Lyon 38–52.

Holloway, Lynette. "Parents Explain Rejection of Privatization at Five Schools." *New York Times on the Web* 13 Apr. 2001. 24 Apr. 2001 <http://www.nytimes.com/2001/04/13/nyregion/13EDIS.html?searchpv-site11>.

Klonsky, Michael. "Remembering Port Huron." Ayers, Klonsky, and Lyon 23–32.

Laurence, David. "Employment of 1996–97 English PhDs." *ADE Bulletin* 121 (1998): 58–69.
Lee, Valerie E., and Julia B. Smith. "Effects of High School Restructuring and Size on Early Gains in Achievement and Engagement." *Sociology of Education* 68 (1995): 241–70.
———. "High School Size: Which Works Best, and for Whom?" *Education Evaluation and Policy Analysis* 19 (1997): 205–27.
McLaren, Peter. "A Pedagogy of Responsibility: Reflecting upon Paulo Freire's Politics of Education." *Educational Researcher* 28.2 (1999): 49–56.
McMullan, Bernard J., C. L. Sipe, and Wendy C. Wolf. "Charters and Student Achievement: Early Evidence from School Restructuring in Philadelphia." Report. Bala Cynwyd: Center for Assessment and Policy Development, 1994.
Meier, Deborah. "The Crisis of Relationships." Ayers, Klonsky, and Lyon 33–37.
———. *The Power of Their Ideas: Lessons for America from a Small School in Harlem*. Boston: Beacon, 1995.
Pittman, Robert B., and Perri Houghwout. "Influence of High School Size on Dropout Rate." *Education Evaluation and Policy Analysis* 9 (1987): 337–43.
Raywid, Mary Anne. "Current Literature on Small Schools." *ERIC Digest*. Charleston: Clearinghouse on Rural Educ. and Small Schools, 1999.
Smith, Alison T. "Secondary Education: Still an Ignored Market." *Profession 1996*. New York: MLA, 1996. 69–72.
Stockard, Jean, and Maralee Mayberry. *Effective Educational Environments*. Newbury Park: Corwin, 1992.
Wrigley, Julia. "Centralization versus Fragmentation: The Public School Systems of New York and Los Angeles." 2001.
Zolbrod, Paul G. "Teaching on the Margin: Notes from a Classroom at Navajo Community College." *Profession 1999*. New York: MLA, 1999. 180–92.

APPENDIX
Suggestions for Further Reading on the Small-Schools Movement, Critical Pedagogy, and Other Issues Related to Alternative Public Education

Applebaum, Deborah. *Critical Encounters in High School English: Teaching Literary Theory to Adolescents*. New York: Teachers Coll. P, 2000.
Ayers, William, Jean Ann Hunt, and Therese Quinn. *Teaching for Social Justice*. New York: Teachers Coll. P, 1998.
Ayers, William, Michael Klonsky, and Gabrielle Lyon, eds. *A Simple Justice: The Challenge of Small Schools*. New York: Teachers Coll. P, 2000.
Berliner, David C., and Bruce J. Biddle. *The Manufactured Crisis: Myths, Fraud, and the Attack on America's Public Schools*. New York: Addison, 1995.
Clinchy, Evans, ed. *Creating New Schools: How Small Schools Are Changing American Education*. New York: Teachers Coll. P, 2000.
Fine, Michelle. *Chartering Urban School Reform: Reflections on Public High Schools in the Midst of Change*. New York: Teachers Coll. P, 1994.
Fine, Michelle, and J. Somerville, eds. *Small Schools, Big Imagination: A Creative Look at Urban Public Schools*. Chicago: Cross City Campaign for Urban School Reform, 1998.
Freire, Paulo. *Pedagogy of the Oppressed*. Trans. Myra Bergman Ramos. New York: Continuum, 1984.

———. *Teachers as Cultural Workers: Letters to Those Who Dare Teach.* Trans. Donaldo Macedo, Dole Koike, and Alexandre Oliveira. Boulder: Westview, 1998.

Kozol, Jonathan. *Savage Inequalities: Children in America's Schools.* New York: Harper, 1991.

Meier, Deborah. *The Power of Their Ideas: Lessons for America from a Small School in Harlem.* Boston: Beacon, 1995.

Rousmaniere, Kate. *City Teachers: Teaching and School Reform in Historical Perspective.* New York: Teachers Coll. P, 1997.

Shor, Ira, ed. *Freire for the Classroom: A Sourcebook for Liberatory Teaching.* Portsmouth: Boynton, 1987.

Sizer, Theodore R. *Horace's Compromise: The Dilemma of the American High School.* Boston: Houghton, 1984.

Weiler, Kathleen. *Women Teaching for Social Change: Gender, Class, and Power.* New York: Bergin, 1988.

Why I Teach in an Independent School

BRENT WHITTED

I have been an instructor of English literature at Marlborough School for almost two years now, and I am writing to let graduate students in literary studies know about the intellectual opportunities that teaching English in a preparatory school can offer. With a national shortage of teachers looming, schools like Marlborough—a private urban prep school for young women in Los Angeles (grades 7–12)—are keen to attract and retain teachers with professional degrees who love to teach. This is not to say that such schools do not support research; they just don't require it. Marlborough School has been very supportive of my continuing research projects: its professional development budget has financially backed my attendance at three academic conferences so far, including one in Cambridge, England. It has supported the purchase of books and other research-related materials, including a UCLA library card. It is also hosting an academic conference a colleague of mine and I are convening next year. The salary is also competitive with that of most assistant professorships. In addition, I have been most impressed with the level of insight; the degree of enthusiasm; and the capacity for creative, rigorous interpretation among the students I have encountered across all grade levels. The pace is intense, and the intellectual demands are constant and significant.

My first exposure to an independent school was in the tenth grade, when I entered the Albuquerque Academy as a sophomore. One of the first things I noticed was that the faculty members seemed more at liberty to teach what they thought was appropriate or what moved them personally. They did not seem constrained by a structured, state-mandated curriculum in the way my

---

The author is Instructor of English Literature at the Marlborough School in Los Angeles.

previous teachers had been. They were adventurous, spontaneous, and even willing to take risks in their presentation of the material they were teaching. The experiences I had in the classroom all seemed personal, eccentric, powerful. This distinctiveness somewhat characterized my fellow students as well; they were encouraged to be different. After three years at the school, I decided that the newfound liberality I found so refreshing was something I wanted to be a part of in the future, perhaps as a teacher. The excitement and provocation that derived from our class discussions in English had an especially profound effect on my sensibilities. I was moved by the earnestness, the joy, and the satisfaction that my teachers displayed and evoked in us through their personalities. It seemed that they were enjoying their autonomy as instructors, relatively uninhibited by ponderous notebooks of the curricular units that channeled the day-to-day work of my previous teachers.

Since high school, during the ten years I spent at college and graduate school (culminating in the doctorate), I always knew that I wanted to return to a similarly enriching environment, a place where I could work with motivated and motivating young people and colleagues like the teachers who had such an impact on me in the late 1980s. I professionalized myself for a tenure-track job at the University of British Columbia (going to conferences, learning how to interview, publishing papers, writing the letter of application, going to the MLA). Though I became caught up in the successes and failures of the process, I knew in the back of my mind where I would like to see myself professionally. So alongside the stacks of university job files on my desk, I always maintained a file devoted to the search for the ideal post in a preparatory school. I attended a job conference hosted by Carney, Sandoe, and Associates in Boston (these conferences are basically the same as the MLA's Job Information Center at the annual convention),[1] sent out masses of letters to schools that interested me, and followed up the occasional leads with my best phone interview efforts. All this strategizing eventually led me to Marlborough School, which put me through two rounds of intensive interviews for the position of instructor of British literature.

I thought I was prepared for the job—and in many ways I was—but there are three things (there are more) that especially challenged my transition from graduate school to high school.

The pace It took a little more than a year for me to get a handle on the incredible pace at which the young women I teach process, query, and articulate information—not only about the work we're discussing but also about themselves, one another, and even me. The school runs a fast-paced schedule, so interactions must often be quick, to the point, and clear the first time around. There is indeed time for longer conversations, but these must be scheduled in advance. I have had to learn how to make split-second decisions and to voice them as I make them. While at times this mode of exchange can try my patience—especially at points in the semester when I have the plots, themes, and critical apparatuses associated with seven or eight novels running through my head and ready for instant recall—I have found a way to get a rush from this intellectual dance.

Being a public rather than a private scholar The final two years of my doctoral degree were, naturally, socially isolating. To escape the all-too-intimate relationship I was having with the library and my computer, I found solace in a tight group of friends. The juxtaposition of this world and my place on the hot seat in front of bright, uniformed, sophisticated young women in a classroom four hours a day could not have been more shocking. In theory, I was prepared for the change, but I soon realized how much help I needed to acquire quickly the skills necessary to translate my ten years of experience with literature into an effective classroom presence. I also discovered that the range of classes I was teaching—ninth, eleventh, and twelfth grades, with class sizes ranging from eight to sixteen students—would require me to adjust this presence. Luckily, the school gave me a professional teaching coach, a hired consultant, to sit in on all my classes and respond personally after each one with constructive criticism based on the specific episodes and interactions that she witnessed. This guidance has proved invaluable, for it enabled me to begin to craft my own public face on the mysterious, enigmatic persona that was so enveloped in the identity of my thesis.

Student ambition This challenge is a cross-section of the first two. The young women I teach, generally, are extremely motivated to get into the most prestigious universities in America. This lofty goal most often translates into a willingness to work hard; for us in the English department, it is manifested in a serious devotion to the writing process. Almost always, we read and comment on both the rough and final draft of each essay a student writes. The process makes for a lot of written and spoken commentary, but the results are impressive, largely because of the students' desire to improve their ability to think and write effectively. The students see this ability as a ticket to the kind of collegiate and professional environment to which they aspire.

These three challenges would have been significantly more difficult if not impossible for me to overcome without the support and kindness extended by my nine colleagues in the English department. My peers (two men and seven women) represent a wide range of interests, literary and otherwise; we are a congenial group—inquisitive, humorous, and devoted to the craft of teaching. Most of us have done graduate work in English, and three of us have recent doctorates (another is just about to finish one). Meeting weekly in teaching teams, we regularly share ideas about the content of the courses we offer and the techniques that have worked (or not worked) in our presentation of the literature and the writing process. All of us have duties outside the classroom; some serve as faculty representatives on student leadership councils, one member organizes the yearbook committees, another facilitates the annual literary magazine, and all serve on one faculty committee or another. There are also growing opportunities for team teaching and interdisciplinary work. This year witnessed the beginning of a two-semester American studies course, which is taught by one member of the English department and one member of the history department.

My course load has concentrated on the two-semester British survey course and the year-long ninth-grade composition course. The survey covers nearly all the major literary movements from the Anglo-Saxon epic to the theater of the absurd. I was, and still am, sufficiently challenged by the pace and scope of this course, for I hadn't taught many of the works when I was a teaching assistant in graduate school. Having run through the curriculum twice, helping to make adjustments here and there along the way in consultation with my two colleagues who also teach the class, I feel very excited about the intellectual journeys my new crop of eleventh graders and I will share in the autumn. The ninth-grade class is an entirely different world, not only because of the two-year age difference but also because the composition course allows us to spend much more time working through a text, such as *Othello* (a month), *Catcher in the Rye* (three weeks or so), or Jamaica Kincaid's *Annie John*. These fifteen-year-old students more than make up for the slower pace of our reading schedule with their ability to ask twenty questions at once—most of them very good ones.

In addition, I have taught semester-length electives, which are seminar-style, theme- or genre-based classes. One of the more positive aspects of teaching in a school like Marlborough is that teachers can often construct the course of their dreams. The semester-long advanced placement seminar I taught last year, entitled Supernatural and the Macabre, features a curriculum that changes from year to year according to the instructor's desires; my choices included *Macbeth*, Jane Austen's *Northanger Abbey*, Henry James's "Turn of the Screw," E. M. Forster's *Passage to India*, Toni Morrison's *Beloved*, and Leslie Marmon Silko's *Ceremony*. After I read these works the summer before, I drafted an overview of the course that I gave to my students on the first day of class:

The Text as Mystery

In 1981, the renowned scholar of Renaissance English literature and culture, Stephen Orgel, invited us to ask, "What is a text?" Eighteen years later, in *Shakespeare after Theory*, David Scott Kastan contributed to the ongoing process of answering this question by making the following conjecture: "The meanings of the literary work are [...] not intrinsic to it, not properties solely of its internal structuring, but functions of its mediation of and by the cultural contexts in which it is located" (48). Literary scholarship in the last twenty years or so has regarded the imaginative text (the play, the novel, the poem) as a product of collaboration; the text we read is not a "pure" rendering of a solitary artist's aesthetic process but instead an interweaving of social forces and interests of which we are ourselves products. Furthermore, by engaging the text either as students, editors, or professional literary critics, we transform its meaning, so in a sense we ourselves are agents in the text's transformation. Every material transformation of a text (or reassessment of it in the light of our shifting values) contributes to the ongoing remaking of its cultural significance. Most of us have heard about the "death of the author," but Kastan wishes for us to finesse this notion:

> The author is, of course, not dead (the theoretical claim to the contrary hardly worth the effort of refutation and spectacularly rendered fatuous by the Ayatollah's fatwah pronounced against Salman Rushdie in 1989). But if we must, of course, grant that the author is a historical agent and no mere instrument or effect of a linguistic order, we must also recognize that the author is not autonomous and sovereign, neither the solitary source nor the sole proprietor of the meanings that circulate through the text. This is not to dismiss or denigrate the claims of authorship, only to observe that the act of writing is inevitably fettered and circumscribed. An author writes always and only within specific conditions of possibility, both institutional and imaginative, connecting the individual talent to preexisting modes of thought, linguistic rules, literary conventions, social codes, legal restraints, material practices, and commercial conditions of production. (32–33)

Just as the text is a kind of mystery, so is the author, enmeshed as he or she is within the perplexities of human in(ter)vention.

Given these intellectual promptings, what can we conclude about literary works across the centuries that accentuate the ambiguities of human existence? Who or what controls our actions? Are we influenced by external unknowns, or do we project these unknowns onto our mental and physical landscapes? Does our past "come back to haunt us"? Furthermore, how can we relate these questions to the problem (or the mystery) of authorship? Are literary works that explicitly treat the supernatural and the macabre doing this merely to "scare" or "thrill" us—or is something more obscure and complicated going on here? Are these "ghost" stories, to one degree or another, tapping into our fears in this way to test or subvert our sense of autonomy, of being in control? Do writers use the supernatural figures/places in their works to exorcise the specter of their own authorship, their autonomy as creators (or lack thereof)? Perhaps these devices serve as an author's clever means of admitting the ambiguity and contingencies of his or her own authorial voice, made ghostly once a manuscript escapes into the publisher's hands.

The four months I spent with the sixteen enrolled seniors taught me that the course I had envisioned was just a starting point. While the original overview of the course gave the students in the seminar fuel for the first three texts we read, it did not readily gesture toward possible answers to perhaps the more interesting (and basic) question they asked while we were reading *Passage to India*, *Beloved*, and *Ceremony* (three texts that became for us a kind of trinity): What is so supernatural about this text anyway? Some of the students had admittedly come to the course expecting something by Stephen King (and we did indeed watch *The Shining*)—not necessarily the kinds of works we were reading, which contain supernatural elements that seem somehow central to larger cultural issues.

The racial diversity among the students in the class helped us all apply some of these touchy issues to ourselves: Is it possible to be truly multicultural? Is it possible to perpetuate racism among one's race and mask it as something else? Is it possible to allow the fictional worlds created by our readings of these works to radically warp our sense of what is natural and supernatural? That the class included students from a wide range of racial and national backgrounds, with several students from a multiplicity of backgrounds, and that the class as a whole was comfortable enough to extend the very sensitive conflicts of the fictions we were reading to a discussion of the students' own sensibilities—their collective sense of what seemed natural or not—drew something tangible and personally meaningful out of a course description that eventually, in retrospect, appeared too abstract.

Basically, our discussions of the three final texts led us to a point of common ground about what unites the radically different worlds into which Forster, Morrison, and Silko invite us (India under British imperialism, Reconstruction-era Ohio, and the Acoma Indian Reservation near Gallup, New Mexico). This common ground easily led us to the final exam question:

> It would seem that only a few of the works that we've read in this course entertain the "supernatural" in a form that we might recognize as traditional or conventional (things that go bump in the night). Yet our discussions have enlightened our awareness of more complex notions of what the supernatural might be. With emphasis on Forster's *Passage to India*, Morrison's *Beloved*, and Silko's *Ceremony*, offer an intellectual meditation on the different ways writers use the notion of the (super)natural as a motif to articulate their ideas about human existence. Are there any similarities between the ways Forster, Morrison, and Silko fashion this notion?

Students had two hours to respond to this question.

What led us collectively to it was the sense that, in each novel, the natural and supernatural are inverted. Each novel presents a force of domination (the caste system, imperialism, slavery, reservation life) that is a norm—from the perspective of both those in power and those oppressed. The oppressed have been forced to discover strategies for rationalizing and internalizing their situation as somehow acceptable and natural. Over time, these strategies develop into forms of intracultural oppression, whereby oppressed groups apply toward their social hierarchies the forms of domination they experience externally. What we soon discovered as we read was that the novels fashion these forces of domination—forces that keep different groups separated from one another—as supernatural, for they derive from an inner fear of difference. The product of this fear is the aggressor's establishment of the cultural and physical stasis of the oppressed (the demographic configuration of imperialist Chandrapore, the residence at 124 Bluestone Road, Tayo's reservation), yielding a psychic limbo zone in which the natural growth and intermixing of individuals and communities are permanently stultified. What would ideally be natural in these situations seems unattainable, so what becomes natural is what normally would be supernatural: the caves' benign mysteries (*Passage*); Beloved's resurrected rage (*Beloved*); and the revised, updated ceremony (*Ceremony*). Forster, Morrison, and Silko present these entities as integral parts of natural cycles that demand to break through the supernatural stasis maintained by the imposition of misguided, awkward power relationships (the very idea of Anglo-India, the pseudofreedom enjoyed by ex-slaves in the northern states during Reconstruction, and the sense of hopeless loss often experienced by the inhabitants of American Indian reservations).

What this class of culturally sensitive, intellectually adventurous high school seniors found so fascinating is the distinctive ways that Forster, Morrison, and Silko each use their fictions to illustrate how the psychological impulse to create and maintain supernatural (stagnant) social configurations is even more frightening than the conventional forms of the supernatural (ghosts and the like), for this impulse comes from inside all of us. We all have the ability in us to destroy ourselves; this potential is the most frightening part of being human, especially because we have the unique ability to mask our destructive potential as oppressive regimes we all too easily deem normal or natural. My students also came to appreciate how they could manage to draw strikingly similar thematic parallels among three novels representing radically different cultures.

May this brief account of my experience as a prep school English teacher help current graduate students understand the broader range of professional options available to them—options that will very much demand the skills they are acquiring as readers, thinkers, writers, researchers, and teachers.

NOTE

[1]Carney, Sandoe, and Associates is a placement agency for teachers and administrators seeking jobs in independent schools in the United States and abroad. The agency can be contacted at 136 Boylston Street, Boston, MA 02116 (800 225-7986).

WORK CITED

Kastan, David Scott. *Shakespeare after Theory*. New York: Routledge, 1999.

Teaching the Urban Underprepared Student

CELESTINE WOO

A colleague of mine, swapping grad school war stories with me, told of an adviser who'd proclaimed that if you failed to write an article a week and get several published, you'd "end up at a community college!" God forbid. Community colleges are considered anathema not only by many job seekers but also by their faculty mentors in graduate school. The low level of the students' academic preparation, the four- or five-course load every term, the presumed indifference of the department toward faculty scholarship, and other factors render the community college a last resort for many a recent PhD, despite the abysmal state of the market. The same objections probably obtain in one's consideration of four-year urban commuter campuses: schools populated by underprepared students from less than ideal high school and family backgrounds. These students, undisciplined, undermotivated, and typically unappreciative of literature and the humanities, are more often seen as a burden than as a blessing by aspiring professors. I have worked in both these supposedly undesirable environments and have two objectives in discussing them here: first, to provide a detailed picture of what life is actually like in such places; second, to attest that immense satisfaction and growth, on a professional and personal level, are possible in environments that the average candidate may initially be loath to consider.

I worked for a year full-time as a combined faculty member and administrator at a small urban commuter college that serves adult students (the average age is thirty-five), most of whom are African American or West

---

The author is Assistant Professor of English at Fort Lewis College.

Indian. My duties there were many and varied: I developed and taught a course in film and literature, taught a course in advanced composition and introductory literary analysis, hired and mentored adjunct faculty members in the humanities, directed the writing center, ran the developmental English program, oriented faculty members to educational technology, advised students, served on an assessment committee, ran a literary club, chose textbooks for all humanities courses, and developed curriculum. I thus fulfilled duties that at a larger, more established place would not have been given to a junior faculty member: hiring faculty members, performing faculty observations and evaluations, determining course offerings across the spectrum of the humanities, shaping the requirements for the English major, delineating programmatic assessment strategies, and more. Because this was my first full-time academic appointment, all these responsibilities served as an initiation rite (or perhaps a baptism by fire) into the profession I was so eager to enter, and they confirmed for me that I would indeed enjoy this career. Small, understaffed urban campuses, then, can not only test one's ability to handle heavy amounts of responsibility and juggle numerous tasks but also propel one up the ladder of authority sooner than at a large institution.

I fulfilled yet other duties, such as registering students, orienting potential students, handling grade appeals and other disputes, helping students with financial aid and with documenting mitigating circumstances, and filling out and submitting tutor time sheets. In other words, I wore a dozen hats: I alone was the humanities department, with no full-time faculty members and only minimal secretarial support. The position was extremely arduous but nonetheless one of the most exhilarating experiences I've had. The rewards of such a job come under the rubrics of social relevance, cultural understanding, and the chance, simply, to introduce students to the joys of reading literature. In the idealized setting of an advanced seminar of sophisticated English majors, where you are preaching to the converted, I imagine it is easy to lose sight of what caused you to love literature in the first place; in an urban non-humanities-oriented setting, those factors are perforce kept at the forefront of your teaching.

An institution that serves a low-income, inner-city population cannot count on alumni to provide the generous donations possible in richer areas: hence the creation of hybrid, overloaded positions such as mine. The intimidating catalog above paints a sobering picture of the overlapping and exhausting responsibilities that were my daily fare. And yet the job offered me a unique and intimate insider's view of African American culture; of the stark realities of life on New York City streets; and of the ways in which I could daily, tangibly contribute to people's social betterment. Never again will I secretly wonder at the usefulness of choosing a career in English: the ostensible divide—engrained in my Baptist-bred soul—between pragmatic social service (good) and rarefied imaginative musings (bad) has for me irretrievably collapsed. For my students, there was no question that English was both pragmatically relevant *and* a luxury; they could see not only that improving their communication skills was crucial to bettering their lives but also that understanding the issues that have inspired passionate writing across barriers of geography and chronology empowered them to apprehend their own culture and lives more fully.

In *Profession 1999*, Paul G. Zolbrod usefully delineates the challenges he faces at a community college on a Navajo reservation. My own early experiences were analogous: having a student population composed of adults who are academically underprepared, are far from wealthy, and live in a tough urban environment creates immense obstacles to teaching. For one thing, as the administrator in charge of finding textbooks for all the humanities courses, I was required to limit my choices to thirty dollars total for each course. I also taught one course a term and so learned the benefits and challenges of teaching this population. One benefit is that students are highly motivated, having learned the hard way the importance of education to their career goals. However, instead of offering the usual irresponsible excuses for being tardy, my students would explain that their boss threatened to fire them if they didn't stay two hours overtime or that the babysitter arrived over an hour late or that their son was stabbed at school and had to be rushed to the hospital. Balancing the need to maintain academic standards and policies with the need to be compassionate in an endless stream of urgent situations was my constant battle—a battle that forced me salutarily to ponder how to make pertinent what we did in the classroom, how to render the experience of education weighty enough to match the tremendous sacrifices my students willingly made.

Not only did the intrusive realities of my students' lives impress on me the need to make learning relevant for them but also their variegated experiences transformed the classroom for me into a place for reflection on institutional injustice. Learning the details of students' experiences in high school—such as when a woman mentioned being told at the age of sixteen by her high school counselor that she'd never amount to anything and ought to quit school, and when many others in the class said that the same thing had happened to them—conveyed to me the importance of affirming anyone's ability to learn. Seeing ex-felons come to understand the complex sociopolitical and historical forces that shaped their experiences, mothers on public assistance study to begin or to further their careers in social work and public education, and high school dropouts eagerly ask me for more grammar homework is nothing less than inspiring. The majority of my students possessed a fervent vision of community transformation, and the college's philosophy allowed them great freedom in crafting their academic projects to bear on their real-life concerns. I had the privilege of participating in this empowerment, through discussing William Blake's rhetoric of whiteness in "The Little Black Boy" and analyzing today's rhetoric of color, through contrasting American notions of privacy and gender roles with those depicted in Chitra Divakaruni's "Doors." In a classroom of English majors, pointing out modern-day analogues to issues in literature might seem pedestrian; for my students, doing so infused the literature with life.

Working with academically underprepared students brings a certain satisfaction of beating the system: you are educating those who have been told for many years that they are stupid, those of whom little achievement has ever been expected, those who expect to fail every test and actually work harder when told that a C is not a good grade and that they can do better. At the same time, these students are not passive, naive victims: many of them recognize the mistakes they made in high school and are in college to rectify them. Educating these students is not more meaningful per se than working with traditional students, but since the stakes are higher, the interrelations between education and society seem to be confronted more ineluctably.

Whenever faced with an other, you tend to see yourself more clearly. For me, there was something indescribably valuable about being a person of color in a place filled with other people of color—but of a different hue. I came to understand more deeply our shared experiences of discrimination as well as our very different experiences of education. Although I was at this college only one year full-time (I left it for a position at a community college because I craved more time in the classroom), I will remain grateful for the glimpse I gained of African American culture; it would probably never have come my way otherwise. One anecdote: I was talking to a man who expressed his admiration for the ethnic pride he ascribed to some Asian American teens who were participating in some function in Chinatown. I replied that though I did not disagree with him, it seemed to me that from my limited observation, African Americans tend to feel unabashedly proud of who they are (and he agreed), whereas many Asian Americans (of a certain generation, anyway) have struggled with shame and embarrassment about their ethnic heritage. The event in my eyes was more ambiguous than it had seemed to him; nevertheless, it was enlightening to hear his reading of it.

Another ongoing cultural lesson for me came from noticing how some students and staff members integrated their Christian faith into their learning and lives: the college provided a very different picture from what I was accustomed to, having been raised in a Chinese Southern Baptist community. I thought of faith as a private, slightly embarrassing thing that one shared with others out of somewhat shamefaced duty. At this campus, by contrast, people talked openly of the devil, of Christ, of biblical precepts in conjunction with academic concerns. On Fridays, staff members played gospel music as they typed their memos, demonstrating to me how faith and work can coexist unself-consciously. I could not help noticing and analyzing the molding of Christianity by the culture in which it is interpreted: I doubt that the Chinese fundamentalists I grew up among were literally dancing in the corridors and exclaiming, "Praise Jesus," at the news of President Clinton's acquittal from the impeachment charges, as my coworkers did. Exposure to other cultures aids my understanding of my own identity formation, and I come away enriched.

I have also realized the necessity of acquainting myself with the other cultures of the institution and department I am in and of recognizing the nuances of the subcultures that inform identity and educational behavior. At my graduate institution, for instance, the pedagogical model espoused for teaching expository writing encourages (rather vehemently) the decentering of traditional trappings of authority, by, for example, letting students address us by our first names. This approach proves effective for a student body of privileged, jaded teens who thrive when presented with ways to defamiliarize traditional academic structure and for whom education is a given. However, at institutions where students have to combat the tendency of their family and environment to devalue education, I have concluded that it does the students a disservice to ignore or undercut the traditional markings of respect for a teacher.

I moved on from the urban college to a suburban community college, where I was asked by one of my students what kind of a doctor I was; he was astounded to learn that one could be called doctor by studying English. Coming from a culture that venerates money and athleticism over academic achievement, he struggled to find a way to pursue his educational goals without being ostracized by his friends. Another form of alterity I encountered there was the fact that most of my students came from schools and homes where studying hard is criticized, ridiculed—and was even sufficient cause to be beaten up. Students regularly complained to me that they learned nothing in high school. While I did not take their complaints as any accurate measurement of what goes on in local high schools, what struck me was that these were complaints: that these students (sometimes) possessed a burning desire to learn but could not find a culturally acceptable way to express this.

For others, the situation was more dire: I had a student from Jamaica who left her family to come here to study. She supported herself and lived with a grandmother who regularly said that the student was spending too much time selfishly studying and not enough time caring for her. The student's relatives in Jamaica chimed in, asking why she wanted to waste her time on school and ignore her family. The student asked me one day, "How do you study?" She had no idea how to find time to study while working simultaneously: the concept was so foreign to her, she didn't know where to begin. I realized that knowing how to study is an aspect of educational privilege. My student's questions also put me in mind of Virginia Woolf's notion of a room of one's own. I never had to contend with the lack of a place or time to study. For first-generation college students, the cultural hurdles to be overleaped are of this sort; the lack of a mechanism, a paradigm, by which to make academics a higher priority in their lives can significantly counter the highest level of motivation.

What is satisfying about being at a community college is the very real sense of making a difference in people's lives and of affirming worthwhile decisions that students make. For many, college is the first time they have ever committed themselves to doing something positive and to thinking about their future. Some have overcome significant obstacles to attend college. Some have undergone traumatic events and so have to contend with severe anxiety attacks. I had very bright, insightful students who were hampered by learning disabilities. I had a student who was newly liberated from an abusive family situation; she reveled in her ability to choose, for the first time in years, what she wanted for her life. Another student never cared about school until his brother was thrown in jail for a multitude of crimes, including attempted murder; my student reacted by deciding to pursue a degree in criminal justice and to become a positive role model for his younger siblings. He became one of my top students. Having to deal with students' financial aid in my first college job exposed me to hair-raising experiences that made me feel privileged indeed: one student whose apartment was burned down lost everything, one student had three deaths in the family in a single semester, one student was attacked by a pit bull who chewed her legs so badly that she couldn't walk for months, one student was shunted from shelter to shelter along with three children to avoid a vengeful batterer. For people such as these, the mere fact that they were able to attend class was a triumph. Working with them underscored for me just how meaningful my vocation is.

Of course teaching at a community college entails difficulties. Some students may want to amend their high school ways but have yet to learn the extent to which change is necessary. I found myself reduced to using elementary school disciplinary tactics, occasionally beset with despair on days when after repeated warnings a student continued to chit-chat loudly in class instead of doing the task at hand. Having spent most of my own student life in honors classes, I was shocked at this lack of respect and total ignorance of or apathy toward academic behavior: many of my students never took notes, were completely indifferent when told a certain concept would be on the midterm, interrupted me and carried on conversations while I was speaking, flatly disobeyed direct requests to move to another group, and so on. Once again, the lesson I gleaned was cultural: in the culture of this English department, it was necessary and laudable to police students—check homework daily, penalize them for incomplete work—whereas at my graduate school this treatment would have drawn accusations of being tyrannical and juvenile. One must recognize the needs of students in a particular context and the societal forces that inform those needs.

Donald E. Hall accurately stated in *Profession 1999* that "far too little discussion occurs within graduate programs and the MLA about professional life at 'teaching schools'" (193). My remarks here are meant as a step toward addressing this dearth of information. Hall also points out that faculty members at PhD-granting institutions are obviously not experienced themselves at teaching heavy loads in such less prestigious locales and thus do not and cannot provide much helpful advice to their graduate students on this score. Indeed, I have heard tell of tenured faculty members' horror at the news that a favorite grad student of theirs was considering a job with a three-three load—whereas anyone who has been a job candidate for a few years in recent times tends to consider three-three a light load. I know of community colleges on the quarter system that require a five-five-five load: fifteen courses a year!

Graduate programs, then, ought to recognize that since in the near future most of their graduates who land academic jobs at all will do so at teaching institutions, their job placement programs need to garner more specific and abundant information about life in these places. I am sharing my experiences here in the hope of encouraging future job candidates to consider that a post at what may seem an undesirable school may not be as bad as they think. After all, my first position entailed many responsibilities that are expected to accompany an entry-level assistant professorship: committee work, advising, curriculum development, writing-center work, and so forth. All in all, the time I spent in these "undesirable" schools, as well as the semesters I spent as an adjunct, has given me a wealth and range of professional experience appropriate to the launching of a bona fide academic career. And the rewards of my teaching remind me of why so many of us choose this often lackluster, seldom lucrative career: because we love imparting literature's insights to others.

WORKS CITED

Hall, Donald E. "Professional Life (and Death) under a Four-Four Teaching Load." *Profession 1999*. New York: MLA, 1999. 193–203.

Zolbrod, Paul G. "Teaching on the Margin: Notes from a Classroom at Navajo Community College." *Profession 1999*. New York: MLA, 1999. 180–92.

Settling for a Great Job

JENNIFER M. STOLPA

Obtaining a position teaching English at the postsecondary level has been my goal since the somewhat surprising age of eleven. Since that time, at no point did I seriously entertain the idea that I would someday teach at a community college, technical school, or other two-year institution. However, the University of Wisconsin, Marinette, where I now teach, is a two-year campus. Although UW-Marinette is similar to four-year institutions in that it offers course work in the liberal arts and not the practical arts, the only distinction that ever meant anything to me was the one between a two-year and a four-year institution.

While I was a graduate student, when people would ask where I hoped to teach when I finished my degree, I was quite decided that I did not want to teach at a research university. I would identify instead, as did many of my fellow graduate students, a small, idyllic liberal arts college where I could make a difference in students' lives and only publish when I had a strong desire to do so. Because of my awareness of the tight job market for English PhDs, I usually added that I would even consider teaching at a two-year institution. I did not recognize it at the time, but the language of my response, especially the word *even*, was significant.

Once I began applying for positions in the fall of 1999, I quickly discovered that including two-year institutions allowed me to double the number of opportunities I had to obtain a job. As the year passed and my search became more intense, I was grateful for interviews at any institution, anything

The author is Assistant Professor of English and Spanish at the University of Wisconsin, Marinette.

that would give me an indication that I was a viable candidate for a post-secondary teaching position. In fact, all the telephone and campus interviews I had were at two-year institutions. In March 2000, I was delighted to accept the position at UW-Marinette, in large part because it meant that I had a job. In the market I had been led to expect, and in the market I had found, securing a tenure-track position at all was a great accomplishment.

It was only after I had accepted the position of assistant professor at UW-Marinette that I truly began to reflect on the choice I had made. As I shared my good news with family, friends, and professional colleagues, I was called on to describe the university at which I would be teaching. In answer to questions about the university's specialty, I was forced to acknowledge that it had none, that it was "just a two-year institution."

As I examine the way in which I answered these questions and as I continue to consider my new position, I find that my response to working in a two-year institution is more complicated than I would like to admit. I would like to be able to say that I was happy to have a job, and indeed I was. I would also like to be able to say that I saw no difference between the position I held at UW-Marinette and a comparable tenure-track position at a four-year institution and that I was pleased to be teaching only freshman composition as opposed to both composition and literature. As a consolation for not teaching literature, I was grateful for the opportunity this particular position offered me to teach second-year Spanish courses as well, drawing on my bachelor's degree in the language.

To a certain extent, however, I viewed accepting a position at a two-year institution as settling for something less than I had hoped for or expected. Perhaps I felt this way because I had no experience as a student or instructor at anything but four-year universities. While a few of my fellow graduate students had worked as adjunct instructors at two-year institutions, there were fewer still who professed a desire to land a tenure-track position at such a place. During graduate school, I believed that two-year institutions offered only instructional workloads prohibitive of any research, an intellectually inferior faculty, and a student population with lower abilities than those of students at four-year universities.

Surrounded now by intelligent colleagues who are often filled with the fervor of teaching well, I am chagrined to admit my initial prejudices of two-year institutions, their faculty, and their students. While I acknowledge that not enough time has elapsed for me to fully judge my lasting satisfaction with my current position, I contend that in no way has my position at a two-year institution failed to give me what I for so long had imagined receiving at a four-year institution. In comparing my current position with the one I imagined at a four-year university, I sometimes need to remind myself that teaching full-time was always my eventual goal. While a graduate student, my focus was on research and scholarship, but now that I teach full-time, these aspects of my life—research and teaching—become complementary.

Even with the responsibilities of teaching three sections of two different freshman composition courses and one section of second-year Spanish, I have still had time to do my own research and writing, both branched off of my dissertation in Victorian literature and related to teaching composition. I know that even as a tenure-track, probationary faculty member at that small, idyllic four-year liberal arts institution that I had long imagined, I would likely be teaching four classes, perhaps three composition classes and one literature class; indeed, many of the positions at four-year institutions for which I applied had four-four teaching loads. Furthermore, teaching English or any subject well is a labor-intensive process. All teachers struggle to find time for their own work, and I believe my struggle at a four-year institution would be much as it is now.

Additionally, I have happily landed in a situation where my colleagues and the administration are supportive of my efforts to continue my scholarly work. Thanks to the Internet and to readily accessible texts through quick and efficient interlibrary loan systems, my research is not hampered because I work at a two-year institution rather than at a small four-year university. Professional development funds are as available to me now as I believe they would be at a small four-year institution.

The skills I honed in graduate school are essential to my teaching work now, despite the absence of literature courses from my current slate of duties. Although I was trained in the final years of my graduate education as a Victorian specialist, I was also trained as a specialist in reading and writing. In composition courses, I teach students to read and understand more of the author's intended meaning as a way to help them become better writers. Thus, I am able to use the skills for approaching written texts that I developed throughout graduate school. If I am ever tempted to complain that I do not now have the chance to teach Victorian literature or other general literature courses, I consider the situation of many high school instructors. For example, my sister teaches high school mathematics. Although Karen has her master's degree in mathematics education and although during her undergraduate and graduate career she studied advanced levels of calculus, abstract algebra, non-Euclidean geometries, and other areas of higher-level mathematics, she teaches primarily advanced algebra and, once a year, an introductory algebra course geared to at-risk and learning-disabled students. The mathematical concepts she teaches certainly do not reach the level of education she has in the field. If I wish to complain that the grammatical concepts I teach are not equal to the education I have in literature, what do I say to her? She is the norm among high school instructors, who rarely teach the advanced material in their field that they studied during the last years of college and often years of graduate study for continuing education and licensing purposes.

I am, of course, conscious of the potential for burnout one faces when teaching the same material for many years. However, to a certain degree, my teaching of composition can become stagnant only if I allow it. After eleven years of teaching the same courses, Karen has responded to the possibility of stagnation not by fighting to obtain the right to teach calculus or advanced math but by adding to her curriculum reading and writing about the history of mathematics and important historical figures. Her advanced algebra students leave not only with an awareness of essential algebraic components but also with a stronger sense of the people behind mathematical discoveries, of ongoing research topics, and of the larger picture of the many and varied fields of mathematics. I expect that Karen would have little sympathy for me if I constantly complained about being unable to teach Victorian literature.

The students I teach at UW-Marinette provide the same challenges and offer the same rewards as those students I taught at four-year institutions. I have dedicated students who amaze me with their abilities, and I have students who struggle with the rigors of college life. I have students who are committed learners and actively engage in vibrant class discussions, and I have students who have yet to find their public voice. I have students who successfully balance work, family, and a full course load, and I have students who are struggling to balance three college classes. Teaching at a two-year college has given me the opportunity to work with a remarkably diverse student population.

Additionally, coming from a family of educators, I grew up knowing that the daily challenges of teaching are the same in any institution and even at any level. As a graduate student, I witnessed this reality when I worked part-time as an instructor at Sylvan Learning Centers, teaching children from third grade through college in the fields of mathematics, reading, writing, and study skills. The same teaching skills I had gained in the college classroom were applicable (with modification for grade level, of course) to students from various age groups. I remind myself now that teaching is teaching, no matter what the institution.

Ironically, even as I began to resolve my prejudice against teaching at a two-year institution, I was reminded by my students of the perceived difference in quality between a four-year and a two-year institution. I was unpleasantly surprised by a number of students who said to me that they see UW-Marinette as inferior to any four-year institution, not simply because of the obvious difference between the degrees one can achieve but also because of the lower level of education they believe they are receiving. One student considered the education he received from the professors at UW-Marinette as "an extension of high school curriculum" rather than the "high-level education" he would have obtained at a four-year institution. Others have made comments about why students are at UW-Marinette and not at a *"real* university," offering such reasons as an academic struggle in high school or the lack of financial resources. While some students may make such remarks because of their desire to leave their hometown (and their parents' home), these comments also suggest an underlying belief that one would attend UW-Marinette only because of extenuating circumstances, certainly not by choice.

At first I was surprised, even shocked, that students would choose to attend a school of which they thought so little. I was also disappointed and finally angered. At the center of their statements deprecating the education they were receiving was, I believed, their perception of the faculty members as inferior to those who taught general education courses at four-year universities. I told these students that in my class they were receiving the same level of education and were held to the same standards I had when teaching at four-year public and private institutions. In the end, however, I could not truly blame them, for had I not held the same assumptions about the faculty members and students at two-year institutions? Accepting my position at UW-Marinette has forced me to confront the elitist assumptions behind such statements.

I am not suggesting that grappling with these issues is behind me. I fully expect to have students each semester who question the legitimacy of the education they are receiving and who belittle the caliber of the students attending with them. I fully anticipate a continued struggle in myself over my decision to teach at a two-year institution rather than hold out for a similar position at a four-year institution. However, if I have indeed settled, it is for a tremendously rewarding and challenging job. The job-search process and my first year teaching full-time have taught me that what matter more than the type of institution at which one teaches are the faculty with which one works, the support staff that is available, the environment in which one teaches, and, most important, one's attitude toward the institution. My experiences throughout this transition from graduate school to teaching at a two-year institution have led me to believe that as professional educators we need to lead the way in changing how people outside academia view two-year institutions. We must review our own assumptions about such institutions, their faculties, and their student populations.

A number of articles have recently appeared in *Profession* and other journals regarding the struggles of English PhD recipients to find tenure-track positions at universities in the United States.[1] Few voices, however, have addressed the reality that there are numerous positions open at two-year institutions; such positions are seldom seen by graduate faculty members and students as viable professional options. The specific challenges and rewards of teaching at a two-year institution ought to be discussed in English graduate programs so that PhD recipients are better able to make informed decisions as they enter the job market.

What issues should be discussed in English graduate programs? Job-search seminars in the English department of Loyola University, Chicago, where I received my PhD, commendably always included discussion of how to tailor cover letters to better fit the mission statements of two-year institutions. Graduate students ought to be encouraged to consider teaching at two-year institutions as a viable professional option, and the benefits ought to be made clear. For example, two-year institutions often offer faculty members interdisciplinary opportunities. Many, including mine, are interested in the practice of learning communities, which allow instructors to broaden the parameters of what they teach. In *Border Talk: Writing and Knowing in the Two-Year College*, Howard B. Tinberg argues that faculty members at two-year institutions are uniquely "predisposed to cross borders" and are able to engage in "transdisciplinary conversations without feeling as if [they] have betrayed departmental or disciplinary affiliations" (68).

Tinberg also outlines his own decision to move from a four-year to a two-year institution, in large part to teach a more diverse student population. Texts and articles similar to his could be used in job-search seminars and professional topics courses to help graduate students understand the challenges and rewards of teaching at various types of institutions. There should also be an open dialogue among graduate students and faculty members about how positions at two-year institutions are perceived in higher education and the larger educational community.

This dialogue should take place both within graduate departments and across the discipline. At the 2000 NCTE convention, I attended a session entitled "Connections and Differences: Teaching at Two-Year and Four-Year Institutions," led by Mark Reynolds of Jefferson Davis Community College in Brewton, Alabama. The purpose of the session was to discuss how the challenges and opportunities provided by teaching at a two-year institution differ from those at a four-year institution. One of the attendees was a member of the graduate faculty at a PhD-granting institution, and he repeatedly asked what he could tell his students about teaching at a two-year institution. What could he say to them to convince them that such teaching was not simply a stepping-stone to a later position at a four-year university but could be in itself a truly rewarding career? While those of us at the session did not find any definitive answers, these important questions should be addressed by graduate English departments with and for their PhD students.

We continue to read about the changing face of education, with an increased reliance on distance learning and Internet courses. Age-old arguments, such as whether public or private institutions are better, remain of interest to many. The debates that surround the academic job market—about the use of adjunct instructors, about retirements and the subsequent loss of tenured faculty lines—are heated. As graduate students of English and as teachers of composition and literature at the postsecondary level, we must add to these discussions a dialogue about the professional opportunities that two-year institutions offer to recent PhD recipients. While teaching at a two-year institution is no solution for someone who truly wants to work at a research university, we should examine carefully how long-standing assumptions about two-year institutions may prevent people from considering such positions as professionally sound choices. As I hear of my graduate school colleagues finishing their doctorates and entering the job market, I hope they too will confront the assumptions they may hold about two-year institutions. I know I am better for having done so.

NOTE

[1] For example, John Guillory discusses graduate students' concerns over the increased job market expectations for them. Lisa Botshon and Siobhan Senier lament the growing presence of the "advice article" for recent PhD recipients and the status quo implications of the survival advice offered in such articles. Linda Hutcheon cogently describes the confusion graduate students face in deciding what preparation is necessary in order to obtain a tenure-track position after graduation. She also notes the creation by the MLA Executive Council of the Ad Hoc Committee on the Professionalization of PhDs to consider some of the issues involved in evaluating candidates for tenure-track positions in the field. As just these three articles evince, many important subjects regarding the current and future job market for English PhDs have already been broached.

WORKS CITED

Botshon, Lisa, and Siobhan Senier. "The 'How-to' and Its Hazards in a Moment of Institutional Change." *Profession 2000*. New York: MLA, 2000. 164–72.

Guillory, John. "Preprofessionalism: What Graduate Students Want." *Profession 1996*. New York: MLA, 1996. 91–99.

Hutcheon, Linda. "Professionalization and Its Discontents." *MLA Newsletter* 32.4 (2000): 3–4.

Tinberg, Howard B. *Border Talk: Writing and Knowing in the Two-Year College*. Urbana: NCTE, 1997.

Pagers, Nikes, and Wordsworth: Teaching College English in a Shopping Mall

MARTIN SCOTT

> *Our Dean of Something thought it would be good*
> *For Learning (even better for P.R.)*
> *To make the school "accessible to all"*
> *And leased the bankrupt bookstore at the Mall*
> *A few steps from Poquito's Mexican Food*
> *And Chocolate Chips Aweigh. So here we are—*
> —R. S. Gwynn, "The Classroom at the Mall"

My first month as a full-time instructor at Houston Community College, Northline Mall Campus, was marked by a fight and major loneliness. One day while I was giving my American literature students a nice, quiet exam, the sound of banging and thrashing came through the thin pasteboard walls of the classroom. I walked next door to investigate and found two students throwing punches and desks at each other while screaming death threats. I foolishly placed myself between them and, when security finally came (a well-armed off-duty Houston policeman), I learned what this violence on campus was all about. One of them claimed the other had stolen her pager. Or rather, she had loaned it to the other to get it activated, which evidently had not happened. Therefore, she was going to kill her and her children, too. I left the room and the two boxers as they were giving their statements to the cop.

The author is Instructor of English at Houston Community College, Northline Mall Campus, and a published poet and essayist.

The loneliness came from the way almost no one would speak to me in the faculty workroom for the first year. The instructors seemed intent on preserving their private pain and entered the room collating their personal humiliations. They sat down on the hard plastic chairs to coddle these hurts like insane, deformed kittens. If we had spoken, we would've had to admit to one another how broken and defeated we were. It got better when they hired some more new (read naive) people and remodeled the workroom into gray but spiffy carrels. Nevertheless, we all kept staring into the dead end right before our seats and, try as we might to make fun of it, felt the dust of death settling on our shoulders like a permanent dandruff.

I guess we all sensed, rightly or wrongly, that we were made for better things than this: for students who would come to class prepared, who came from decent high schools, and who could understand what we were saying if we said it clearly. Instead, we had students on the sophomore level who did not know the moon causes the tides or who, halfway into a semester of political science, would ask the instructor, "But what is *government*, anyway?" They weren't questioning authority; they did not know what authority was. And after surviving the ego thrashing required to receive a PhD, if we couldn't feel entitled to teach at Harvard or even a good state school without publishing more, maybe we could at least have offices and be treated as if we were highly trained professionals who knew what we were doing. But such was not the case: faculty meetings were all about how we were not turning in some form on time or not giving out our home number to students when we called to tell them their class was canceled. Or perhaps the issue was we were not happy about our twisted teaching schedules (five classes a semester—and most of us taught overloads as well—at widely spaced campuses). Judging by the faculty meetings, one would think that education, what goes on in the classroom, had no place in a community college. Cynicism is perhaps unavoidable anywhere, as I'm sure some Ivy League professors feel they have much to complain about, but the danger here at Northline was bitterness and the sense that life had taken something from you for which you were not compensated. I didn't want to be warped into bitterness.

After a few months of trying to get a good discussion going at Northline in class, I gave up. I had extensive teaching experience in the Houston area, and I had always prided myself on my ability to get ninety percent of any class to contribute to the flow and debate, but Northline beat me down. It wasn't that my students were mean or bad people; they were mostly friendly and attractive. They just didn't understand. Anything, it seemed. So I had them write in class much of the time and stopped asking too many probing questions or expecting probing answers. I think this was a good solution, because they certainly needed the writing practice, but something was lost. What can you do with a college class that doesn't know what *hierarchy* or *enchantment* means (I mean the literal definitions—they've never heard the words)? My questions in class now have to do with vocabulary and basic reading comprehension. My sophomore literature classes are now all about basic reading skills. Anything beyond that is asking many students to use an analytic thought process beyond their grasp, which cannot help being a little depressing if you have had a few classes of bright and articulate students in the past. For me, moving up to full-time employment meant leaving better schools behind.

So there are definitely times in your teaching career when you must balance ambition with reality and make some kind of compromise agreeable to both intellect and pocketbook. That is, you have to come to terms with the fact that even though there aren't brilliant graduate students lined up in the halls to confer with you, you still do some good with the community college undergraduates (should one call them "students," "clients," "customers"?) who sometimes come to class. The people you serve as an instructor at such an institution are important to society, or so our democratic system encourages us to think, but it is also clear that the status bestowed on "instructor, community college" is quite beneath that of "professor, major university." The underclass never merits the attention or prestige of the middle class, though, ironically, the pay scale for community college teachers is often significantly above that of university professors. I guess we like our top professors a little bit desperate, so we can yank the chain on them, if we need to. And we need to keep our instructors on the bottom solvent, or who would bother to teach those all-important accounting and reading classes to the workforce of the new service economy?

Before I acquired my full-time job teaching at Northline, I was a freeway flyer. That is, I pieced together a schedule of classes at three or four different colleges working for the reduced pay given to adjunct professors. When I was lucky and had a full schedule of eight to ten classes, I would spend up to two hours on the freeways each day, commuting among the different campuses spread all over the Houston area, the radio turned way up. This was the early nineties, so I got very familiar with alternative music, Nirvana and Hole, Pearl Jam and Bush. It was not unusual to begin my day on the extreme west end of town, in Sugarland at the Wharton County Junior College campus, and end up on the extreme east end of town, the north campus of San Jacinto Junior College. Sometimes I would listen to cassettes of John Lee Hooker or Robert Johnson during the long trips out to nowhere and back. Every night I'd stop in at the same convenience store for a package of Twinkies and some Diet Coke, the only compensation I could afford to balance off the blues of moving from campus to campus.

> Descend, O Musak! Hail to thee, World Lit!
> Hail, Epic ("most of which was wrote in Greek")
> And hail three hours deep in Dante's Hell
> (The occupants of which no one could spell)—
> As much as our tight schedule might admit
> Of the Great Thoughts of Man—one thought per week. (72)

So R. S. Gwynn has it, crying out from Beaumont, Texas, to the rest of the mall-teaching world. There is something fundamentally wrong with mixing the sale of Nikes and cheap imported clothing with education, but if one considers that education dollars are in competition with Montgomery Wards, one realizes just how far the groves of academe have been overgrown with poison ivy. A class including Milton and Wordsworth costs a little less than a pair of the coolest basketball shoes, but you can see and feel the shoes on your feet while they last. The whole internal education thing requires abstraction and discipline, two qualities not encouraged by our culture. Empiricism has won the day, undercutting even empiricism's child, science. The world is one black box tucked inside another, at least as far as our students are concerned.

O you who would judge me for my cynical attitude, come sit with me in some community college class down the street from the chemical refineries, where the sulfur and the plastic weigh heavy in the atmosphere and you breathe in mental hell with every assignment. As if in reverse compensation, the administration of the worst schools is the most oppressive, watching the least move of every instructor, since it is clear to administrators that teachers would not do their job if not coerced. You can feel the IQ points pouring out your ears as you try to talk to people whose ideas of college come from advertising slogans ("Learn more to earn more!") and their fathers' bitterness about factory work. Even the administration wants to take it out on the faculty, the smarty-pants and the eggheads, the pretty boys and the spoiled brats, as if those with their fresh PhDs hadn't already just got their asses kicked in the hazing of comprehensives and defenses and large student loans. I remember one administrator circulating through the building, making sure that none of us released our class five minutes early. The back wall of my classroom was glass, and every night she passed by, checking off her list. There was always this stern look of disappointment on her gray face, as I was too responsible and she could not have the pleasure of docking my pay.

Everyone's got a reason to be bitter: I've known elder statesmen poets and fiction writers who had published many books and won many awards but could not hide their bitterness at the world for not giving them more. They never had to teach at a community college, but the universities weren't giving them the chairs and fellowships they deserved, and no one ever gets enough applause and brownnosing. Out of bitterness flows politics, and out of politics flows bitterness—when someone outmaneuvers you.

I remember there was a time when I felt like education was sacred, that the initiation into the inner meaning of texts and concepts was an ecstatic occupation. Reading Wordsworth and Nabokov for the first time was like discovering new territory of the heart and mind, as if one were ascending to a new level of being. "Resolution and Independence" and *Pale Fire* are like nothing else, a pure intellectual drug. I still think about the high I got reading them the first time, and I search for that same feeling elsewhere in obscure or classical texts, the terror and beauty of the unknown book. The beauty is the aesthetic of the surface dimension of the text, and the terror is the depth of the symbolic and metaphoric: the waxwing flies into the mirror of the window, just as the leech gatherer wanders off to streams unknown. "By our own spirits are we deified" (Wordsworth, "Resolution" 155)—or so we will believe in solitude, but not in the company of unprepared students or perplexed administrators, who would rather we be less than human in perspicacity. The rush that brought us into teaching has little to do with class time and committees.

But there are moments when even the dullest classroom full of students is paying attention to every word you say, and the rapt look on their faces tells you they are getting your explication of Roland Barthes's essay "Toys"; are really moved by Whitman's compassion for a bird in "Out of the Cradle Endlessly Rocking"; or, during a personal conference, are beginning to understand just what a comma splice is and how to fix one. And then those very sweet moments when you say something funny and the whole class laughs for thirty seconds nonstop—they got something intellectual, and they laughed. These victories are hardly large, but they are real, and they do mean something to students. They make you feel that you're not speaking into the void the way you thought, that you *are* having an effect on how people think about life and reading. Then there are those students who manage to get into four-year private colleges or nursing schools because of the recommendations you wrote for them and the very optimistic lies you told about their performance in class. My students are all working to break out of the overworked, the underclass, or the criminal world, and a lot of them really do make it. And maybe I'm a part of that escape.

I can't say that what I do is sacred, though there have been times I've felt like a priest when students wanted to tell me their personal problems. Sometimes you have to listen—their fathers died and they are sure an unanswered telephone ring was from him in his last hour, or they were orphans growing up on the streets of Mexico City and did things to stay alive they would rather not remember. They broke up with their boyfriends or their girlfriends; their children have been murdered by their boyfriends or their girlfriends; their parents will not go into rehab but are the only ones who can baby-sit their children. Sometimes they cry and confess their sins in class; sometimes their husbands or their boyfriends stalk them on campus and even come into the classroom and you have to shoo them off. Sometimes their pagers and cellular phones go off over and over in one period. Sometimes you think the demons are hovering around their tender lives and you wish they'd just back off for one semester. It's a wonder they ever hear anything you say, but when they do, it's heaven.

I want my poor class to be the place where one can find

>   That blessed mood,
> In which the burden of the mystery,
> In which the heavy and the weary weight
> Of all this unintelligible world,
> Is lightened:—that serene and blessed mood,
> In which the affections gently lead us on,—
> Until, the breath of this corporeal frame
> And even the motion of our human blood
> Almost suspended, we are laid asleep
> In body, and become a living soul [. . .].
>   (Wordsworth, "Lines" 67)

Maybe literature is religion, or at least the best of it we have left to us. I don't know what it is that I'm supposed to be doing, but I know what my students need: a reason to go on and read a bunch of really hard texts. Then go home and face a hard life they cannot leave behind. I've heard all about it: violent fathers and husbands, the creeping hand of disease and murder, disloyal friends and the hamstringing cut of poverty and loneliness. It is the "still, sad music of humanity" (68) one hears in community college, in the papers and the discussions, in the journals and the conferences. This is the life the young Wordsworth lived and turned into poetry. It is the shudder of unbearable pain, the illness that tells us we must believe in something:

>   Nature never did betray
> The heart that loved her [. . .]
> [. . . . .]
>   [. . .] neither evil tongues,
> Rash judgements, nor the sneers of selfish men,
> Nor greetings where no kindness is, nor all
> The dreary intercourse of daily life,
> Shall e'er prevail against us, or disturb
> Our cheerful faith, that all which we behold
> Is full of blessings.   (69)

The reason to live and get educated is that words contain some hint of where salvation is to be found, and why should anything else matter to anyone? Maybe the walls are falling apart, but we have to believe that in the ruins lie the secret plans to the new temple and the heart of flesh on which the law is written like a tongue of flame. "Thanks to the human heart by which we live" (Wordsworth, "Ode" 145)—we make a family and a life out of everything we have been thrown into, as if there were a plan to this, a plan that we cannot possibly believe in but that we cannot possibly do without.

WORKS CITED

Gwynn, R. S. "The Classroom at the Mall." *Rebel Angels*. Ed. Mark Jarman and David Mason. Brownsville: Story Line, 1996. 72–74.

Wordsworth, William. "Lines Composed a Few Miles above Tintern Abbey." Wordsworth, *Poems* 66–70.

———. "Ode: Intimations of Immortality." Wordsworth, *Poems* 139–45.

———. "Resolution and Independence." Wordsworth, *Poems* 153–58.

———. *Selected Poems*. Ed. John O. Hayden. New York: Penguin, 1994.

The American Dream as a Life Narrative

MARGARET MORGANROTH GULLETTE

Narratives may have most power over us when they are most invisible: that is, infinitely repeatable but unnoticed and unanalyzed. The American dream is actually—whatever else it may be—such a narrative. As such, it still flourishes in the garrulous, half-lit, preconscious realm of conversation and writing, where all the other master narratives also once dwelled.

It is an example of a life-course story told by ordinary people in their everyday lives, over time, about work: first to themselves as a prospect, then in medias res, and finally in retrospect. Usually there's a motive or a pressure to tell a particular American-dream narrative to others. I first heard one told by my mother, spontaneously, as she was sitting at the kitchen table doing her lesson plans for her first-grade class. I must have been in mid adolescence, so she was then in her early forties. She'd say, "Well, there was the base pay I started with, $———— [giving the dollar amount of the first salary she had earned], then there was an increase of 3.2% the first year, the second year an increase of [she gave the percent increase each year since], so that's $————, plus the extra for the in-service courses, plus the extra for the extra degree [she had an MA], so that makes $————." Every year the numbers got bigger, and the implication was that they always would. (They did, thanks to the American Federation of Teachers.) My mother loved the litany. She also loved children and teaching; later, training apprentice teachers; the friends it made her—it was all John

---

The author is a writer and resident scholar in the Women's Studies Research Center at Brandeis University.

Dewey, conviviality, and mission. Talk about narrative pleasure! I have heard many self-delighting talkers in my time but never more solid satisfaction than in this oft told version of an incremental progress tale anchored to a rising age-wage curve.

My father, by contrast, when pressed, told economic stories that featured exciting and puzzling events—running booze to Trenton for a bootlegger during the depression, working for a "haberdasher"—as well as an episode of failure, six months of unemployment (mentioned once and never again). He had a daily story, certainly: up and out at six in all weather, home late, hard work. He was a small businessman who went in those years from repairing oil burners to co-owning a landscape nursery, delivering beverages, running his own parking lot. There was accumulation, there was saving; I knew he made the mortgage payments. But he told no longline economic story; he lacked a plot with narrative unity. What he earned was never mentioned; I assumed it veered up and down from year to year. This situation was frustrating and unsatisfying. I wanted my parents to have matched narratives; I wanted yet another happy progress story as a model and portent. Either his was incomplete or he didn't have one.

Frank Lentricchia talks about unpublished anecdotes that "stand in for a bigger story, a socially pivotal and pervasive biography" (321). My parents' storytelling inducted me young, as must happen to children, into what may be the biggest of those stories. What hers matched and his did not, I can now see, was the cultural archetype of success, with its nifty graphic shape (exhilarated storytelling in the kitchen, shopping expeditions made possible by the annual surpluses) and its personally applicable telos (my future going to college, my obtaining some unknown career that would go curving above theirs to empyreans of the elite). It was a family life-course story involving at least two generations.

My mother's autobiography had idiosyncratic elements, of course, but because she was permanently hooked into a seniority system, it was also a story of the ideal working life that many Americans wanted to tell about themselves and still do. (The local gender oddity was that my mother had the perfect story, my father the ad hoc, shapeless, deprived one. This difference gave me at first odd ideas about men, and later, a relation to feminism that was deep but orthogonal in a way Carolyn Steedman would immediately recognize.) Eventually, with effort, I figured out how to tell my father's story too, but for a long time my understanding of his entire life was hampered—empathetically obstructed—by the lack of fit between what he had to say about his work and the requirements of the dominant narrative.

Whether as spur, delusion, or reward, the so-called American dream is a model national biography that shapes subjectivity and (auto)biography.

Working Americans of all hyphenations strive in some relation to it. It is an economic life-course story that seems personal, although it can be realized only through the opportunity structures of a particular material world in historical time, in relation to such factors as class, race, ethnicity, gender, age, access to education, unions, et cetera. It requires extrinsic measures like steady employment, salary, security, and a rising age-wage curve as its infrastructure, but it conceals this material infrastructure, as well as the number and qualities of those who "fail," under an innocuous patriotic label that is also apparently ahistorical.

Moreover, as I show next, the narrative called the American dream comprehends and may affect many other meaningful and intrinsic life stories we can tell during those years: about selfhood and development, the fate of the family life course, friendship, community, avocations. As an economic life-course story, it privileges only the part of the life course that coincides with workforce participation: life from the first paycheck—from part-time hourly work as early as twelve or sixteen—until retirement. An economic life-course story also has a reflux effect on the earlier and later phases that appear to surround the working life, childhood and old age. Both phases are cast as unproductive and dependent, as capitalism requires. Old age in particular can be treated as a shard of life detached from the main site, an archaeological fragment that ought to be lovely in itself but is likely to drift into inconsequence, even abjectness. The comfort (or misery) of old age depends in part on earlier acquisitions—pensions, Social Security, savings—tied into one's economic history. Yes, our dominant economic narrative is central to life-course (auto)biography. This centrality has always been distressing in some ways. All the more now, because American-dream work and its narrative are both being undermined by contemporary attacks on employment conditions, especially seniority.

SENIORITY AND SENIORITY ENVY

Seniority makes rich promises for the life course: becoming more highly valued as you learn the ropes; getting respect, a pension increasing in worth, a reliable social life, friendships, trust, and salary raises that recognize your greater powers and the greater value of your generativity and institutional memory; feeling secure enough both to grow and to mentor others. The older you get, the higher your wage rises: ideally, your age-wage peak comes at retirement. That graph of respect pays off in your family too, in your ability to help your children financially as they grow up; and it pays in community currencies—in your ability to make ethical decisions, speak with authority, do good. Seniority, looked at this way, is a system for producing a certain narrative of the life course. Our dominant culture is not traditional with respect to aging into old age; quite the contrary. But our fundamental dream narrative tells the young that theirs will be a progress story, with youth, relative ignorance and powerlessness, and apprenticeship as the ephemeral starting points and with all the peaks saved for the middle years as a reward for growing older.

If seniority is a progress narrative, academic tenure was arguably the best of the twentieth century's institutional inventions for conferring the ability to tell it. But tenure is by no means the only one: unions provide similar supports, legal and customary; city, state, and federal governments (including the military) provide others. Standard jobs in corporations, businesses, and even in some factories—ladder jobs, with benefits—contribute elements of the same progress story. There's no need to position the academy as a separate sphere; there's excellent reason to observe it as akin to others, primus inter pares. That polyvalent and overworked term, the American dream, thus depends on structural chances: on getting the kinds of jobs—once available at many economic levels—that make a long-term progress narrative possible. When parents said they hoped that their adult children would do better than they did, they didn't mean better merely in educational attainment or at the entry level in a job; they meant what the adult children would potentially achieve later on, in their own middle years. The midlife high.

Critics have seen negatives in the seniority system—its exclusiveness, first of all. A dream is always premised on a lack; and why give disadvantaged people illusory hopes of a future, so that they stifle demands for their own progress out of hope that their children may achieve it? But because of the civil rights movements, affirmative action, and nondiscrimination laws, women, newer immigrants, African Americans, gays, people with disabilities, and others began to break into the system more often, riding the age-wave curve upward toward their own midlife highs, translating skills and experience into value added over time. So the story's constitutive tilt toward temporality as progress broadened historically, democratizing access to the narrative. (The uncomfortable fact that the midlife peaks are so different for the CEO and the janitor is obscured—both by the triumphalist story of American opportunity and by the smooth current boast that American inequality is the highest in the world.) As seniority accrued more progressive aspects, some of its other negatives were unconsciously eroded. So-called meritocracy doesn't seem so class- or race- or gender-biased or so personality-based if *aging* is the main proxy for experience-based merit. Hierarchy has less sting if it's a version of aging into the midlife that allows you and eventually your kids to climb its ladders.

I'm really telling a metastory: a brief, apparently Whiggish, history of the narrative of seniority from the point of view of those on the bottom in the postwar era. Seniority became a righteous story—to tell or to dream. Not just good enough: very good and likely to become better.

But some peculiar things, discursively and economically, have been happening since the 1970s. Now the young are being told that job security with seniority is something they don't want and that anyway it's going out of style. The implication is, it doesn't exist anywhere; forget about it. Yet what this media discourse purports to explain is an untruth. Seniority is as desirable as it ever was, and when younger people are offered a choice between a steady paycheck with a future or some short-term job with a remotely possible windfall in it, many take the security and the promise, despite what the media in the 1990s said they were asserting ("We like being contingent!" [Stirling]). In the academy, people who get offered tenure usually take it, and unless they are belittled beyond bearing as unproductive in their middle years and offered early-retirement packages, they usually keep that tenure.

The great problem is that in many areas of the economy people no longer get the choice. Once they've decided their likeliest field of work, it comes with a given limiting structure. A younger person can see it ahead: it's not going to be a steady long ascension with some kind of tenure after a probationary period but rather the shifting dunes and ruts of contingency year after year. Thirty percent of all American workers hold "nonstandard" jobs (Kalleberg et al.); such jobs are the trend. The working stiff on that track of the economy is isolated in the workforce: an adjunct in the academy, a temp or consultant outside. Whatever your title is, you put in your time, moving headlong closer to the impossible 24-7—but your effort doesn't translate into reputation, perks, or a future. Even when you've amassed a résumé, keeping up your personal and economic value seems like Sisyphus's task. You roll a rock up a hill, alone, every day, without help, and see it rolled down again overnight. That's a trope of endless repetition, exhaustion, anxiety, affront, and other assaults on self-esteem (Beckett provides its structure, Dilbert its daily details)—a trope for lives lived without seniority. *Of course* those who still have seniority are envied.

Envy does not, by itself, explain the virulence with which tenure is being attacked for everyone from first-grade teachers to university professors. The contempt expressed in the business and mainstream media has a financial motive. The managerial class is driving wages down by making as many workers as possible "flexible." The business mentality applied to the universities has accomplished this economy at the cost of creating a demeaning two-tier system, where adjuncts earn one-half to one-quarter what tenured or tenure-track people earn for doing the same work. In K–12, we see this bottom-line approach in state after state; it presses for posttenure review and charter-school evasions of seniority—making teaching at those levels an increasingly less attractive profession. As tenure is being weakened or terminated in nominally unionized school systems, the process isolates higher education as the imagined sole repository of seniority, threatening tenure up the line.

The undermining of the seniority system in all walks of life is a long-term effect of corporate restructuring (e.g., downsizing, outsourcing, exporting jobs overseas) and Republican policies, such as the decades-long attack on unions and on so-called big government, including Social Security. Education is the third target. The main fault of all three is that they provide security, seniority, and pensions. Some nonunion businesses offer decent remuneration but not as rights guaranteed by the employees' manual. Education, unions, big-hearted government where it still exists—these are the remaining systems that support workers through the life course and give them a claim on telling the American dream.

But envy is a factor in this undermining that not only teachers at all levels and labor unionists but all working people ought to worry about in their philosophical moments. Management under globalization can destroy the concept of seniority and the memory of its life-course benefits only if the public becomes passive or hostile. One way to produce these reactions is to convince people rhetorically that there are no alternatives to lifetime insecurity. The complementary way is to eliminate the existing alternatives by making people feel that Sisyphus's situation ought to be more broadly shared. If my rock rolls downhill every night, let everyone else suffer equally! Let there be no one able to move a rock a little way up the hill and ratchet it there. Why should anyone rest? Especially in higher ed! Tenure was once simply the best form of seniority, the one toward which other forms could aspire; it was justified by the awe paid to those capable of earning a PhD, by the nobility of teaching the young, by the dignity of accepting low pay. Those values remain, but now tertiary education is made to seem the only provider of seniority and, by this sleight of hand, the last and unjust realm of outmoded privilege.

The appearance of being singular and passé is untrue (think of generals and CEOs with stock options), and the implication of unfairness is faulty. Envy doesn't see that the seniority systems of education, the government, and the unions serve Americans both as a standard and—in Shakespeare's words from *Coriolanus*—"a world elsewhere" (3.3.135). As long as these institutions support the system and the narrative, the young or the disenchanted can move into them instead of shouldering the rock up the hill. Knowing the existence of that option, business must somehow compete with the modest but secure standards set by these institutions. Other workers in the Sisyphean economy, aka global capitalism, thus benefit. End the "world elsewhere," and nothing can stop the drive to the bottom.

Envy is another "corrosion of character"—like loss of trust, one of the feelings that Richard Sennett talks about in his remarkable 1998 book about the effects of postindustrial capitalism on selfhood. We can see envy of tenure being built up through the supposed superiority of generation X in the New Economy and the alleged reports of members of that generation shouting, "Down with baby boomers!" (Gullette, "Xers"). Envy is a nasty, isolating emotion that blinds us to the truths of job degradation and even to our own anxiety and fear. It's a self-defeating emotion and divisive enough to assist the triumph of antilabor and middle-ageist forces.

The crises in higher education (the reliance on the business model, the loss of tenure lines and the proliferation of adjuncts, the weakness of the job market for graduate students and for most faculty members) have led to attacks on tenure from within our own ranks. The young are being turned against their elders. They sometimes innocently mouth the middle ageism borrowed from the media, with its ignorant assumption that *deadwood* is an age-related term. Age-cohort differences are reified; historical change is ignored in favor of pop demography. Even inside feminism—usually so suspicious of binaries—those markers of excess difference, second-wave and third-wave, may wash us apart. Those with tenure are led to feel guilty about retaining it, and those without it are led to think that the only way to get a job is to have a midlife person leave one.

Working people—among whom I include those in the teaching profession at all its levels—need solidarity. We need more security, not less. Attacks on tenure are being rebutted, especially in the new *Academe* under the editorial direction of Ellen Schrecker. But the arguments narrowly limit themselves to the so-called ivory tower. Nowhere except in my essay "The Politics of Middle Ageism" have I seen a broad-based case made for seniority as a countervailing system against globalizing forces. Such a case provides a new weapon for wider resistance to these trends—a weapon available to, and for the sake of, everyone in the working world. Here I want to urge as well that we argue—in the language of the humanities—on behalf of the intimate, precious, and precarious life-course narrative that, under the name of the American dream, relies on seniority to survive.

Academics can resist in our institutions by supporting tenure and the expansion of tenure to adjuncts, by joining AAUP or a union (as even doctors are doing). We can support other seniority systems, donate to a group that is unionizing (graduate students, temps, Nicaraguan textile producers), join a group that tells people where the danger spots are—like Teachers for a Democratic Culture; Scholars, Artists, and Writers for Social Justice (SAWSJ); or, at the international level, the Campaign for Labor Rights.[1]

The Long March toward Age Studies

Why has the American dream not been recognized as a life-course narrative? Why didn't I for one recognize it as such earlier? My mother's story had been so important to me; my father's, in other ways, no less. I have considered myself a partisan of age studies since the early 1990s. Moreover, on the long journey of raising my age consciousness (and trying to figure out what age consciousness meant if it didn't mean fretting about skin, hair, and bones), I fortunately started as a fiction critic working on narratives about midlife characters. My *Safe at Last in the Middle Years: The Invention of the Midlife Progress Novel* distinguished "midlife Bildungsromane" from the "Bildungsroman of youth," the midlife "progress" genre from the "decline" narrative, and even noted, of nonwriters, "we're not used to the idea that our own personal life story is likely to have a genre" (xvi).

I can begin to answer this question about conceptualization by noting what interdisciplinary and theoretical developments of the 1980s and 1990s provided elements essential to it. In the humanities, many besides me needed the insights of feminist cultural studies before we could look at the everyday and begin to descry the history of the present. All resistant critical theory (race, queer, feminist, legal, age) asks us to seek out marginalized or silenced stories. Marxist theory enables us to tie narrative together with labor conditions—to see the American-dream narrative as an economic life-course story supported or endangered by specific, historical, namable forces. But the fundamental conceptual need, I would argue, was to recognize that age (in literature, the age of the author, the age of the protagonist or prior self, the age of the assumed reader; in culture, relevant age discourses) makes a tremendous difference to narration. In her monologue, my mother taught me one meaning of time passing; my father, through his allusions and reticences, another. All around us, if we learn to observe it, we can notice people talking and writing in similarly subtle ways about age and aging.

But the study of life-course narrative, in particular, has not been a named emphasis in literary and cultural studies, even in identity theory and (auto)biography studies. Identities are recognized to be multiple only simultaneously, at one static point in time, when in fact they are also multiple sequentially, over time. "Life writing" is now an alternative name for (auto)biographical writing and its study (Jolly). Kathleen Woodward in her essays on Freud (*Aging*) and Simone de Beauvoir early demonstrated how age-wise critique can shake up our clichés about the naturalness of telling age. But in general little life writing is focused on age in a critical way. The *Journal of Narrative and Life History* emerged from the field of psychology rather than literature (they dropped "life history" from the title and now call themselves *Narrative Inquiry*). In the humanities some concerned with age were encouraged by age-conscious work going on in anthropology (Barbara Myerhoff, Judith K. Brown [Kerns and Brown]), psychology (Abigail Stewart [Stewart and Healey]), and history (Tamara Hareven, Thomas R. Cole). Roy Schafer, by observing how some psychoanalytic theories construct life stories, brought me closer to understanding that some subset of narratives might serve as explanatory systems for life in particular historical conjunctures. Life stories could come in different rhetorics, flavored by their disciplinary or media origins, by their different distorting metaphors, or by their relentless expectations.

Specifically, age theory needed to develop a historicized, narrativized, and demystified midlife studies. Without that, the long middle of adulthood remained unmarked, despite the dissemination since 1900 in England and the United States of the new age class: the middle years. (In literary studies, the emphasis still often falls on the "season of youth," to echo a title of Jerome Buckley's. The expansion of the canon has, from this point of view, mainly added many different kinds of young people—still venturing no further along than the so-called coming of age.) Once the midlife was critically marked, the term filled in the life course as a discursive and cultural construction from the first "Happy birthday to you" until the living will.

By then I understood the term *age* not as a euphemism for old age, not as the object of gerontology's disciplinarity, not as a mere social science variable. Suddenly age could join gender and race, class and sexuality, disability and religion, as a set of categories, terms, practices, beliefs, relations, institutions, et cetera. Age is then universally relevant not because it is a biological fate but because it is implicated, startlingly, in all formulations of life's events.

Age studies is an emerging approach that will have exciting, perhaps immense repercussions in the humanities. But that future is a subject for another time. All I need add in relation to my theme of seniority and the American-dream narrative is that we needed a feminist, materialist, critical-cultural, and historically minded age studies in the humanities before we could have a notion of temporality that foregrounded narrative as life history. And we needed the concept "age studies" to transcend "aging studies," gerontology's bailiwick, and the other "slice-of-life studies" (Gullette, "Age Studies as Cultural Studies" 219–30) before we could see the whole life as a field for storytelling.

NOTE

[1] The addresses for these groups are: Teachers for a Democratic Culture, c/o Stephen Parks, English Department, Temple University, Philadelphia, PA 19122; Campaign for

Labor Rights, 1247 E Street, SE, Washington, DC 20003; SAWSJ, Labor Relations and Research Center, University of Massachusetts, Amherst, MA 01003.

WORKS CITED

Buckley, Jerome Hamilton. *Season of Youth: The Bildungsroman from Dickens to Golding*. Cambridge: Harvard UP, 1974.

Cole, Thomas R. *The Journey of Life: A Cultural History of Aging in America*. Cambridge: Cambridge UP, 1991.

Gullette, Margaret Morganroth. "Age Studies as Cultural Studies." *Handbook of the Humanities and Aging*. Ed. Thomas R. Cole, Robert Kastenbaum, and Ruth E. Ray. 2nd ed. New York: Springer, 2000. 214–34.

———. *Safe at Last in the Middle Years: The Invention of the Midlife Progress Novel*. Berkeley: U of California P, 1988. Lincoln: iUniverse, 2001.

———. "'The Xers' and 'the Boomers': A Contrived War." *Review of Education/Pedagogy/Cultural Studies*. Forthcoming.

Hareven, Tamara, ed. *Transitions: The Family and the Life Course in Historical Perspective*. New York: Academic, 1978.

Jolly, Margaretta, ed. *Encyclopedia of Life Writing*. 2 vols. London: Fitzroy, 2001.

Kalleberg, Arne L., et al. *Nonstandard Work, Substandard Jobs*. Washington: Economic Policy Inst., 1998.

Kerns, Virginia, and Judith K. Brown, eds. *In Her Prime: New Views of Middle-Aged Women*. 2nd ed. Urbana: U of Illinois P, 1992.

Lentricchia, Frank. "In Place of an Afterword—Someone Reading." *Critical Terms for Literary Study*. Ed. Lentricchia and Thomas McLaughlin. Chicago: U of Chicago P, 1990. 321–38.

Myerhoff, Barbara. *Number Our Days*. New York: Dutton, 1978.

Schafer, Roy. *Language and Insight*. New Haven: Yale UP, 1978.

Sennett, Richard. *The Corrosion of Character: The Personal Consequences of Work in the New Capitalism*. New York: Norton, 1998.

Steedman, Carolyn Kay. *Landscape for a Good Woman: A Story of Two Lives*. New Brunswick: Rutgers UP, 1987.

Stewart, Abigail J., and Joseph M. Healy, Jr. "Linking Individual Development and Social Changes." *American Psychologist* 44.1 (1989): 30–42.

Stirling, David. "The Search for Database Marketing Talent." *Direct Marketing* Aug. 1997: 28.

Woodward, Kathleen. *Aging and Its Discontents: Freud and Other Fictions*. Bloomington: Indiana UP, 1991.

———. "Simone de Beauvoir." *The Private Self: Theory and Practice of Women's Autobiographical Writings*. Ed. Shari Benstock. Chapel Hill: U of North Carolina P, 1988. 90–113.

Languages and Language Learning in the Face of World English

JOHN EDWARDS

English in the World

These are difficult times for some languages—the small ones, the stateless ones, those of lesser-used or minority status, and so on. An exchange taken from a recent conference transcript is illustrative here:

> "What do you think of Gallic now—be honest!"
> "Well, it's a language that may still do you some good in the Highlands and Islands, maybe still in parts of Cape Breton, but outside those little areas, it isn't going to take you very far . . ."
> "Isn't it used in any other settings, then?"
> "No, it's simple, really—no one to speak it with. Who did you have in mind?"
> "Maybe Scots abroad . . . ?"
> "Listen, outside Scotland, Gallic speakers hardly use the language at all, even amongst themselves."
> "OK, but what d'you think of the language itself—is it a good sort of language, or what?"
> "Actually, I'm not too keen on it, as a language per se. It has become pretty bastardised, you know, bit of a mixture really—different dialects, English borrowings . . ."

This little discussion surely has a familiar ring to it: a "small" language struggling against larger forces, a variety increasingly confined geographically and

---

The author is Professor of Psychology at Saint Francis Xavier University. A version of this article appeared in the Winter 2001 issue of the ADFL Bulletin.

socially, a medium whose intrinsic status is often seen as degraded and impure. And, if it proves difficult to maintain such a language in something like its native state, what attraction does it possess for language learners elsewhere? Why would anyone study it at school or university? The elementary catch-22 operates here: How can you induce the learning of a language when its community of use is negligible, but how will that community ever grow unless more join it? The dreary downward spiral seems fated to continue, resulting in a native community that is small and a secondary community that may become the preserve of a tiny band of consciously committed enthusiasts.

I have been deceitful here. The exchange about Scots Gaelic never took place. It is modeled, however, on this earlier passage:

> "What thinke you of this English tongue, tel me, I pray you?"
> "It is a language that wyl do you good in England, but passe Douer, it is woorth nothing."
> "It is not vsed then in other countreyes?"
> "No sir, with whom wyl you that they speake?"
> "With English marchants."
> "English marchantes, when they are out of England, it liketh them not, and they doo not speake it."
> "But yet what thinke you of the speech, is it gallant and gentle, or els contrary?"
> "Certis if you wyl beleeue me, it doth not like me at al, because it is a language confused, bepeesed with many tongues: it taketh many words of the latine, & mo from the French, & mo from the Italian, and many mo from the Duitch [. . .]." (Yates 32)

This is taken from John Florio's *First Fruits*; published in 1578, it is a textbook and manual for the teaching of Italian to English gentlemen. The fruits *"yeelde familiar speech, merie Prouerbes, wittie Sentences, and golden sayings. Also a perfect Induction to the Italian, and English tongues [. . .]. The like heretofore, neuer by any man published"* (as Florio modestly points out in his fuller title). John Florio was, of course, an exceedingly interesting character who played many different roles, language teacher and translator among them. He provided, for instance, an engaging—if sometimes rather loose— translation of Montaigne's *Essays*, a translation read and used by Shakespeare. In his time (c. 1553–1625), French, Italian, and Spanish were the powerful international languages, widely studied in Tudor and Stuart England. Italian challenged the supremacy of French in both the cultural and the commercial worlds, and many prominent Elizabethans studied it. Indeed, the queen herself was a student, along with luminaries like Edmund Spenser and the earl of Southampton, Henry Wriothesly—a literary patron to Florio and, more famously, to Shakespeare (Yates; Acheson).

Very few people in the sixteenth century would hav[e predicted world] status for English, a language with four or five millio[n speakers, well] back in the linguistic sweepstakes. The point is a simp[le one: varieties] of language rise and fall; the variety that today wields [an influ]ence on a scale never before seen was once of very secondary im[po]r[tance] and restricted utility. It is easy to lose sight of this immediately demonstrable fact—particularly, of course, at a time when historical knowledge and the contextualization of current events to which its application must inevitably lead are commodities of little priority. It is sometimes imagined that the global power of English represents a new phenomenon. It is, however, only the most recent manifestation of a very old one, although its strength and its scope are arguably greater than those possessed by earlier "world" languages: the difference, then, is one of degree rather than of principle. I don't mean to argue that all this somehow lessens the impact of English on other varieties; I simply want to suggest that social and linguistic struggles to resist the encroachments of English are not battles against demons never seen before. I would also not wish to belittle the anxieties felt by those whose languages and cultures are under threat. I only wish to say that all these things have happened before and will no doubt happen again: it is an old play we are looking at here, a play whose plot endures while the cast changes.

Languages of "wider communication" have no special linguistic capabilities to recommend them; they are simply the varieties of those who have power and prestige. It seems necessary to repeat this truism quite frequently, and not merely for the benefit of those languishing in ignorance outside the academy. I find in the Fall 1999 *ADFL Bulletin*, for example, a piece that suggests that current linguistic dominance

> lies very simply in the fact that English is more responsive than any other language to the growing knowledge base that is the hallmark of these postmodern times. It is this ability to be eclectically open to new thoughts, new ideas, new concepts that has predisposed English to be the major medium of modern communication. (Eoyang 27)

It is undoubtedly the case that, more than (some) other languages, English has been an open and "loose" medium—ready to take what was needed from other varieties, to be flexible in the face of modern necessity, and so on. It is an egregious mistake, however, to think that such "openness" accounts for its dominance. The truth is rather more brutal. (I note in passing here that one occasionally reads a defense of some threatened "small" variety that is based on its elegance of phrasing, its regularities, its linguistic "purity," its marvelous literature: this language is just as good as the

...king neighbor next door. Unfortunately, as Mae West once said, apropos of diamonds, goodness has nothing to do with it.)

The reasons for the relative "openness" of English are not entirely transparent, but they certainly are entwined with many historical threads. There exist, today, a strength and practicality about English that make a relaxed stance easy; that is, a secure and powerful medium need not worry very much about borrowings and hybrids, about localizations and colloquialism, about purism and prescriptivism. But even if we go back to periods in which English was not dominant, back (say) to the sixteenth and seventeenth centuries, when "standard" national languages were beginning to emerge in Europe, we find English linguistic reflexes to be unlike those elsewhere. The most notable example is the lack of a language academy whose purpose is to help standardize, yes, but usually also to protect, to keep out foreign influence, to manage neologisms, and so on. Some years ago, Randolph Quirk pointed to an "Anglo Saxon" aversion to "linguistic engineering," a disdain for language academies and their purposes—goals that, he felt, were "fundamentally alien" to English speakers' conceptions of language (68). This is putting things too strongly, perhaps, but it is certainly noteworthy that the United Kingdom and the United States are virtually the only countries not to have (or to have had) formal bodies charged with maintaining linguistic standards. It is also interesting to consider that—given the obvious need for standardization, even in English—both countries essentially appointed one-man academies; the great lexicographers Samuel Johnson and Noah Webster produced dictionaries that became the arbiters of standards and of "correctness."

One aspect of English "openness," and another indication of its strength, can be found in the degree of its localization around the world, and—more important, perhaps—the attitudes attaching to this localization. Compare the recent history of English with French in this regard. The latter has seen its influence shrink dramatically, and it is unsurprising that the current stance is often one of protection and defense. Part of this involves a renewed vigor—for the basic tendency was always there—in what might be called linguistic centralism. French is certainly interested in expansion—in bringing Antoine Rivarol's language of clarity to more people—but this is to be accomplished in a guarded and centralist way. English, however, is much more *de*centralized, less guarded, and more expansive. Local varieties achieve considerable status (Indian English provides perhaps the single best example of a developing and accepted indigenized model) and, indeed, some predict an increasing divergence, reminiscent of the birth of the Romance languages; but it must be noted that there are strong countertendencies to this. In any event, a language once tainted by imperialism is rapidly becoming one of "our" languages in many parts of the world. It is suggestive that we see books devoted to the "new Englishes," that there are journals called *World Englishes* and *English World-Wide*, and that these have essentially no equivalents in French scholarly circles.[1]

It is obvious that even "big" languages now worry about English—examples can easily be found of English usages common in France, in Japan, in Germany. It is worth noting, though, that these usages do not simply fill *new* needs or avoid translations for words in common international exchange; they can also push aside already-existing equivalents. It is one thing, then, to refer to *das Web-Design* or *der Cursor*, and perhaps another to employ *der Trend* or *der Team* or *der Cash-Flow*. External pressures often lead to internal division. "E-mail" is commonly used in French, for example, even though the Académie Française has endorsed *message électronique* (or *mel*, an abbreviated version), and Quebec's Office de la Langue Française has plumped for *courriel*. It is not very surprising, either, that within the wider language community the more threatened sectors will tend to be the most linguistically watchful. Canada's sovereigntist Parti Québécois recently accused France of not being French enough, of not sufficiently guarding the barriers, when it was announced that Air France pilots would now speak English to air-traffic controllers in Paris. This is in line with international practice, which makes English the norm in aviation, but French has been allowed in Quebec airspace for twenty years, and its place there has considerable symbolic importance. French pilots may inform ground control that they are about to commence *le fuel dumping*, but their Québécois counterparts are more likely to refer to *délestage*. All this suggests that there now exists a division in the ranks of "big" languages: English is the sole occupant of one category, while French, German, Spanish, Russian, and other languages jostle among themselves in the second.[2]

Learning Languages in North America

It has always been more difficult to teach and to learn foreign languages in North America than in Europe. Within Europe, the difficulties have—in recent times, at least—been greater in Britain than on the Continent. Do we observe here some genetic anglophone linguistic deficiency? Are the British and the Americans right when they say, "I'm just no good at foreign languages"? Are they right to envy those clever Europeans (or, indeed, Africans and Asians) who slide effortlessly from one mode to another? The answers here obviously involve environmental conditions, not genetic ones, but I present these rather silly notions because—to the extent to which they are believed or half-believed or inarticulately felt—they constitute a type of self-fulfilling prophecy that adds to the difficulty of language learning. I use the word *adds* here because the real difficulties, the important contextual conditions, the soil in which such prophecies flourish have to do with power and dominance. Anglophone linguistic laments perhaps involve some crocodile tears or, at least, can seem rather hollow: the regrets of those who lack competence, but who need not, after all, really bother to acquire it.

Given what I've said earlier about the status of English in Florio's time, for instance, we could assume that English speakers, when not globally dominant, were actually assiduous language learners. This is a view endorsed by Norman Davies in his recent popular history: before the twentieth century, the idea that the British were somehow innately ill-equipped to speak foreign languages would have seemed ludicrous, and most educated people (not just the royals, not just Victoria and Albert chatting away in German) were, in fact, bilingual or better. There are counterindications, however, and, indeed, one of those takes us back exactly to Florio's day. In *The Merchant of Venice*, Portia complains of Falconbridge, one of her suitors, that "he understands not me, nor I him: he hath neither Latin, French, nor Italian" (1.2). All her admirers, including a Scot, are criticized, but only the English one is slated for linguistic incompetence. (Nick Oulton provides the Shakespearean example here—noting that perhaps the pre–twentieth-century competence attributed by Davies to the "British" might exclude the English!)

Well, we need not take Shakespeare as an infallible guide to language abilities here, but, in any event, there is no real paradox. Educated English speakers were, at once, more broadly capable in foreign languages than they are now and increasingly less capable—because of the growing clout of their maternal variety—than their Continental colleagues. A related and relevant point is that as we approach the modern era we find that linguistic competence becomes more and more associated with formal educational instruction and less driven by mundane necessity. Of course, this is a very general statement, and there are all sorts of exceptions to it. Nonetheless, the correlation between the social, political, and economic dominance of the English-speaking world and the decline in its foreign language competence—for those reasons already touched on—means that language learning becomes more a matter of the classroom than of the street. And this has clear implications for both students and teachers.

These implications are, if anything, rather more pointed in North America than they are in Britain (or should I say England?), and they rest on an interesting point. It is commonly accepted that favorable attitudes and positive motivations are central to successful second-language learning. There is, indeed, a very large literature on this theme (see, e.g., Edwards,

Multilingualism; Noels and Clément). The importance of favorable attitudes, however, *varies inversely with real linguistic necessity*. Historically, most changes in language-use patterns owe much more to socioeconomic and political pressures than they do to attitudes. Some have suggested that one sort of motivation may play a part here. A mid-nineteenth-century Irishman, for instance, could well have loathed English and what it represented, while still realizing the mundane necessity to change. This *instrumental* motivation is, of course, a grudging quantity and quite unlike what has been termed an *integrative* one—that is, one based on genuine interest in another group and its language, perhaps involving a desire to move toward that group in some sense. There might also be a useful distinction to be drawn here between *favorable* and *positive* attitudes (to cite the adjectives I used above). To stay with the Irish example, one could say that the language attitudes toward English were typically instrumental—and positive in the sense of commitment or emphasis—but not necessarily integrative or favorable. Of course, attempting to separate instrumentality from "integrativeness" may prove, in practice, to be difficult and, as well, the relation between the two no doubt alters over the course of language shift. But there *is* a distinction between, say, the English needed by Japanese engineers and that sought by Japanese professors of American literature; the difference is one of depth of fluency, to be sure, but it goes beyond that (Edwards, *Language*).

Similarly, the language teaching of most interest here is something that goes beyond language training, although it must build on that and although some students are primarily interested in acquiring what we could now call an instrumental fluency. It has been argued that since attitudes (favorable ones, at least) are often of little consequence in real-life situations of language contact and shift, they are trivial elsewhere, too. My point is simply that attitudes may assume *greater* importance in many teaching settings: if the context is *not* perceived to be very pertinent in any immediate or personal way; if the participant is *not* there out of real, mundane necessity, then attitudes may make a real difference. In this way—leaving ability out of the equation, of course—language classes may become just like all others.

In a society that rewards narrow and immediately applicable learning, in educational systems that are increasingly corporatized, in the thousand-channel universe that confuses information with knowledge (awash in the former and inimical to the latter), and in a world made more and more safe for anglophones, language learning and all its ramifications lose immediacy. Not only does instrumental appeal lessen, but the more intangible and more profound attractions—to which instrumentality leads and with which it is entwined—also inevitably decline. These are the social constraints within which language teaching and learning occur, and they tend to dwarf more specific settings. At a recent seminar, Janet Swaffar made some suggestions (which were reprinted in the *ADFL Bulletin*) "to help foreign language departments assume command of their destinies," and the usual suspects were pedantically rounded up: a redefinition of the discipline ("as a distinct and sequenced inquiry into the constituents and applications of meaningful communication"); more emphasis on communication and less on narrow grammatical accuracy; the establishment of standards, models, and common curricula (for "consistent pedagogical rhetoric"), and so on (10–11). All very laudable, no doubt, but why do I think of Nero? It has always been difficult to sell languages in Kansas; wherever you go, for thousands of miles, English will take you to McDonald's, get you a burger, and bring you safely home again—and a thorough reworking of pedagogical rhetoric doesn't amount to sale prices.

Broadly speaking, there are two paths through the woods, although occasionally they share the same ground. The first is for foreign language teaching to satisfy itself with that shrinking pool of students intrinsically interested in languages and their cultures. These are, after all, the students nearest to one's own intellectual heart. The problem is that the natural constituency here might prove too small to support a discipline at desired levels, and it is hard to nurture it in any direct way. The other is to hope and work for a renewed instrumental interest, with whatever longer term fallout that might lead to. On the one hand, this is dependent on a context that extends well beyond national borders and on alterations in global linguistic circumstance that, while inevitable, are not always easy to predict. On the other hand, things might be done at home—a home that is, after all, culturally diverse, in which the loss of a hundred native languages to English is seen as uneconomic, in which the rights of immigrants (particularly those who are entitled to vote) attract social and political attention, and so on. In a word, we look at Spanish.

The importance of the study of Spanish in the United States is self-evident. It is a language that has a lengthy cultural and literary tradition with many interesting branches to the original trunk, and it remains a widely used variety around the world; with something like 300 million speakers, it runs fourth (behind Hindi, Chinese, and English) in the usage sweepstakes. Academically, then, it is the ideal second language. More immediately, recent reports show that there are over 30 million people of Hispanic background in America (about 12% of the population); that this group is the fastest-growing minority; and that in fifty years' time its proportions will double, so that one in four Americans will be of this ethnic origin. (These are informed speculations, of course, and there is room for variation: Carlos Fuentes recently said that by 2050 three out of every five Americans will speak Spanish.) The figures, impressive as they are on their own, take on more weight when we consider their traditionally concentrated nature: millions of people living more or less together are a different sociological phenomenon than if they are scattered among others. At the same time, not all Hispanic people live in the Southwest or the Southeast. In the last ten years their numbers have more than doubled in Iowa (to take one example), and they are now more numerous than black Americans there (Bohrer; see also Fuentes). All in all, a powerful and growing population.

Considering both the global and the national presence of Spanish, it is little wonder that the language is the linchpin of modern language teaching in the United States. The whole discipline, however, remains weak: even though recent (1998) MLA statistics suggest an overall increase of about 5% in foreign language enrollments since 1995, only 1.2 million college students are represented here, fewer than 8% of the total. There have been, indeed, steep declines in some quarters; enrollments in German were reportedly down by 7.5% (90,000 students altogether), and those in French decreased by 3% (to about 200,000). But for Spanish, the figures are better: enrollments are up by about 8%, which translates to some 660,000 students. And to complete this part of the story one can see that students of Spanish thus constitute 55% of *all* language students. Is Spanish learning in a healthy situation, then, or does it only seem so in comparison with weaker sisters?[3]

This may be an impossible question to answer. How many students *ought* to be studying Spanish—or archaeology, or quantum mechanics, or sculpture? Still, one might expect that language study would be more immediately related to extraeducational factors, for example, jobs, mobility, and opportunity, and, if that is so, then one might wonder why the strength of the American Hispanic community does not bolster the educational effort more.

In fact, despite America's multiethnic status in general, and its powerful Hispanic components more specifically, the country remains resolutely anglophone in all important domains and, indeed, the chief supporter of English as a global language. Historically, the melting pot has been most effective at the level of language, that is, while aspects of cultural continuity can be discerned in various groups, languages other than English typically last no longer than the second or third generation, and the normal pattern has meant moving from one monolingualism to another. This is true, even for the two special cases, francophones in New England and hispanophones in the Southwest—special, inasmuch as they, unlike all other arrivals, remain close to their heartlands, the borders of which are easily and frequently crossed. The timing of language shift is naturally dependent on such variables, but the overall shape of the curve is remarkably similar across groups.

All this makes Carlos Fuentes's remarks rather naive, even though they are eminently understandable, reflective of the views of many, and, indeed, attractive in their impulse. He asks why most Americans know only English and sees their monolingualism as a "great paradox": the United States is at once the supreme and the most isolated world power. Why, he continues, does America "want to be a monolingual country?" All twenty-first-century Americans ought to know more than one language in order to better understand the world and deal with problems. And so on and so on. Obviously, monolingualism is not a paradox, and to say that Americans "want" to be monolingual would seem to miss the point—it is simply that English serves them across domains.

In more subtle ways, though, it could be argued that Americans do "want" to be monolingual—or, to put it more aptly, see no reason to expand their repertoires. They therefore resist the institutionalization of other languages. In a climate like this, especially a long-standing one, such an outlook—arguably based on perceived practicality—can expand on less immediate and more unpleasant levels. Not only do languages other than English appear unnecessary, their use can be seen as downright un-American, their speakers as unwilling to throw themselves wholeheartedly into that wonderful pot, their continuing linkage to other cultures as a suspect commodity. It is surely not surprising that, given the right context, these sorts of views would find formal expression, that organizations like U.S. English would flourish, that many states would enact English-only legislation, that bilingual education would be progressively deemphasized and, in one or two notorious cases, scrapped entirely. Nor is it surprising that the central part of that "right context" would be an increasingly worried sense that the non-anglophone "others" are becoming too potent. English only, therefore, typically means not-Spanish. And so another circle is completed: the very language community that, by its power and numbers, ought logically to blaze the way in foreign language teaching and learning is under attack by powerful bodies that are either nostalgia-ridden yearners for some selective status quo or, worse, carriers of the most abhorrent social virus. And, even if these bodies were absent from the political landscape, one could only expect from the public at large a lukewarm and uninformed stance.

I have aimed here only at some slight elucidation of the social context relevant to languages and language learning. Large forces and weighty histories are at work, and their presence should be acknowledged and thought about. I didn't intend to write a jeremiad although I know that, for many, English is a lowering villain depriving other mediums of their rightful inheritance. I would simply reiterate that the factors at work here are neither unfamiliar nor unpredictable. We have seen transitional linguistic and social times before—and transition is, almost by definition, a painful and wrenching experience for those whose lives are directly affected.

It is a truism to say that the teaching and the learning of languages are influenced by the state of affairs outside the walls of the academy. It would be heartening—in a world in which, for all the power of English, bilingual or multilingual competences are still the norm—if the North American academy were dealing with a constituency that acknowledged and accepted such repertoires. The products on offer would not then require such advertising; the demand would arise naturally and would not itself have first to be suggested to the consumers. But this is a setting in which some linguistic analogy of Gresham's law seems to operate. As well, one recalls the (perhaps apocryphal) remark of that school superintendent in Arkansas who steadfastly refused to have foreign languages taught at the secondary level: "If English was good enough for Jesus, it's good enough for you" (qtd. in Ricks and Michaels xvii).

We should recall, though, that there remains on this continent a rich linguistic and cultural diversity, and in many instances this continues to be a visible and powerful quantity. We have also engaged, over the last few years, in an unprecedented debate about multiculturalism and pluralism, about identity and citizenship. The field here remains terribly disputed and highly politicized, but the debate is far from over and the valuable middle ground has yet to be charted. Although the most active participants in the discussion have not been those whose primary concerns are linguistic, the latter have a role to play and a contribution to make.

NOTES

[1] On academics, dictionaries, Rivarol, and journals devoted to "Englishes," see Edwards, *Language* and *Multilingualism*.

[2] For recent French and German developments, see Séguin, "France," "Reverse Role"; Freeman; Gagnon; Ribbans. See also Edwards, "Language."

[3] See recent editorials in the *Times Higher Education Supplement*, 17 Dec. 1999, commenting on the meetings of the MLA: "German—Fewer than 100 Jobs" and "Literature Moves to a New Latin Rhythm."

WORKS CITED

Acheson, Arthur. *Shakespeare's Lost Years in London, 1586–1592*. London: Quaritch, 1920.
Bohrer, Becky. "U.S. Hispanic Population the Fastest-Growing Group." *Globe and Mail* [Toronto] 13 May 2000: 12.
Davies, Norman. *The Isles: A History*. London: Macmillan, 1999.

Edwards, John. "Language and the Future: Choices and Constraints." Conference on Language in the Twenty-First Century. Whitney Center, Yale U, June 1999.

———. *Language, Society and Identity*. Oxford: Blackwell, 1985.

———. *Multilingualism*. London: Penguin, 1995.

Eoyang, Eugene. "The Worldliness of the English Language: A Lingua Franca Past and Future." *ADFL Bulletin* 31.1 (1999): 26–32.

Freeman, Alan. "The English Patience of France." *Globe and Mail* 1 Apr. 2000: 22.

Fuentes, Carlos. "A Cure for Monolingualism." *Times Higher Education Supplement* 17 Dec. 1999: 4.

Gagnon, Lysiane. "Back in the Trenches of the Language War." *Globe and Mail* 3 Apr. 2000: 18.

"German—Fewer than 100 Jobs." *Times Higher Education Supplement* 17 Dec. 1999: 6.

"Literature Moves to a New Latin Rhythm." *Times Higher Education Supplement* 17 Dec. 1999: 4.

Noels, Kimberly, and Richard Clément. "Language in Education." *Language in Canada*. Ed. John Edwards. Cambridge: Cambridge UP, 1998. 102–24.

Oulton, Nick. Letter. *Times Literary Supplement* 17 Mar. 2000: 21.

Quirk, Randolph. *Style and Communication in the English Language*. London: Arnold, 1982.

Ribbans, Elisabeth. "Germans Bemoan Popularity of English." *Globe and Mail* 27 Apr. 2000: 11.

Ricks, Christopher, and Leonard Michaels. *The State of the Language*. London: Faber, 1990.

Séguin, Rhéal. "France Not French Enough, PQ Says." *Globe and Mail* 29 Mar. 2000: 4.

———. "Reverse Role Model Made in Canada." *Globe and Mail* 1 Apr. 2000: 22.

Shakespeare, William. *The Merchant of Venice*. *The Riverside Shakespeare*. Vol. 1. Boston: Houghton, 1974. 254–85.

Swaffar, Janet. "The Case for Foreign Languages as a Discipline." *ADFL Bulletin* 30.3 (1999): 6–12.

Yates, Frances. *John Florio*. Cambridge: Cambridge UP, 1934.

Degrees of Success, Degrees of Failure: The Changing Dynamics of the English PhD and Small-College Careers

ED FOLSOM

I have taught for twenty-five years at the University of Iowa, and in that time I've mentored doctoral students who have gone on to entry-level positions at the following colleges: Luther, Saint John's, Bethel, Elon, Carleton, Grinnell, Central, Wooster, Drake, Wittenberg, Mary Washington, Augustana, Hope, Wartburg, Cardinal Stritch, College of Saint Mary, Mount Holyoke, Puget Sound, Gustavus Adolphus, Hobart and William Smith, Saint Olaf, Kalamazoo, Lafayette, Millsaps, Mount Mercy, Findlay, Viterbo. This Whitmanesque catalog of small-college America is an incomplete one—I could in fact add many more. In the same period, I've had students take positions at the following AAU institutions with prominent English PhD programs: Wisconsin and Berkeley. That is a complete list. A few others have taken jobs at large institutions with graduate programs in English, like Kansas State and Texas Tech, but most of my doctoral students became professors at small colleges. And, perhaps not surprisingly, most of them did their own undergraduate work in small colleges.

What is surprising, at least to many of my colleagues, are the implications of an important change in dynamics over the past ten years at institutions like Iowa. We once were happy to build our graduate classes out of the best English majors from small colleges in the Midwest, students who for the most part were excited about taking jobs and forming careers in

---

The author is F. Wendell Miller Distinguished Professor in the Department of English at the University of Iowa. A version of this article appeared in the Fall 2000 issue of the ADE Bulletin.

small Midwest colleges. It was, after all, their experience as undergraduates at those colleges that made them want to become professors in the first place, and the models that most of them brought with them to graduate school were their own undergraduate professors. But then came the era of professional itinerant university administrators, who conceive of their careers not unlike ivy as they climb through the minor leagues into the, well, Ivy League. At Iowa, the last two presidents, neither of whom had Iowa associations previously, left to become presidents of Ivy League schools. Iowa was a place they climbed through but did not cling to. They were both impressive figures, and their own professional aspirations inevitably became generalized as the aspirations for the institution as a whole: it was no longer satisfactory to be the University of Iowa, an institution that had gained its identity by being unlike other places, that had created the Writers Workshop and International Writing Program precisely because no one else had them or anything like them. We were instead encouraged to adopt the goal—along with, as far as I can tell, about three-quarters of the major state universities in the country—of becoming "a top-ten public research institution," whatever that is.[1]

To formulate institutional aspirations in terms of a top-ten list has a perverse brilliance to it, especially at large state institutions like Iowa, which tend to have formidable athletic budgets and big-time football and basketball teams. We are accustomed to checking the polls weekly to see how the university team stacks up against those of our peers, and many of us are gratified by the team's appearance in the top ten. But what AP or UPI poll do we consult, and how often, to find out who is currently on the list of top ten public research institutions? That list, if it existed, wouldn't seem likely to change quite as often or as capriciously as the football or basketball polls, but by casting institutional goals in terms of polls, we are all led to believe that the strategy for turning around a faltering football program is applicable to the whole institution and that there are five-year reallocation plans that will alter our ranking as dramatically as a new coaching staff hopes to alter the football team's poll position.

If the university pays enough for an inspirational new coach, so the theory goes, one who has perhaps been a top assistant at a winning program, he or she could increase the school's visibility and reputation by getting more out of current personnel and by recruiting top-class talent, the kind of talent that wouldn't have looked at this place before but might consider it now that the program is on its way up and aiming at a national ranking. No matter that this coach might just use our program as a stepping-stone to a head coaching job at one of the perennial winners, where national championships are a tradition and where recruiting top talent is a given. As long as this head coach, in the interim, can make our program noticeable and competitive, we'll be happy. We can't expect anything so sentimental as loyalty from a head coach any more than we can from the increasingly fickle student-athletes that the head coach is bringing here from all over the country. The better the players and coaches are, so we assume, the more volatile things become: to recruit the best means we'll lose some of our prize players to the pros and some of our coaches to the richer and more successful programs. We will have to get used to beginning the rebuilding process again and again, each time coming up with better facilities, higher salaries, nicer amenities, all specified in a new plan—a strategic plan—the rejection of which would indicate that we're satisfied to live with mediocrity and doomed to decline.

We at state universities are used to hearing that a strong football program is good for the whole institution, that it makes alumni feel better about the school and increases donations not just to the athletic programs but also to the libraries and scholarship funds. Iowa's gigantic and opulent new Center for University Advancement, which houses a large fund-raising staff in quarters that English and foreign language professors could not even dream of, is itself an impressive monument to the truth of such fund-raising axioms as "to raise money, you've got to spend it" and "no one likes giving to a losing cause." "It's the economy, stupid": expensive new facilities breed success; success breeds increased revenue; increased revenue funds stronger programs; stronger programs, as the football and basketball teams demonstrate, can lead to top-ten (or at least top–twenty-five) recognition.

If it works for athletics—and, occasionally, it demonstrably does—then why shouldn't it work for the whole institution, especially at a big state school in the Midwest? We could be in the top ten, our strategic plans began to tell us. And so along came *U.S. News and World Report*, tapping into this weird new institutional desire by conveniently providing a kind of yearly poll that we now all read and scoff at even while we celebrate and publicize our rise in the rankings or worry about our slippage. Each year, the magazine slightly alters or recalibrates the factors that it uses to arrive at its ratings, thus creating an illusion of institutional movement (and incidentally making it necessary for everyone to buy this year's issue). If the rankings stayed steady, not only would there be no need to buy annual issues, there would be no reason for administrators to buy into the notion that universities' reputations can rise and fall as variably as the reputations of their football teams. At least football rankings are informed by weekly results of actual competitions that are decided on a field of play: it is difficult to discern whether meaningful overall institutional rankings can ever be arrived at in the first place, let alone change by the year. These *U.S. News* polls, dismissed by many as mere popularity contests or statistical sleights of hand, have nonetheless already become entrenched as indicators of institutional strength, cited by the media and university public relations offices and, more ominously, by administrators looking for signs of strength.[2] The polls appeared at exactly the right moment, feeding the voracious need of institutions to have some publicly accessible measure, however specious, of whether they are moving toward their strategic goal of a top-ten ranking.

This goal, by definition, puts an institution in an imitative mode. Once we determined at Iowa that the top ten was our objective, we realized that we had to be more like the institutions we were told were somehow better. Instead of remaining a unique Iowa, we were sold on the advantages (or necessities) of being a second-rate Michigan or Berkeley, which, given the disparities in resources, we were, of course, dooming ourselves to become. I imagine these campaigns—which come suspiciously complete with bumper-sticker slogans, accompanying strategic plans, and benchmarks—are handed out in kits at university-president retreats. And I suspect we are not far from the day when some office at the university will begin issuing actual bumper stickers to advertise our campaign to join the ranks of those elusive top-ten public research institutions. We have recently been informed that our administration has hired a consulting firm to "improve communications" at the university; this firm specializes in teaching institutions how to package information effectively and decorate it with catchy slogans.[3]

I can precisely date the change at Iowa—from unique institution with its own identity to top-ten wannabe—because two of my junior colleagues, now both associate professors, were halfway through their probationary periods when the administration announced a "toughening of tenure standards." Both my junior colleagues described the change in their professional environment as chilling: for their first three years as assistant professors, they said, they were treated as full colleagues, took active part in the service mission of the department, and taught a wide variety of courses and were appreciated for doing so. Then, overnight, the probationary status of their appointments was underscored; they were reprimanded for spending too much time on committees, warned about the dangers of not repeating the same courses, and scolded for not publishing enough fast enough. Like children of loving parents who were nurtured by being encouraged to experiment and question and explore but who suddenly awoke one morning to find mom and dad wielding belts, imposing curfews, and generally laying down the law, they were confused. One of my colleagues chose to proceed as if the place really hadn't changed; the other retreated to her library carrel. Both colleagues received tenure, although neither did so easily, and both have since become invaluable members of our faculty. But it was the beginning of a new era. We were told we were on the road to academia's sweet sixteen or better—our strategic plan even said so—and so we should start behaving more like the stereotypes of the departments that were our superiors (so we were led to believe), even if (or maybe because) those departments were often miserable, divided, unstable, and paranoid. If the entire university was now striving for the top ten, then each unit had to do the same, and *U.S. News* again came to the rescue with an increasingly large variety of new rankings, including graduate programs in specific disciplines and specialized areas within disciplines. Now even the Victorianists had their own poll to worry about.

To better compete, we reduced service assignments to the minimum for junior faculty members, giving them more time for their research and emphasizing their isolation from the departmental community and from decision making. We gave them early, pretenure leaves that allowed them more free time and removed them from the department for two-thirds of a year at exactly the period that was crucial for their bonding with the departmental community. We lowered teaching loads to give them more time to themselves and to inculcate the universal formula for rewarding accomplishment in academia: the better you do, the less you teach. (I've proposed a teaching award that would reduce by one the number of books expected from the winner over the next five years—a book reduction instead of a course reduction—but I've so far been unable to generate much interest.) All these new amenities, we were told, would help us recruit strong new faculty members, the very candidates who were now going to the more highly ranked institutions. And once we enticed them to come to Iowa, we were responsible for enforcing a new regimen that would mold them into the kinds of stars that would convince the poll voters to rate us higher. We began to require samples of published materials at the third-year reviews instead of at the tenure reviews. We sowed the seeds of division, paranoia, and instability that seemed hallmarks of the departments we now aspired to emulate. We joined in, in other words, with the much discussed preprofessionalization of our discipline, where we just kept pushing expectations for one rank back to the next lower rank. Now our graduate students worry, when they go on the job market, about not having a teaching and publication file equal to what was expected for tenure candidates fifteen years ago.

Meanwhile, our administration came up with money for Graduate Iowa Fellowships, which paid handsomely and allowed the fellows to pursue their graduate work with "fellowship years" that drastically reduced their teaching obligations. The fellowship competition was overseen by the graduate college, which wanted to press departments to recruit students who otherwise would not normally come to Iowa, especially students from institutions whose reputations we now aspired to. More and more Ivy and near–Ivy League students entered our graduate program, financially rewarded for doing so and required to teach fewer courses than the usual Iowa graduate student coming from the less-lustrous small schools that had been our trusted source of graduate students for years. Graduate students were given an early sense of a two-tier system: those who taught three courses a year while trying to complete their own coursework and those who in effect had two years' paid leave from teaching so that they could polish their graduate work into the publishable articles or books that would presumably get them a job at a big research institution. It was never too early, it seemed, to begin sorting out those who would help Iowa's ranking from those who might harm it.

What happened, of course, is that the big research institutions that were now sending us some of their good undergraduates who could get a great fellowship at Iowa seemed not to work up much enthusiasm for hiring our new breed of PhD. In fact, with a few exceptions, we kept placing our PhDs in the same array of small schools as in the past. But the first to get jobs now, not surprisingly, were the students who had taught less and published more. They had already imbibed a graduate-student version of being a research professor, but they were going off to small schools they knew little about and whose missions and ways of living a professional life often seemed alien. The sense of a career that is in decline even before it begins is an important facet of the relation between small colleges and research institutions.

For many years, Iowa produced a kind of PhD who was well adapted to life in most small-college departments. Our PhDs had gone through a program that required them to teach many classes while also carrying out their own coursework and writing graduate papers. Because of our large general education program, they also had taught a number of different courses, and they had usually served on committees to review courses or booklists or to help mentor new graduate instructors. The classes they taught were limited to twenty-two students each, so that they learned to work with small classes and to emphasize discussion. One chair of a small-college department who had hired two Iowa PhDs commented to me that Iowa PhDs seemed three years more professionally mature than candidates from most other programs since our PhDs had been forced to balance a heavy teaching load with service and scholarship and had already made the kinds of decisions and necessary compromises that often befuddled other first- and second-year professors. While most candidates give hypothetical answers to interview questions, this chair told me, candidates from Iowa give experiential answers—they've actually done the things they are asked about. Iowa's program traditionally found students who liked the idea of beginning their graduate work by taking an intensive seminar in teaching and who, before they entered their first graduate course, were already thinking about what was involved in teaching a good undergraduate course. And they were, for the most part, students whose own undergraduate experience had taught them the value and attractiveness of small-college life. What they went through at Iowa mimicked in some ways what they would face professionally when they returned to some version of their own small college as a professor.

But here's the rub: while we still produce the same kind of PhDs we produced ten years ago, we have also geared up for producing another kind—one more sheltered from the heavy burdens of teaching, more primed for a research career, and often armed with an impressive portfolio of publications to take to the first job interview. This PhD is the result of the altered dynamics I have outlined, a PhD prepared for a research institution position but produced by a university whose niche has always been to turn out good small-college teachers. I suppose Iowa administrators believed, along with the administrators at the other Big Ten (or Eleven or whatever) schools that bought into the same basic scheme, that they would begin to produce PhDs who would compete with those at the Ivys and their clones. When I attended each year a meeting of Big Ten English department chairs, we would all tell each other how astonishingly good our PhD programs had become, how we were all bringing in students who were far more impressive than those we used to get (and who were even coming from Ivy League schools), how they were publishing almost before they finished their first courses, and how lucky any research institution would be to hire our new breed of PhD. But I recall one Big Ten chair meeting when I made a sobering request: I asked each of us to list the institutions from which our newly hired assistant professors came. Slowly, the sad truth revealed itself: while we were celebrating the unprecedented strength of our PhDs, we had virtually stopped hiring one another's PhDs. Instead, to teach in the new high-powered programs that were out to challenge the big guys, we were hiring from the programs we were imitating, not from our fellow imitators. With very few exceptions, the catalog that day was predictable—Columbia, Duke, Harvard, Yale, Virginia, Stanford, Berkeley, and so on. While once upon a time Big Ten institutions regularly staffed one another, the situation had changed, and although we were now all proud to be producing our best-ever PhDs who could compete with those from the Ivys and near-Ivys, the Ivys weren't hiring ours, we weren't hiring ours, and we were hiring the Ivys'.

So the Ivy-modeled PhDs went to jobs where Iowa PhDs had traditionally and happily gone for many decades: to small colleges largely in the

Midwest. But the small colleges were now finding some extraordinary differences in the qualifications of these new Iowa PhDs: they had impressive publications, maybe a book in press; they had impressive undergraduate pedigrees, often from elite schools on the East or West Coast. And they tended to be hired, understandably, over the PhDs who were in the more traditional model—applicants who had done lots of teaching and solid graduate work but who were more developed as well-rounded departmental citizens than as emerging scholarly stars. And why would anyone hire the unpublished young PhD over the published one? That probably should not be the rhetorical question it has come to be, because, as I discovered in my last couple of years as chair at Iowa, there may in fact be good reasons to do just that: for the first time, I began hearing about Iowa PhDs who seemed unhappy in their small-college jobs. I heard from chairs about new hires who were grumbling about too much teaching and not enough support for their "own work." I heard from chairs who said they had always counted on Iowa PhDs to understand the nature and values of small colleges but now found them eager to leave for a job at a more research-oriented institution.

If I were going to start a new English PhD program or try to revitalize an existing one, I'd set it up as a program for small-college teaching. Part of the program would involve summer seminars taught by small-college professors, who would be brought to campus to work with graduate students on how the profession works in a small-college setting. The program would recruit the best students from small colleges and send them back to small colleges—broadly educated in the field, theoretically sophisticated, immersed in the latest cutting-edge debates, eager to enter into those debates as time allowed, ready to carry out a full and satisfying and energetic professional life in a small college. The objective would be to theorize the generalist and seek a new definition of the term, a definition that would fit the vastly expanded canon, the proliferating sites of Anglophone writing, and other developments in the field. But is there any way that such a program would not be seen as hopelessly provincial and retrogressive instead of cutting-edge? Is *that* a rhetorical question? Should it be? Would any institution strategically aspire to become a top-ten producer of small-college professors? Why are you laughing?

NOTES

[1] In the university's current strategic plan, *New Century Iowa*, the top-ten goal appears early in the document as the institution's sole "aspiration": "The University of Iowa aspires to become one of the ten most distinguished public research universities in the

nation." This aspiration has evolved over the years from the original, slightly hazier 1989 desire "to reach a level of quality comparable to top-ten public institutions, with selected areas in which the University is a leading institution nationwide" (*Achieving Distinction* 10). The aspiration got rewritten for the executive summary of the 1989 strategic plan, where the call was simply for the university to "become one of the best ten public universities in the nation" (1). The next strategic plan "strongly reaffirmed" the "commitment" of "the University's bold and lofty Aspiration" to "raise the quality of the University to a level comparable to that of the best ten public institutions in the nation" (*Achieving Distinction 2000* 4). This "soaring aspiration" (1) was again articulated more directly on a widely distributed card—published by the president's office and sized for easy carrying in faculty members' pockets—that was to serve as a continuing reminder of Iowa's "core values and institutional goals": "To prepare students for the 21st century, The University of Iowa has challenged itself to become one of the ten best public research universities in the nation."

[2]Even some alumni are apparently getting annoyed by the tendency of many universities to boast about rankings like those in *U.S. News*. In a recent issue of the alumni magazine of the University of Rochester, the alumnus Thomas V. Miller wrote, "I wonder if it isn't about time the University gave up proudly referring to those tiresome and fatuous pronouncements by *U.S. News & World Report* that it now ranks 19th in this and 42nd in that, or whatever—improved from last year! I see other publications are starting to do something similar; it must sell a lot of magazines. So while the industry will no doubt keep on doing it as long as it finds it worthwhile, is it really an exercise that serious institutions such as Rochester should take part in?" The editor's reply indicates how the university public relations machinery just can't help itself anymore: "We quite agree that minutely graded rankings are not a very accurate way of measuring the intrinsic worth of any one institution. But, like them or not, these rankings are now 'news.' [. . .] Incidentally, for what it's worth, in its fall listings this year, *U.S. News* ranked Rochester as 32nd among top national universities [. . .]."

[3]President Coleman's letter explained, "I am writing to make you aware of an important new strategic communications initiative." A minor tempest occurred when reporters and some faculty members asked how much this initiative was going to cost, and the administration refused to provide figures. As I write this, representatives of Lipman Hearne, "a leading communications firm based in Chicago, that serves the non-profit sector," were on campus talking with various faculty, staff, and administrative groups. One recurring question they asked was, "What words do you most often use to describe the University of Iowa to colleagues from other institutions?"

WORKS CITED

Achieving Distinction: A Strategic Plan for the University of Iowa. Iowa City: U of Iowa, 1 Dec. 1989.
Achieving Distinction 2000: A Strategic Plan for the University of Iowa. Iowa City: U of Iowa, 17 Dec. 1996.
Coleman, Mary Sue. "Dear Colleagues" letter. 5 Nov. 1999.
Miller, Thomas V. Letter. *Rochester Review* 62 (1999–2000): inside front cover.
New Century Iowa: Bridges to the Next Horizon: A Strategic Plan for the University of Iowa 2000–2005. <http://www.uiowa.edu/president/strat_plan.html>.
Reply to letter of Thomas V. Miller. *Rochester Review* 62 (1999–2000): inside front cover.

Redefining the Mission of the English Department at the University of Louisville: Two Years Later

DEBRA JOURNET

Three years ago, I presented a paper at the ADE Summer Seminar in which I talked about a series of changes that we were preparing to institute at the University of Louisville. The response to my talk was encouraging. Many people asked questions both at the seminar and afterward, and David Laurence was kind enough to include my paper in the *ADE Bulletin* and Phyllis Franklin to reprint it in *Profession 1999*. In that talk, I described how my department had responded to a set of difficult issues concerning staffing and teaching by moving all professorial faculty members into first-year composition. In return, the administration gave us eight new tenure-track positions. This change promised both exciting possibilities and difficult challenges. I ended my talk by saying that I had staked a lot on the success of this proposal and that in a couple of years I might be back at the ADE seminar licking my wounds. I want to report that I am still relatively healthy. The changes in our department have not been without difficulties and have necessitated tact, persuasion, and even bribery. Not everyone has climbed on board, to shift the metaphor a bit, but, for the most part, our experiment has been a success. This paper tells what has happened at the University of Louisville's English department in the last two years. It begins with a brief explanation of why we decided to redefine our mission in the way that we did, then talks a little about what worked and what didn't. Finally, I offer some general comments about what I have learned as a department chair instituting a change of this magnitude.

The author is Professor of English and Chair, Department of English, at the University of Louisville. A version of this article appeared in the Spring 2001 issue of the ADE Bulletin.

The University of Louisville is a Research I institution, and its priorities include increasing its research stature and maintaining its commitment, as the state's only urban university, to a diverse undergraduate student population. The English department, as one of the few departments in the College of Arts and Sciences that offers a doctoral degree, as a major player in general education, and as a department with a large major, has one of the most complex missions of any department in the university. In addition, we are greatly understaffed—still the third smallest English department in the Kentucky system, despite the fact that we have as many English majors and graduate students as the English department at the University of Kentucky, the largest. These circumstances make resource allocation—staffing classes, supervising graduate students, advising students, running programs, conducting research—complicated.

In the summer of 1997, the University of Louisville faced a number of institutional changes and challenges: a new provost and dean of the College of Arts and Sciences, our regular ten-year accreditation review from the Southern Association of Colleges and Schools (SACS), a new set of initiatives designed to strengthen the research profile of the university through enhancement of targeted doctoral programs. These changes and challenges provided an opportunity to rethink old practices and explore new ideas about the faculty and curriculum—an opportunity we in the English department were able to take advantage of. In response, we proposed to commit all professorial faculty members to teach first-year composition at least once a year. In return, the administration gave us eight new tenured or tenure-track positions, including two senior hires.

When I spoke at the ADE seminar, the University of Louisville English department consisted of twenty-seven full-time faculty members, none of whom regularly taught first-year writing. This year, we are a department of thirty-five full-time professorial faculty members, and every faculty member has taught and continues to teach a section of first-year composition each year. The assistant professors we hired have brought a wide range of new interests and abilities into the department—from Renaissance Jewish studies to humanities academic computing. In addition to the new faculty members, the department has received a number of other kinds of support. We have been given two new state-of-the-art technology classrooms. We have been allocated resources to implement a university-wide writing center. And although we have been fortunate not to have to deal with budget cuts in Kentucky, we have gone through internal budget reallocation. During a time of intense reinvestment in the university, we have been able to protect our teaching loads and our relatively small class sizes. We are in line for an endowed chair in rhetoric and composition. We have the full support of the administration, which sees us as a kind of poster child for the well-rounded department. We were even the subject of a television ad spotlighting some of the university's sites of excellence, which shows during football and basketball games. We were the only humanities department to be so featured. The ad consists of a series of shots of faculty members teaching writing, over which the president explains how at the University of Louisville every English faculty member, from first-year assistant professor to endowed chair, teaches first-year composition. The president ends by saying, "For students, for everyone, it's an exciting time to be part of U of L."

All this sounds really good, but of course there have been problems. As some people have noticed, the television ad does *not* say that at the University of Louisville every first-year student is taught composition by a professorial-rank faculty member. The reality is that out of the 180 or so sections we offer, less than 25% are taught by the professorial faculty (though the percentage now is an improvement over the less than 1% in the past). And despite constant juggling, we have seen a reduction in the number of upper-division courses we can offer, because of the need to commit faculty members to first-year teaching. The biggest issue, though—at least for me as chair—is institutional culture and what it has meant to ask faculty members, most of whom are literature specialists, to move, many for the first time in years, to the regular teaching of composition. Since it is this change that has had the greatest impact on the life of my department, I devote the rest of this paper to looking at faculty response over the last two years as we implemented this plan.

The two CCCC panels I chaired—the first in 1999, the spring of the first year of this change; the second in 2000, the spring of the second year—offered a glimpse into the life of my department as we came to understand the consequences of what we had committed ourselves to.

The Conference on College Composition and Communication, a constituent of the National Council of Teachers of English, is seen by many as a friendlier version of the MLA convention, one where composition faculty members attend lavish publishers' parties and go to sessions, many of which center on teaching. For me, as a rhetoric and composition specialist who has taught at a number of institutions, CCCC is a place where I regularly meet old friends. Thus, I was happy when a group of my colleagues asked me if I would like to chair a session devoted to faculty responses to the first year of regular composition instruction. The year 1998–99 was a difficult one for me, and in the spring, when I was scheduled to teach 101, a set of complicated personal circumstances kept me out of the classroom and out of the office for much of the semester. So I was—and I was not unaware of the irony—the only faculty member that first year who did not teach composition. (The irony wasn't lost on some of my colleagues either.) How out of touch I was, however, did not become clear to me until I was sitting in a room at CCCC in April, listening to Beth Boehm, the director of graduate studies in my department and one of my closest friends, deliver a paper entitled "Fear and Loathing in English 101."

Boehm's paper reported on the responses to a survey she had sent to all professorial faculty members asking them to comment on their experiences in the composition classroom that first year. I had not heard her paper until that afternoon, but I knew something was afoot when, at the beginning of her talk, she explained that over two-thirds of the department had returned the surveys, compared with the six faculty members who responded the year before to the graduate committee's survey about proposed changes to the MA program. "More significant than the number of responses, however," she said, "was the thoroughness of the responses: half the respondents provided single-spaced, two- to four-page typewritten essays, and most of the handwritten responses, while shorter, were similarly thoughtful." I thus heard, for the first time, some of the stories my colleagues had to tell about teaching composition. But what I heard was not, as Beth explained, the "conventional conversion narrative" we so often get in stories about classroom experience; instead, my colleagues told stories that revealed an "extraordinarily complicated set of issues" surrounding the changes we had enacted (48).

Many of the issues Boehm described were familiar to me. Because we spread our searches out over three years, we have been playing catch-up, and I was all too aware of the heavy workload entailed in searching for multiple positions and the pressures on our curriculum and our faculty members. What surprised me was Boehm's claim that many faculty members noted that they were demoralized by their experience in the first-year classroom. I was pleased to hear that despite these problems with morale, most said that they stood by the decision they had made a year earlier. However, the need to face morale issues became painfully obvious to me when Boehm concluded her paper by quoting a colleague who remarked that "I think it would be a good idea if the chair would do more to recognize that this is a morale problem, rather than acting as though people ought to like this, and are bad if they don't" (52).

My response to this paper was mixed. As I sat there, looking out at an audience of friends from other institutions who were interested in what we had achieved, I felt pretty defensive. After all, I thought, asking people to teach one composition course a year was not the same as sending them to hell. As a department chair, I think I have a better sense of what academic hell is, and I was trying my best to steer my department away from what I saw as the hellish consequences we faced in a time of increased demands for accountability, assessment, and productivity if we did not do something of this sort. I was also cognizant of how privileged many of my faculty members were, at least in relation to what other people did in many other institutions—for example, teaching more and teaching more writing as a regular part of their professional lives. Beth's presentation was followed by two others that offered even more pointed remarks about the kinds of dissatisfaction people were suffering in their first attempts to teach 101. As I sat there with forced smile and queasy stomach, I kept trying to remember that critique and self-examination are integral parts of our profession.

The next CCCC I attended told a different story. The panel, which this time I put together, focused on the positive changes that can occur when senior faculty members enter the first-year writing classroom. The rationale for my session was that senior faculty members bring with them a wealth of experience as classroom teachers and that they can draw on that experience in diverse ways to enrich the teaching of composition. Participating on the panel were three University of Louisville professorial faculty members, all of whom were new or newly returned to the teaching of composition. For two, it was the first CCCC they had attended. The presenters described their first-year writing class and discussed how the course had come out of research, administrative, and teaching experience. One presenter, a full professor who is an expert on nineteenth-century fiction and who edits the *Henry James Review*, described how she organized her course, an honors section of first-year writing, around nineteenth-century journals and asked students to do primary research on a journal of their choice. Another, a full professor who is also an associate dean for undergraduate education in the College of Arts and Sciences, talked about the way her course, which was tied to a section of History 101, dovetailed with general education goals. The third described a course that incorporated Web authorship and centered on issues of literacy and textuality. What these talks showed were some of the very best consequences of the changes we'd enacted. Integrating senior and experienced professorial faculty members into first-year composition, we all agreed, has not only meant a greater investment by faculty and administration in the English department and its writing program, it has also allowed our department to explore the wide range of resources experienced teachers bring with them to the classroom and to consider how those resources can be used creatively to rethink the material and pedagogical conditions of the first-year composition class. (This panel, presented in Minneapolis, was entitled "Who Teaches Composition? [and How? and Why?]: Re-imagining an English Department's Mission and Integrating Senior Writing Faculty into the First-Year Writing Class." The participants were Susan Griffin ["Victoriana in the First-Year Writing Classroom; or, Can This Book Order Be Right?"], Julia Dietrich ["First-Year Composition as General Education"], and Marc Bousquet ["Read/Write Enabled: Student Web-Authorship in Cyber Compliterature"]).

By ending with this more optimistic version of the changes my department has enacted, I am, of course, inscribing that very conversion narrative that Beth Boehm rejected in her paper a year before. Of course I want to believe the story of my CCCC panel, even though I am more clearly the author of its narrative than I was of Boehm's CCCC panel, where I was the public listener. Nevertheless, I believe that things have got better and that in many ways what I predicted would happen has happened. When we first proposed these changes, I knew that most of my colleagues are excellent classroom teachers, that no one wants to fail in the classroom, especially year after year, and that consequently we would find a way to make the teaching of composition more effective and efficient. We seem to have found a way. Morale seems to me (and to some of my spies) to be better. Student evaluations are up. And many faculty members have come to realize that, as some of us tried to explain earlier, teaching writing is *not* teaching grammar, that responding to student papers is *not* copyediting a manuscript. Of course problems remain. One or two members of my department remain openly hostile to the ongoing requirement to teach a section of 101. And some people are, for a variety of reasons, not particularly good at teaching writing, though they are probably better at it than they realize.

As I have thought about Boehm's paper, though, I have come to understand that many of the concerns and much of the unhappiness articulated by my colleagues in response to her survey have to do with more than "merely" the burden or responsibility of teaching composition once a year. As Boehm put it, "We need to address the morale problem not only as one that is produced by local circumstances but also as one that reflects a changing academy and a changing understanding of what constitutes English studies" (52). In truth, my department is responding to a set of pressures and demands that are common to many English departments, at least those in public universities. As another colleague said, "One of the most pernicious effects of the academic labor system is the creation of a triumphalism among literature faculty even as their object of study moves further and further from the center of the curriculum." The role of composition in an English department is only part of the issue, as English departments debate and define what constitutes literature, tradition, and even a text. These challenges, along with increased demands for accountability by legislatures, administration, and other stakeholders and the increased professionalism of our students, are making us rethink our mission in a number of complicated ways. The way careers themselves are defined is also changing. Now, at least at the University of Louisville, we tend to talk about the department's mission and how it coincides with the university's rather than about the research profiles of individual faculty members. Perhaps not much has changed except the rhetoric;

nevertheless, in requests for sabbaticals or new lines or research assistants or whatever, it is not enough now simply to talk about the contribution to disciplinary knowledge. Instead, justifications have to be made in terms of institutional priorities—priorities that are based in large part on the economic realities of the Kentucky legislature. This is a very different culture from that in which many of us were trained, and for some the shift has been difficult.

My department is changing in many ways—some welcome and some worrying or even frightening. Because of all our new hires, the age, experience, and expectations of my departmental colleagues are different from what they were ten years ago. The cultural shift that I have described is itself foreign to many new PhD graduates, who are being educated in more expansive traditions, and consequently we have brought into the department new colleagues, both in literature and composition, who have training and experience in the teaching of writing quite unlike that gained by faculty members of my generation. The English major is changing, as more and more of our students plan to use their degrees for entrance into professions quite different from those for which we prepared ourselves. My university is changing, as success in the competition for resources is based more and more on institutional priorities that are largely defined in terms of economic and social contributions to Louisville and the state. Education in Kentucky is changing, as both schools and universities are increasingly asked to define and assess goals based on performance and the achievement of specific skills necessary to public values. During a time when many institutions are facing these pressures as well as undergoing serious cutbacks and shortfalls, teaching English 101 once a year seems to many, including me, a small price to pay. But I think it has been for many members of my department the most concrete sign of how higher education is changing and will continue to change. I understand the concerns of my colleagues, but as chair I sometimes have to see things differently. I also understand that we must define our priorities in ways that reflect the priorities of the institution—in part so we can continue to do the things *we* want to do. Teaching first-year writing has allowed us this freedom. And while for some it has been a curse and for others a blessing, I believe that effecting this change has been the most important work I have done as department chair.

WORKS CITED

Boehm, Beth A. "Fear and Loathing in English 101: What Happens When English Faculty Members Reenter the First-Year Composition Classroom?" *ADE Bulletin* 128 (2001): 48–52.

Journet, Debra. "Rethinking General Education and Increasing the Number of Professorial Faculty Members; or, When Opportunity Knocks." *ADE Bulletin* 112 (1999): 27–30. *Profession 1999.* New York: MLA, 1999. 79–85.

My Life as an Infomercial: On Time, Teaching, and Technology

PAT MILLER

What if I told you that you could teach your course in such a way that your class's final average would improve by nearly one full letter grade, that your course evaluation average would improve by seven percent, and that you could do so by spending one-third less time in the classroom? Conjures up visions of Suzanne Somers in her latest guise of wide-eyed innocence marveling over some incredible product that makes her life meaningful while actually reducing cellulite, doesn't it? I'm loath to say that I find myself the academic equivalent—at least at the small southern university where I teach print journalism as part of the English department's professional writing track.

A bit of perspective. Two years ago I received a small grant from my university to develop a Web-based component for my news writing course. My idea was simple: Put the information portion of the course online (just how many times can you explain newsroom organization without inducing spontaneous combustion?) and use class time to develop the actual skill of writing news stories. In short, the elements that bored me—primarily my lecturing on the same material ad nauseam—and that bored my students I put in interactive modules using a program called *WebCT*. (Let me, in good debate style, answer my opponents' objections. It's not that I'm a lousy lecturer or don't update material or try fresh approaches. It's simply that the restriction of having to communicate a certain amount of information in a particular time frame limits the methods of presentation. It's the classic

---

The author is Professor of English at Valdosta State University.

case of "if I had world enough and time." In addition, students' learning styles have changed as the technology that drives our society has changed. Students, especially those first-generation students I often have, aren't geared to listening to and discerning what's important in a lecture.) *WebCT* allowed me to create a site that integrates my lecture notes with readings from a textbook and sample stories. The reading material directly correlates with exercises designed to reinforce the theory just presented and with quizzes that qualify students to take exams. I set up a system that encouraged students to do what they were going to do anyway: I allowed them to work together on exercises and quizzes but required that they make an 80 or better on each quiz in order to qualify to take the related exam. The exam, logically, required them to demonstrate a knowledge of both theory and practice. I encourage them to work together because that's what they'll do when they enter the profession. Writers, editors, and designers collaborate.

To their great (both anecdotal and statistical) delight, the students didn't have to attend class on days designated as *WebCT* lessons, an arrangement I cleared with administrators. In practice, this meant they met, on average, twice rather than thrice a week on a Monday-Wednesday-Friday schedule. A typical *WebCT* lesson asked them to read the chapter in the textbook associated with the topic—how to structure a news story, for example. Then they read my concise essay on how to do whatever was being studied; read examples; completed exercises; and, finally, took the online quiz. They always had two opportunities to take a quiz. I encouraged them to take it directly after they finished the lesson. If they failed to make an 80 or above, I encouraged them to print the quiz, find the answers, then take it again. When they came to class, the emphasis was on application: they wrote news stories (and grades indicate that they wrote them better than their non-*WebCT* counterparts). The course design also meant that they could work at their own pace as long as they met the deadline for completing each lesson and that they could work ahead. They had ample opportunity to e-mail me questions or talk to me during office hours. I kept the computer lab open during class hours to ensure that students had access to computers, though surveys showed that access was rarely an issue. When they did meet, they were either writing or workshopping stories, taking exams, or watching one of my brief demonstrations based on material they'd already covered—like how to write effective leads.

A bit more perspective. The workload at my small southern university, at the best of times, is heavy. I teach four courses and advise a weekly student newspaper. Then there's the rest of what almost every faculty member does: committee work, advising, student conferences, service, the occasional foray into actual research. Thus I'm forced to look at the return on investment for every endeavor that threatens to take a significant amount of time. Learning software and developing online courses take a significant amount of time. Maintaining those courses takes somewhat less time but still a considerable chunk. So I've learned to ask two governing questions to help determine return on investment: Will this endeavor make me a better teacher? Will it make me a better faculty member?

I'm a natural cynic—which is what you learn to say when various pressures make you use business terms to describe something as vital, in all senses of that word, as the art of teaching. But the statistics more than indicate that the use of technology to teach (meaning to communicate information) is well worth the investment for this course and, by extrapolation, for others that inherently intertwine theory and skill. Students are satisfied with the course change. They rated the spring 2000 course, the first time I used the *WebCT* component, at a 4.7 on a 5-point scale, compared with 4.4 for the spring 1999 course. Equally significant, eight out of thirteen respondents gave the course a perfect 5 for all categories. Students particularly liked having the class notes available at all times, especially when they needed to review for exams. They liked the immediate feedback of the online quizzes.

Their grades were better after the change. The class average for the spring 2000 course was 82, compared with 74 for the previous class. Similar though less striking improvements were evident when I compared the course statistics for Maymester 2000 (a three-week intensive course) with those for Maymester 1999. The success has been impressive enough, both to me and the administrators, that I sought and received another grant this summer to develop a *WebCT* component for my grammar and editing course.

Lest you be reading this essay late at night, when your natural skepticism is down and you feel the overpowering urge to sign up for the technology team, let me point out that the practice has some serious drawbacks beyond the basic technical snafus that seem to haunt every system and that can be remedied only by those pasty-faced techies who generally lurk undetected behind computers always several generations ahead of yours. As a pedagogical matter, you must recognize that the computer teaches subject matter; it doesn't necessarily teach human beings. It can't gauge how information is being received. I can. That means that I can adjust to put information in a helpful context for each particular class or subset in the class. Moreover, I can tell stories that put meat on the skeleton of information students receive. In short, personal contact tends to make the information more memorable. I use narrative and humor to tag information for students. Both narrative and humor are potentially explosive when delivered by computer (remember how Hal was misunderstood?), because they can be easily taken out of context. I also worry about the students' loss of listening skills, especially when they're preparing for a profession that relies heavily on interviewing. Equally disturbing (though I realize this comment may simply be saying something about me), I don't get to know the students as well and they don't get to know me. Thus I have a more difficult time figuring out how to help individual students, and they may have a harder time coming to trust that my actions (e.g., comments on papers, grades) are for their benefit. As a practical matter, more students dropped the course when it involved the *WebCT* component—almost twice the normal drop rate in spring 2000. The basic lesson is that the computer neither nurtures nor accommodates. I can do both. I also discovered, since I make no small plans, that my ambition concerning the course may outstrip my students' capabilities.

All of which brings me back to time, teaching, and technology. The day that classes resumed this fall marked twenty years (almost to the day) since I first walked in front of a class as a teacher. And it was twenty years to the day that I first ranted about students' inability to appreciate what I was teaching. I've learned a thing or two since then. We faculty members are under an ever-increasing burden to accomplish more in less time. As a result, we have to find more effective ways to teach information and skills as well as to demonstrate why both are important. In short, the question has long since ceased to be if we should spend more time. The question now is how to use limited time most effectively. The question is not whether to use technology but how to use it so we can become better teachers. Technology is a science, a capable tool. Teaching is an art, capable of transforming us and those we teach.

There's one more serious question: Does using technology make me a better faculty member? As a teacher, my contract is with my students. I'm obligated to effectively communicate the most current and useful material in a setting that recognizes their value and individuality. I'm also obligated to teach them to uphold the standards of the profession they're preparing for. As a faculty member, I'm primarily obligated to my colleagues and to my institution. (Theoretically, my obligation as a faculty member extends to my community, which justifies the service component for tenure, but I'd argue that my role as community member, not as faculty member, is what obligates me. But that's another essay.) In the light of the ability technology has given institutions to go beyond their walls, first, does my success with a Web-based component unduly pressure other faculty members to develop such components, even for those courses that won't benefit from them? More simply, will market forces determine the delivery system no matter what a course's content? Second, given the unresolved debate over who actually owns the content of online courses, do I erode the long-recognized principle of a faculty member's intellectual property? Third, does the mass producibility of such a course undermine the diversity of ideas that leads to progress? Have I, in short, contributed to the creation of the McCourse? However, the better situated (both economically and intellectually) my institution is in the marketplace, the more the faculty benefits. It would simply be naive to think otherwise.

Counter to the rhetorical logic of the infomercial, I can't close by assuring you that this product will transform your life. (I can, however, assure you that this essay is not designed as a plug for *WebCT*. *WebCT* was simply the program available at the time.) I can assert what we know: faculty members must put technology to its best use for teaching. We must incorporate it according to classroom need rather than allow it to be imposed. We must invest that commodity in shortest supply—time—to ensure that we create courses that best fulfill our obligation to students. We must insist on a place at the table when institutions discuss the use (and occasional abuse) of technology, especially in the classroom, walled or Web.

We can't afford to do otherwise.

Are We There Yet?
The Long and Winding Road to Undergraduate Curricular Reform

HAROLD WEBER

In the fall of 1995, I assumed the position of director of undergraduate studies in the Department of English at the University of Alabama, a mid-sized state university with an undergraduate population of approximately 20,000, including about 250 English majors and 400 English minors. During that same fall, our department of thirty-four tenured and tenure-track faculty members spent two weeks participating in the external review mandated every five years by the Alabama Commission on Higher Education (ACHE), a body appointed by the governor and empowered by the legislature to govern higher education in our state.

We received a preliminary copy of the review early in 1996, and, while it contained some praise for the department, it expressed as well a number of strong criticisms, including an external consultant's rather devastating assessment of our undergraduate curriculum:

> The undergraduate curriculum presents a challenging and urgent set of problems. Like the curricula of other institutions, it appears to have developed by accretion, on a foundation of literary history. Both foundation and superstructure have become shaky, lacking serious analysis or interrogation for many years. For both intellectual and economic reasons, the curriculum now demands intensive examination as a whole. [. . .] I make no specific recommendations myself—this is clearly a matter for local determination. Collective meditation on the major, though, seems urgent.
> ("Program Review" 3)

The author is Professor of English at the University of Alabama, Tuscaloosa.

Within a semester of becoming undergraduate director I was charged by my chair with directing a process of curricular reform that everyone we consulted—including this external reviewer—assured us would not take less than two years of Herculean effort. Indeed, one reason I have composed this brief, impressionistic account of our labors is to celebrate and memorialize our "success": during the fall semester of 2000, fully three and a half years after beginning the process of curricular reform, we officially began to offer the courses that construct our new English major.

Comparing the outlines of our old and new curricula reveals the distance we traveled and suggests some of the intellectual issues that we tried to confront in the reorganization of our English major. The most important, for it was both the first to emerge from our discussions and the one most explicitly articulated by the department, concerns the relation between British and American literature. Breaking down the strict division between them guided our curricular reform.

At the sophomore level the desire to imagine a trans- or circumatlantic culture led us to construct a three- rather than four-course survey sequence,

FIGURE 1
REQUIREMENTS FOR THE ENGLISH MAJOR, BEFORE AND AFTER CURRICULAR REFORM, AT THE UNIVERSITY OF ALABAMA

BEFORE

4 courses: 200-level surveys (British Literature I & II, American Literature I & II)
2 courses: 300- or 400-level period courses (Shakespeare and one other course in British literature before 1785)
1 course: 300- or 400-level course in critical theory or linguistics
5 courses: 300- or 400-level electives

} 3 must be at the 400 level

AFTER

2 courses: 200-level surveys (Early Literature in English is required; students can then choose to take either Modern Literature in English or Twentieth-Century Literature in English)
1 course: Introduction to English Studies (300-level prerequisite for 400-level courses)
3 courses: 300-level period courses in literature to 1700 (1 course required), eighteenth- and nineteenth-century literature (1 course required), and twentieth-century literature
1 course: 300- or 400-level course in critical theory, linguistics, or writing
2 courses: 400-level electives
2 courses: electives (can include the third 200-level survey or African American Literature, another 200-level course)
1 course: Senior Seminar (400-level course)

Study of a foreign language for two years was and continues to be required of all English majors.

chronology rather than national identity providing its formal coherence. At the junior and senior levels the frequent integration of British and American literatures allowed us to trim a list of sixty-five courses—many of which, because of the unfilled faculty lines that have become the common administrative response to retirements in the last decade, were either no longer taught or taught only every two or three years—to what seemed a more manageable group of thirty-six.

Courses defined primarily by history and genre could now be assembled on the 300 level and distinguished clearly from our 400-level courses. Even the oldest members of the department could no longer identify what in the old curriculum distinguished a 300- from a 400-level course. Why was Shakespeare at the 300 level but Chaucer and Milton at the 400? Why was Topics in American Literature, 1914–45, taught at the 300 level but Topics in Romantic Literature taught at the 400? Decades of geological accretion had created a landscape in which such distinctions had been lost amid the slow but constant addition of yet another refinement of the literary historical division of two separate national literatures.

In the new curriculum, literary history was compressed—through the integration of American and British literatures—and confined to the 300 level, where, as "bedrock reading" ("Undergraduate Curriculum 2000" 3) it could now ground our introduction of undergraduates to the theoretical ferment of the last quarter century, the second intellectual imperative of our new curriculum. Courses at the 400 level were now defined precisely by their explicit deployment of a critical methodology or methodologies. Critical theory also informs the department's new Introduction to English Studies, required for majors. Although there is much we'd like this course to accomplish in preparing our majors for their years of study in our department, its primary objective is to introduce them to the principle of critical diversity and the choices now available to them in interpreting a literary text. We've designed this course as an exercise in team teaching to emphasize the variety of theoretical approaches that the profession now affords.

The final intellectual consideration that left its mark on our new curriculum involved the desire to permit faculty research to play more of a role in undergraduate teaching than seemed possible in the old curriculum. Such research can introduce undergraduates to what is most current in the field as well as animate the classroom with the excitement that faculty members bring to their latest work. Although special-topics courses on both the 300 and 400 levels—two or three of which might be approved each semester— were a part of the old curriculum, its historical rigidity and adherence to national coverage made it difficult for instructors' current research interests to inform their teaching. Particularly for faculty members whose research did not fall within conventional generic, national, and historical categories, there existed a disconcerting gap between the responsibilities of teaching and the demands of scholarship. By defining 400-level courses as either "Advanced Studies in . . ." or senior seminars—required of each major and designed to provide "a capstone classroom and research experience" by allowing students "to bring to bear in one academic setting all the skills they have assembled during their undergraduate careers" (6–7)—the department made it easier for specialized research interests to play a part in the design and teaching of undergraduate courses. By creating a faculty committee to review and approve all 400-level courses—so that student needs and interests could be safeguarded—we hoped that the department could more successfully integrate undergraduate teaching with scholarly research.

The initial question our department had to resolve concerned not the theoretical nature of curricular reform but the more practical matter of how to form the committee that would direct and conceptualize the process (a smaller department, of course, might choose to meet as a committee of the whole). Normally, such a committee would contain some representatives elected by the department and some appointed by the chair, but the department, aware of the potential divisiveness of curricular reform, took the unusual step of asking the chair to select the committee.

Fortunately, our chair decided that a committee made up of everyone who wanted to join would best serve our needs. In retrospect, this decision was clearly the right one, although at the time it generated some complaint. Our chair was criticized by some for avoiding her responsibilities, by others for allowing a "tyranny of the majority" to assert itself. I was disappointed as well, wanting a streamlined, practical, can-do committee.

The ten-person committee that resulted from the call for volunteers provided a group of people, which included the chair and me, who were genuinely interested in matters of curriculum and who held (often passionately) ideas about curricular goals and how to achieve them. They were willing to work hard, and some were willing to dedicate themselves to what eventually became an almost two-year commitment. The volunteer nature of the committee allowed people to leave when they felt that their particular expertise was no longer germane or to join when their specific interests were engaged. All the department's members felt that they could be part of the process if they wished; the openness of the committee assured most that the process was not driven by ideological purity or a party line.

The second tactical decision that now seems crucial to our success was the establishment of an extended period at the beginning during which the department took only nonbinding votes. The question of where to begin presented a problem. With everything on the table except our freshman composition offerings and the number of hours required for a major (thirty-six)—because changes to either required approval from the university or the state—we found ourselves intimidated by the necessity to fix a point of attack. The reiterated question of our first departmental meetings was, How can we decide what our upper-level classes should be like if we don't know what our sophomore surveys will be? Conversely, How can we reorganize our sophomore surveys before we've decided what to offer at the upper levels?

Even after we determined to begin by reorganizing our sophomore surveys, people hesitated to commit themselves to change at one level before knowing what the implications of that change would be at another. The problem was both logical and psychological, and its solution demanded that our initial decisions not be binding until we could all see the larger picture. Straw votes liberated us both formally and imaginatively, and for the first three months of meetings we were thus able to play with our curriculum, proposing first one structure and then another as objections, complications, or unforeseen difficulties arose. The straw vote also recommends itself because people know when its utility has ended. At some point the department became impatient with my repeated formal announcement that a proposal called for another straw vote. When a straw vote ceases to generate comfort and instead creates the collective sense that the department is spinning its wheels, it is time for a real vote.

The final tactic that allowed the process of curricular reform to move forward was our decision not to allow the question of textbooks to influence us, particularly regarding survey courses. After much hesitation, we began to refashion our curriculum by considering the status of our four 200-level surveys, not just because of the foundational nature of the surveys but also because they had been singled out by our external reviewer for particular criticism. Further, since the old curriculum required students to take twelve hours at the 200 level—fully one-third of the major—it was clear that we could add courses at the upper levels and reshape the major only by making changes at the 200 level.

From the start, some claimed that the survey courses we had formulated simply could not be taught, because no textbooks would ratify our commingling of American and British literatures. All the major anthologies, these critics pointed out, were based on the distinction between national literatures that we were attempting to erase. The design of our surveys, they argued, must be dictated by the available textbooks.

This is a powerful argument, because however much the profession has changed, that change has not yet transformed the shape of the anthologies through which almost all departments teach their survey courses. While the contents of those volumes have certainly been modified to account for transformations of the canon, they remain monuments to accepted and conventional distinctions between national literatures and historical periods.

But the textbook problem is not insurmountable. Through a judicious use of the splits now available from Longman and from Norton (Norton has divided each of its two volumes on British literature into three smaller volumes and will soon do the same with its American survey) and of a series of homemade anthologies drawn from literature freely available on the Web, we have succeeded in providing reasonably priced texts for our newly designed surveys. Allowing the problem of textbooks to dictate curricular reform is to stifle the process even before it has begun. Imagine the curriculum you want and then force the mundane, practical world to ratify your vision.

The possibility of failure troubled me throughout the three and a half years that the department engaged issues of curricular reform. That we achieved any success at all is a tribute to the will of the department as a whole. Although the ACHE review provided the initial impetus for curricular reform, only a shared conviction that change was necessary could have sustained us through the years of frustrating, divisive, and often tedious work that followed. Maintaining the full participation of the department was essential to this process; talking all our problems out united us.

That this unity exacts a price is nowhere more apparent than in the new curriculum, which is not always a model of intellectual consistency. We may have banished the split between American and British literatures at the 200 level, but at the 300 level half the thirty-six courses we now offer remain explicitly categorized as American or British. We may have mandated that 400-level courses define themselves by their critical methodology, but the seven categories we've used to organize such offerings are defined not by critical method—such as formalism, gender criticism, cultural criticism, or reader-response theory—but by general, descriptive titles that include, no surprise, American literature, British literature, and literary genre. The new curriculum provides flexibility for those willing to take chances and rethink conventional ways of designing courses and presenting literary studies to undergraduates, but it also allows those who don't want to change the opportunity not to. Such is the price of consensus.

That the new curriculum therefore fully satisfies no one might be regarded as its virtue, for it belongs to the department and not to a particular constituency. Some see it as just another ridiculous manifestation of the faddish critical thinking and political correctness that have disfigured the profession during the past quarter century; others find it offers nothing that could genuinely be called new but merely rearticulates and refashions critical and historical clichés that have been in play for years. It is a quintessential document by committee, and its intellectual compromises make it an easy target for the different factions in the department.

The process of curricular reform is so complex and takes so long to carry out that it cannot help generating mixed feelings in a department of our size. Ripples of criticism and unhappiness inevitably result from each member's dissatisfaction. Such discontent can end up infecting everything related to curricular reform, even the affirmation of departmental identity and engagement that is the other important outcome of the process. The external consultant accentuated this benefit when in her report she noted that "the Department and its leaders must be willing to face the possibility of active conflict in order to achieve a more serious level of collective discourse and collective engagement. [...] The ultimate result of such self-examination—in addition to its consequences for the matters investigated—might be a more intellectually active form of communal life" ("Program Review" 3).

An antiquated curriculum represents not simply a failure to respond to a changing profession but also an inability to harness the collective energies of the individual members of a department. The external consultant was right to suggest that the successful outcome of curricular reform lies as much in a renewed sense of departmental identity and responsibility as in a new curriculum. Our achievement has been less than ideal; if our new curriculum is flawed and provisional, so too is our new departmental community, which remains tarnished by some of the intellectual and personal conflicts either exacerbated by or raised during curricular reform.

I suspect that the two members of the department most satisfied with the curricular reform and with the new community it has generated are the chair and I, who can at least pat ourselves on the back for having accomplished something. I could write at even greater length on the intricate two-year process in which we shepherded "Undergraduate Curriculum 2000" through the bureaucratic ziggurat of the modern university—an extraordinary baroque regulative dance for a new undergraduate director to attempt. But that tale of endless paper pushing and administrative consultation, of forms to complete and librarians to placate, is another story entirely.

NOTE

I am indebted to Salli Davis, Joe Hornsby, Sandy Huss, Francesca Kazan, and Elizabeth Meese for help in writing this essay.

WORKS CITED

"Program Review." Dept. of English and Freshman Composition Program, 1995–96. U of Alabama. Spring 1996.
"Undergraduate Curriculum 2000." Dept. of English, U of Alabama. Spring 1999.

Design and Consent:
Notes on Curriculum Revision

MARILYN FRANCUS

In December 1999, the English department at West Virginia University received approval to institute sixty curricular changes in its undergraduate program—to add twenty-six new courses, delete sixteen courses, redesign six courses, and administer minor changes in twelve courses. The magnitude of this change was unprecedented in departmental history and garnered the English department considerable attention throughout the university. This essay describes the strategies we pursued to achieve the change: what worked, what didn't, and why.

For years the English faculty felt that the undergraduate curriculum needed revision, and for all the reasons one might expect: the curriculum did not reflect current trends in literary or linguistic study; it did not respond consistently to student need; its eccentric shape reflected years of ad hoc change without coherence or a shaping vision. Repeatedly, the department attempted to revise the curriculum but without success. The chair convened two separate faculty committees, each with representatives from various specializations, to study the curriculum and make recommendations to the department. Both committees proffered useful suggestions, but as other projects demanded the attention of faculty members and the department administration, the revision process invariably stalled and died.

The chair, aware of the faculty's ongoing concern about the curriculum as well as the frustrations of the committee members in their efforts to effect change, proposed a new strategy: if the entire English faculty was assigned

The author is Associate Professor of English at West Virginia University.

to curriculum committees in 1997, members could make recommendations to the department as a whole regarding the courses in their area. This organizational model relied on a number of premises; first and foremost was that all faculty members were valued stakeholders in the revision process. Since faculty members were best equipped to evaluate the courses in their area of expertise, their colleagues in other areas would defer to their assessment. Finally, by centering the entire faculty's attention on the task of evaluating the curriculum, the revision process would acquire a momentum that would diminish, if not eliminate, the factors that had undermined previous efforts. As this new strategy was implemented, it soon became apparent that this model did not sufficiently account for the politics of faculty experience, and it too failed. Curriculum is arguably the last bastion of faculty authority in university administration, and faculty members tend to be proprietary about their courses. Accordingly, most of the curriculum committees tried to protect the courses in their field if not maximize the number of their courses, while suggesting course deletions in other fields. Without a mechanism to achieve consensus among the committees, this model emphasized the very divisions in the department that it was looking to overcome. At best, the faculty developed an ideal curriculum for each area of specialization, but there was no shaping vision of the undergraduate program as a whole.

The faculty then engaged in an extended discussion about the revision process: should the department revise its course list and then reshape the major, or should it define the major and then revise the list? In the absence of consensus for a revised course list, the chair appointed a committee in spring 1998 to evaluate English curricula at a variety of colleges and universities and then make recommendations to the faculty regarding the shape and content of the English major. Our existing major required thirty-three credits beyond the university composition requirement: four literature survey courses (two American, two British), a linguistics course, a Shakespeare course, and a minimum of five elective English courses at the advanced level. The committee to evaluate the major analyzed undergraduate programs at twenty-five colleges and universities—main and branch campuses of state universities, private colleges and universities, academic institutions in and outside our region, and so on. This research gave the committee a strong sense of the current state of English studies, while providing models of requirements and course sequences. The committee also discussed remarks by faculty members about the existing English major. Many students had enrolled in advanced literature courses without taking the corresponding introductory literature survey, thereby minimizing the pedagogical value of their experience and frequently frustrating faculty efforts. Many majors, pursuing upper-division courses at random, subsequently had difficulty finding employment or being accepted into graduate programs because of the perceived lack of coherence in their academic study.

On the basis of its review of undergraduate programs and faculty comments, the committee to evaluate the major submitted a report to the faculty recommending that the undergraduate major be structured as a core-and-concentration system: all English majors would be required to enroll in a core group of courses and then choose a focus area of advanced study; the focus area would be constituted by a minimum of four courses. The report recommended eight areas of concentration—American literature, British literature, creative writing, professional writing and media, cultural studies, Appalachian studies, English education, and a self-designed concentration with departmental approval—so that students would be provided with many options, and most faculty members would be able to teach in more than one of these areas. The report also made recommendations on the content of the core, the sequencing of the core and advanced courses in the major, and the establishment of departmental honors.

Committee members were available to respond to questions about the report (in the office and online), but there was no faculty meeting dedicated to discussing it. The committee quickly drafted a ballot, and the faculty voted (and accepted) a new major that maintained the existing required courses as a core and added a new concentration system.

The success of the ballot signaled a number of viable strategies for further curriculum revision. First, before any significant changes could be made, research was necessary to provide a context for committee members (then for faculty members) to make an informed decision. Second, a written report with a compelling narrative was crucial; the narrative offered by the committee persuasively paired curricular sequence with pedagogical effectiveness and student experience with student marketability. Next, any proposed curricular change had to be as inclusive as possible, responding to a multiplicity of fields and academic interests, so that faculty members and students could feel both represented by and invested in a new major. Academic inclusiveness also allowed the English department to position itself clearly as fulfilling the mission of a department on the main campus of a state university. Last, by presenting the ballot to the faculty soon after the report, the committee was perceived as efficient as well as diligent, and respect for the committee's work led to a strong response rate to the ballot. In conjunction with the report, the ballot informed and involved the entire faculty and circumvented much of the departmental politics evident in large-scale faculty meetings. Essentially, the democratic process worked: the results of the ballot were recognized as a consensus even by those who did not concur.

Reaching consensus on the shape of the English major was a considerable advance, but the problems of revising the course list still loomed. Without a new course list, it was not possible to present the new major for university approval, much less implement the concentration system. In summer 1998, I was appointed by the chair to direct the undergraduate program, with the express task of bringing the curriculum revision to completion. Having served on many of the above-mentioned committees (including the committee to evaluate the major) as well as having been an undergraduate adviser for many years, I was well aware of the state of the curriculum and of the faculty and student discussions on the subject. I also knew that in the previous attempts to revise the course list many questions about the curriculum had not been answered or had been answered only impressionistically. Statements like "Course X always draws students" or "Students want courses in Y" could be constructed as fact by one member of the faculty and as rumor by another. Without relevant data, it would be impossible to replicate the success of the major evaluation committee.

In other words, it was time to do more research.

Starting in fall 1998, I went through the department files and established an enrollment database that provided student enrollment and withdrawal rates for every section of every undergraduate course offered over the previous five years, excluding only the composition courses required by the university of all undergraduates. Five years accommodated two full cycles of our course rotation and offered the best approximation of the current state of the faculty. Our department had undergone significant faculty turnover in the 1990s; as a large segment of the faculty retired, the department hired new faculty members every year. The data before 1994 would therefore produce a largely irrelevant set, reflecting a very different faculty from the one in 1998.

More important, the enrollment database addressed an ongoing problem in the curriculum revision process: the need for a mechanism to integrate student opinion into the department's analysis. Student involvement in curriculum revision had been a thorny issue from the start. The faculty had always recognized the importance of student input but did not want the students to expect that they could determine the major requirements or the course list. Student comments were cited at meetings, but to my knowledge undergraduates were not invited to speak with or serve on curriculum committees. As a departmental adviser I had access to a broad cross-section of students, but the only available documentation of student opinion was the departmental surveys of seniors regarding the English major. (Undergraduates regularly complete course evaluation forms, but these forms are considered private, a matter between the faculty members and those who evaluate their performance annually.) The senior survey samples, representing about fifteen percent of the graduating class, were evocative but too small to be definitive. I considered sending surveys to our undergraduate majors, but it was impossible to guarantee an adequate response rate, nor would such a survey provide information for the previous five-year period. The enrollment database compensated for some of these gaps by generating a student profile for each of our courses. Emerging trends among English majors became easier to track across time and across courses. Some course profiles revealed that students were enrolling from unexpected colleges in the university; others showed that the students for whom the course was designed were not enrolling. Both trends indicated patterns of student interest as well as ways to improve the marketing of our courses across the university. Enrollment patterns highlighted courses that were amenable to a large lecture format, courses that seemed to flourish in a seminar setting, and the response to our efforts in distance learning. The database also provided material on the viability of the course rotation and on the effects of course sequencing and course frequency across semesters. In many instances, the database documented and justified the impressions of the faculty and the department administration.

There were, however, limitations to the enrollment database, most notably in the absence of data for some courses and the misconstruction of data. For instance, if a course had been taught only once in the past five years, the enrollment data could be construed as suggestive but not conclusive in any way. The database could suggest commentary about faculty performance but no more. High student enrollment does not necessarily signal pedagogical quality, and low student enrollment does not necessarily reflect poor pedagogy. Every department has courses that faculty members think are important but that do not elicit an enthusiastic response from students, and courses that students love are considered questionable by some faculty members. So it was imperative for us to remember that the database showed simply how the students had voted with their feet—and that it was to be used as a tool for analysis, not as the definitive criterion for curricular assessment.

Enrollment figures told one version of the curriculum story but far from all of it. To learn more, I set up a series of interviews with my colleagues, one on one. In each interview, I asked a group of general questions: Do you like your teaching assignment? What courses would you like to teach? Which courses would you like to see added to the undergraduate curriculum? What kinds of changes would you suggest for the courses that you teach? for the curriculum as a whole? What has been your experience teaching large lecture courses? seminars? teaching the requirements for the major? with distance learning? with integrating technology into the classroom? Does the available enrollment data reflect your experience with these courses? As the faculty members responded, I took extensive notes. Everyone was willing to talk (no surprise there), and while many of my colleagues took the opportunity to vent their frustrations about the department, all provided useful information about the curriculum in action. Basically, the interviews allowed people to locate themselves in the undergraduate program and to voice their issues and concerns. The interviews also functioned as a nonjudgmental venue for the faculty to comment on courses outside their teaching assignments without being perceived as divisive, aggressive, or political. Many faculty members were able to explain anomalies in the database and clarify the curricular context—like the dozen pharmacy students who enrolled in an advanced women's literature course one semester (never to return again)—and gave reasons why courses had not been offered on rotation (e.g., fellowship and sabbatical leaves). Conversely, the database often helped faculty members clarify their perceptions of their student audience over time. During the 1998–99 academic year, I conducted twenty-four interviews with tenure-track, tenured, and long-standing adjunct faculty members; I also held extensive curriculum discussions with three colleagues before the database was complete. Of the remaining nine tenure-stream faculty members in my department, two were on leave and two were largely unavailable because of administrative duties. While interviews with the entire English faculty would have been ideal, it was not possible given the time constraints of the process; I considered a faculty response rate of seventy-five percent to be reasonably good. As time-consuming and detail-oriented as the curricular research phase was, it provided an analytic framework for curricular revision and functioned as a mechanism for faculty inclusion without division, a key toward achieving the much needed consensus.

After completing this research, I wrote a forty-three-page report to the faculty on the undergraduate curriculum. This report presented a summary of the faculty analysis and database information for each of the eighty-one courses (exclusive of the composition requirement) in our undergraduate program. Generally, the strategies for revision fell into five categories: adding a new course, splitting an existing course into two, combining two courses, deleting a course, and making minor changes (such as altering the course title or the catalog description) to reflect the current state of the course. Often a course called for more than one revision strategy and rationale. All faculty suggestions for each course were noted. My report also documented all the new course recommendations, along with the justifications that the faculty provided for the new courses. I included university information that pertained to English courses, citing the courses that were required by other academic units and that therefore could not be changed without their approval as well as the courses that fulfilled (or could potentially fulfill) university distribution requirements for graduation. It was necessary to integrate our efforts with the university's mission.

Without a doubt, this report was the most difficult document for me to write in the curricular process. The magnitude of the subject and the degree of detail were daunting, but finding a viable and consistent rhetorical stance was even more challenging, especially for an audience of English professors trained in rhetoric. I had to be above reproach—honest, fair, and nonpartisan. Departmental politics had been a factor in stalling the curriculum revision process in the past, so it was important that the report recognize the different sectors in the English department without privileging any. Tiptoeing through politics is always a delicate task, but especially delicate when one is perceived to be in a position of power. As I drafted the report, I focused on my purpose, to present information—not to provide a full-scale analysis but to enable the faculty to do so. I tried to keep my commentary to a minimum and express the voices of my colleagues as much as possible. This strategy worked. The successful reception of my report (which generated only one faculty complaint) was a turning point toward the creation of departmental consensus. Members of the faculty felt that they had been heard and represented fairly to one another. After the report was distributed in April 1999, I immediately drafted a curriculum ballot based on the revisions suggested by the faculty. We voted that May, and a course list for a new curriculum was born.

The elements that contributed to the success of the committee evaluating the major recurred in the course-list phase of our curriculum revision: research, inclusiveness, a strong narrative, and efficient timing between the submission of a report and a ballot. The narratives that compelled the faculty—and that would subsequently compel the university administration—emerged during the 1998–99 academic year and were articulated in the curriculum report. The overarching theme was millennial: the desire to create a curriculum that would lead the English department from the twentieth into the twenty-first century, and preferably on time. (Or more ironically: the desire for closure, given that the faculty had had enough curriculum discussion after five years.) "To reflect the current state of the field" was the most frequent justification given for curricular change in the department, and since the field (literary, linguistic, and cultural studies) has been expanding in a plethora of directions at once, most of the new and redesigned courses fit under this rubric. The courses Multiethnic Literature, Postcolonial Literature, and Commonwealth Literature acknowledged new growth areas in the field. Other courses focused on theory—Introduction to Cultural Studies, Introduction to American Studies, Contemporary Literary Theory—for while theory had been a part of our undergraduate literature courses for decades, our students needed more than the existing History of Literary Criticism course to partake in the theoretical and metacritical discourses that currently characterize the profession. We decided to split the existing British and American Women Writers course into two, to respond to changes in women's studies, and added a Topics in Women's Literature course so that we would have the flexibility to offer material in new fields, such as Caribbean women writers or women's literature and art. Many course changes were needed to make sequences consistent; we filled in the historical gaps among our advanced offerings by adding, for example, American Literature to 1800 and Literature of the Middle Ages. The department also added the advanced courses Contemporary American Literature and Contemporary British Literature to distinguish between twentieth- and twenty-first-century literatures. The new genre courses Novel, Drama, and Prose were designed to parallel the existing sophomore-level courses Short Story and Poetry. The new upper-level courses Topics in African American Literature, Topics in Native American Literature, and Topics in Gay/Lesbian Studies complemented existing mid-level courses in these fields. These changes were consistent with the shape of the new major that the department had voted on in May 1998, both in that they created sequences of courses and in that they expanded coordinated areas of advanced study.[1]

After the English course list and the core-and-concentration shape of the new major were approved by the department, the faculty defined five concentrations for the new major.[2] While assigning courses to concentrations, the faculty sought to create overlap whenever possible, so that students could have flexibility as they organized their academic program. For instance, the faculty approved the new Introduction to American Studies course for the American literature, Appalachian studies, and cultural studies concentrations.[3] The faculty agreed that twenty-one courses could be used to fulfill the concentration requirement for American literature, ranging from offerings in literary history (the seventeenth century to the present) to courses in minority studies (e.g., African American Literature and Topics in Native American Literature), regional studies (Southern Writers), gender studies (American Women Writers), linguistics, and theory. The concentration in British literature in many ways parallels the American literature concentration, with twenty-one courses in British literary history (from the Anglo-Saxon period to the present), cultural studies (such as Commonwealth Literature, Postcolonial Literature), gender studies

(British Women Writers), linguistics, and theory. The Appalachian studies concentration consists of nine courses in Appalachian literature, folklore, and theory, while the new offerings Multimedia Writing, Editing, and Topics in Humanities Computing are among the fifteen courses that form the professional writing and media concentration. The cultural studies concentration is perhaps the most eclectic, having twenty-eight courses in cultural studies, minority studies, gender studies, regional studies, and theory. Popular American Culture, Multiethnic Literature, and Sexual Diversity in Literature and Film fulfill this concentration requirement, along with the courses in these fields noted above.[4]

For the administrative units outside the English department that needed to approve the course list for our curriculum, the faculty narrative of intellectual currency and consistency was appropriately professional but not especially riveting. Any department could make such claims to justify curricular change. What was persuasive was how our new curriculum responded to the administration's concerns. Correlations between the department's vision and the university's agenda surfaced during the revision process, and the curriculum report highlighted narratives of student professionalization, academic diversity, and administrative efficiency, which were extremely appealing to administrators.

In a state like West Virginia, which struggles economically even during boom periods for the country, the university maintains a strong focus on undergraduate training for the workforce and economic viability. Our new courses Multimedia Writing, Editing, and Topics in Humanities Computing were the most easily understood response to the university's work-training imperative, being clearly geared to make our students more competitive in the job market. These new technology, media, and writing courses built on our existing courses Professional Writing and Science and Technical Writing, and they were easily marketable to our student base outside the College of Arts and Sciences (hence a perk for our dean). The English department also addressed the concerns of long-term employability, student preparedness for graduate study, and venues of employment (e.g., law, business) that require further academic training. The concentration model, sustained by new advanced courses in theory, cultural studies, and literary studies, showed that our undergraduates would gain the requisite analytic and verbal sophistication to bridge the gap between undergraduate and graduate training.

The English department responded to the university's diversity imperative with a palette of new courses in minority studies, gender studies, and global studies.[5] To graduate, students must fulfill a diversity requirement in these areas, and the English department's new offerings support the university's initiative as they considerably increase student choice and flexibility. These new courses also benefit our English majors by enhancing their options in these growth areas of literary study, and they serve a variety of programs around campus, including the Africana Studies program, the Native American Studies minor, and the Women's Studies program. The integration of our efforts with those of other academic units provided a model of both administrative efficiency and academic coherence. Contacts with faculty members outside the English department, some of whom sat on the committees evaluating the new English curriculum for the college and the university, helped reinforce program alliances and paved the way for curricular approval.

Two other factors influenced the administration in our favor. During 1999, university administrators invoked national discussions regarding the state of higher education as they pursued university-wide reviews of academic standards and expectations. Many recommendations of the often cited Boyer Commission report, *Reinventing Undergraduate Education: A Blueprint for America's Research Universities*, were cognate with our curricular vision. By framing our curricular changes in the light of the national academic conversation, the English department was able to define and explain its efforts by national criteria of academic excellence. The consensus itself of the English faculty turned out to be a selling point for many administrators and curriculum committee members. While the English department is not known for being particularly contentious, it is impressive when a faculty of thirty-six tenure-track, tenured, and long-standing adjunct faculty members, all trained in rhetoric and argumentation, agree to agree.

Shepherding the new English curriculum through multiple levels of university administration in the fall of 1999 was challenging, but I had a great story to tell about the English department, the university's academic vision, and how they worked together—and I had the research, the faculty members, and the documentation to back it up. My colleagues, committed to the vision represented by their vote of the previous May, gladly and graciously provided sample syllabi, course rationales, and catalog descriptions. I maintained the enrollment database for current data; filled out form after form required by the university for curriculum approval; and wrote more memos, answered more e-mail queries, and attended more meetings than I thought possible. When the Faculty Senate unanimously approved the sixty course changes that would constitute the basis of the new English curriculum in December 1999, it seemed like the English department had achieved not only success but closure as well.

Of course there cannot be closure, for curriculum never stands still, nor should it. The next phase was under way in January 2000, as I began negotiating approvals for distribution requirements, instituting a curriculum implementation plan, building a new course rotation, and developing a marketing strategy. The new course list will be fully in place by fall 2001, and with ongoing assessment to determine its viability, the English department will have the means to identify and institute any necessary modifications. But, with any luck, we should not need to alter the English undergraduate curriculum drastically for quite some time.

NOTES

[1] The English department deleted sixteen courses, for three general reasons: to reflect pedagogical practice, to facilitate course redesign, and to clarify the major. Courses that had not been taught or were no longer required were deleted; generally these courses (e.g., Words and Usage and the Practicum in Teaching Composition) had been superseded by other offerings. Since the Study of Selected Authors courses were not perceived as part of current pedagogical trends in the field and because they did not strongly appeal to students, they were eliminated. The department deleted courses that were conflated into new and redesigned offerings—for instance, the existing Modern Literature I and II courses were combined into a single Modern Literature course. The department streamlined its course offerings for nonmajors, deleting courses like Themes and Topics in Literature and Appalachian Experience in Literature. Despite the efforts of the advising staff, the status of these courses confused students: they fulfilled the university's humanities requirement but did not count toward the English major. For students who transferred into the English major, the nonmajor courses they had taken wreaked havoc with their academic program, while some majors thought that they could enroll in these courses for major credit. To minimize these problems, the department decided to offer more sophomore- and junior-level courses that met the criteria for both the university's requirements and the major, while retaining a smaller complement of courses for nonmajors.

[2] Three concentrations, in creative writing, English education, and the self-designed concentration, were special cases. The faculty agreed that the existing creative writing minor, which had already been approved by the department and the university administration, was functionally a concentration and did not require alteration to fit into the new model for the major. (The nine-course creative writing concentration involves three levels of course work—an introductory course; a sequence of courses and workshops in fiction, nonfiction, and poetry; and a final seminar in which students produce a significant corpus of work.) The English education concentration is determined by the College of Human Resources and Education, so the English faculty was not at liberty to change it. This concentration requires Advanced Composition, The English Language, Fiction for Adolescents, and Approaches to Teaching Composition, along with a regional-ethnic-minority studies requirement and an advanced elective requirement that can be fulfilled by any of the upper-division courses in the English department. The self-designed concentration could not be modeled by the faculty, since its function is to meet the individual needs of students as they arise.

[3] Courses in linguistics and theory had the highest crossover rate among concentrations. For instance, the new courses Contemporary Literary Theory, Introduction to

Cultural Studies, and Topics in the English Language were deemed appropriate for five concentrations: American literature, British literature, Appalachian studies, cultural studies, and professional writing and media. The faculty discussed developing a student appeal process through the department advising office for courses not listed in a particular concentration.

[4]These five concentrations are being modeled currently by the English department. Formal approval for concentrations is required by the university, which placed a moratorium on all curriculum changes in the 2000–01 academic year as it converts to a new course numbering system. I attempted to apply for concentration approval simultaneously in 1999 with the new course list, but the associate dean and the College Curriculum Committee felt that the English department would be better served by pursuing separate approvals for the course list and the concentration system, given the complexity and magnitude of the course list. As a result, I used the concentration system as a framework for discussion with administrators and faculty leaders about the course-list changes. I expect that the English department will apply for approval of the new concentrations in the near future.

[5]Students must enroll in at least one course in non-Western culture, minority cultures, or gender studies to fulfill the university diversity requirement. The new English courses American Women Writers, British Women Writers, Multiethnic Literature, Non-Western World Literature, and Postcolonial Literature fit well within these parameters. (The new courses that rotate subject matter, such as Topics in African American Literature, Topics in Gay/Lesbian Studies, and Topics in Native American Literature, may also be eligible.) Formal approval for diversity course designation is granted by the Liberal Studies program, which administers and monitors the diversity requirement.

WORK CITED

Boyer Commission on Educating Undergraduates in the Research University. *Reinventing Undergraduate Education: A Blueprint for America's Research Universities*. 1998. State U of New York, Stony Brook. Ed. Melissa Bishop. 21 June 2001. 28 June 2001 <http://notes.cc.sunysb.edu/Pres/boyer.nsf/>.

And That I Should Teach Tolerance

BETTINA TATE PEDERSEN

The MLA Task Force against Campus Bigotry, in its report that appeared in *Profession 2000*, makes as one of its many thoughtfully considered and articulated recommendations "that the advisory committees of *Profession*, the *ADFL Bulletin*, and the *ADE Bulletin* search out articles that address tolerance in teaching and learning and in the profession, the different forms that intolerance can take, best-case scenarios that offer strategies for resolving conflicts and misunderstandings productively, and so forth" (Royster et al. 234). In thinking about this recommendation of the task force in particular, I have reflected on what addressing issues of tolerance in teaching and learning means to me, what intolerance I have experienced and perhaps enacted as a female learner and teacher, and what strategies I actually use to forward tolerance in the university communities in which I participate. Each of these points of reflection had identifiable and significant influences in my teaching and in my learning, but the nagging question that provokes my response to this recommendation and *Profession 2000*'s call for papers is this: On what grounds or with what authority do I approach my students to teach tolerance?

Because this question is inescapably personal, my answers are markedly autobiographical and confessional. Autobiography and confession are not usually the genres of choice for the MLA's journals, but they are in keeping with the nature of the twenty-four scenarios enumerated in the report illustrating the myriad issues of tolerance, diversity, and bigotry on our

---

The author is Associate Professor of English at Point Loma Nazarene University.

campuses. A confessional autobiography, brief though it may be, also appears consonant with the statement the report makes in response to its question, Why should bigotry be an issue for the MLA? "The humanistic disciplines," the report reads, "articulate variously a commitment to the preservation, development, celebration, and critical exploration of language, literature, and culture; interests in ongoing cultural production; and *concerns for the human mind, body, heart, and soul*" (220; emphasis mine). However underexamined the tenet of teaching tolerance may be in my own mind and teaching practice, I too see it as a matter of the mind, body, heart, and soul. Moreover, it is a precept about which I care very deeply and because of which I engage in a whole host of professional and pedagogical activities and choices. Hence, it is crucial to examine just how the position of teacher, with its attendant roles and authority, may complicate the act of teaching tolerance.

Deconstruction and reader-response theories can help illuminate my position as a teacher of tolerance. While these theories are increasingly making their way into pedagogical praxis, the student populations and constituencies of the universities in which I've taught have continued to see teachers as experts—a position that resists deconstruction and reader-response teaching postures. I teach largely from a pedagogy driven by Rosenblattian reader-response. I directly state that it is my students' ideas about the texts we read that I want to hear in class; I routinely use small- and large-group discussion over lecture format; I consistently teach more inductively than deductively, consciously and repeatedly resisting students' maneuvers to compel me to tell them what the text means rather than to facilitate their own discovery and articulation of what they think, even tentatively, it means. Despite these efforts my students repeatedly ask, What is the real meaning of the text? What did the author really intend? Which of the many responses you transcribe on the board, Dr. Pedersen, is the right one? Some even write on informal and formal evaluation forms, "I'd like this professor to have lectured more, since she's the expert, right?" At the same time it would be disingenuous for me to suggest that my reader-response pedagogy surrenders completely the classroom space or course content to my students. I do, in fact, see myself as having both knowledge and experience that my students do not. However, rather than give them my reading first, thus imposing the "rightness" or fixity of meaning that some of them seem to want, I prefer to work with express direction to shape what textual responses my students offer and create together during class.

When the subject matter is tolerance, the position of teacher as expert becomes an even more serious problem and more in need of deconstructing and reader-response strategies. Assuming the mantle of expert on tolerance suggests an arrogance that contravenes the other-focused, self-interrogative, and self-critical perspective of a truly tolerant person. Further, having the students ascribe such an authority to me may turn the atmosphere of the classroom into a more rather than less coercive one, and I am not at all convinced that tolerance is achieved or even forwarded through coercion. A personal example may help illustrate this point.

It became a well-rehearsed narrative during my years in graduate school that the colonizer was an insidiously evil, self-absorbed, and retrenched subjectivity that could construct only its version of the colonized other; it could never be itself constructed or reconstructed by that other. An understanding of the nineteenth-century imperialist paradigm clearly illuminated the bigotry of such a position and so enlightened me as a student. I was indeed compelled by much of the scholarly discourse outlining such a perspective. Still, as a United States citizen who had lived abroad for extended periods of time, I had experienced a cultural dislodgment that forever changed—deconstructed and reconstructed—me and my worldview. My lived experience did not fully coincide with this theorizing of colonizer-colonized subjectivities. My cross-cultural experience and the disjunction between it and the totalizing effect of these theories drew me to write a paper on the nineteenth-century British *Up the Country*, an account of Emily Eden's travels in India. Reading and writing with the cross-cultural experiences of my own life in mind, I saw several moments in Eden's text that clearly indicated she had been reconstructed by the colonial Indian others she imagined and encountered as much as she had constructed them. This was the reading I offered to the seminar group. It was politely listened to but later dismissed in favor of a reading of *Up the Country* that saw Eden and her narrative as once again reinscribing the imperialist narrative on the Indian other.

Although I was then and still am compelled by theories of imperialism and postcoloniality, what produced the greatest dislodgment of my perspective and behaviors (hence the greatest development of tolerance) was actually living and working with people not from my own cultural position. Indeed, my personal experience of increased tolerance for and acceptance of the cultural other was not accounted for in the very theoretical discourses intended to confront sites and ideologies of bigotry. Moreover, because the theories of imperialism and postcoloniality and their practitioners provided the expert discourse on these matters, my reading, my experience, and even I felt pushed to the colonized margins of the classroom.

If the teaching of tolerance is approached as sheer content—a definable set of theories and concomitant narratives—that relegates students' lived experience to the margins of the classroom discourse, then it may actually appear to our students as coercion to adopt a politically correct set of paradigms, values, behaviors, and so forth. It is precisely this coercion I would like to avoid in my teaching of tolerance, and it seems to me that the only way to begin moving in such an anticoercive direction is to approach my students as a joint learner of tolerance. To address issues of bigotry, diversity, and tolerance effectively, I must dislodge myself from and deconstruct the position of teacher as expert by openly admitting that I am not an expert on tolerance and that I am still learning how to reduce my own bigotry and to increase tolerance personally and systemically along with my students.

To see if my reflecting on the grounds for teaching tolerance bore any resemblance to what students thought about the teaching and learning of tolerance, I asked a class of twenty lower-division composition students to respond in writing to the questions, What do you see as the most effective way to learn to be a more tolerant person? and What do you think are the most effective ways for me to teach tolerance?

Students answered the first question with such responses as "traveling to different places," "learning about other cultures," "through the process of immersion," "hearing about other people's experiences," "seriously taking the time to get to know one another and to appreciate one another," "befriending and getting to know the untolerated person or thing," "finding common grounds with different people and relating to them personally," "getting to know a wide variety of people (whether homosexual, rich, poor, different race, etc.)," "becoming less bigoted through direct contact with whatever I am against." They answered the second question with such comments as "A teacher should engage students in a variety of viewpoints to increase diversity and knowledge," "should help students learn by seeing both sides of a story," "should have them read emotional stories from other perspectives," "should present them with topics of controversy, so they end up being more open-minded and not so narrow-minded," "should show a good example and be less biased to the teacher's own opinions and more open to others' opinions," "should bring the students into contact with different points of view." Some longer responses were:

> For myself experiencing something is the most effective way for me to change something about myself whether it be good or bad. A teacher has a rather hard job to do this [teach tolerance]. He or she must show examples of a topic in order to change a person. The rest is up to the student.

> I become more tolerant when the situation becomes real to me. When I see, read, or become aware of real-life examples, I see the error of my ways. I respond to emotional things. I tend to put things into categories and until it becomes real, I am not very easy to deal with.

> I think that I could become a more tolerant, less bigoted person by having my life to relive. My parents and peers have played such a large part in my racial, sexual, etc. views that I don't think I can change my views. I think that the most effective way a teacher can teach me to be less racist is just by example.

The keynotes of these student responses seem to be lived experience; the fruitful dislodgment that can result from exposure to difference; and the teacher as example (joint experiencer-learner), not as expert. They resonate with my sense that the ground on which I may have authority (perhaps *authenticity* would be a better word or conceptualization here) to teach tolerance depends on my adopting and acknowledging my position as a learner who is also working through the experiences and lessons of becoming a more tolerant, less bigoted person.

Accepting this paradigm and dynamic of mutuality as the foundation for addressing issues of tolerance, diversity, and bigotry suggests certain strategies for teaching that are deeply invested in deconstruction and reader-response pedagogies. These pedagogies do not render my contribution to the classroom as professor and participant unnecessary, unimportant, or unwelcome, but they do suggest that my ideas, opinions, readings, and perspectives should not routinely be the first or most important to be expressed, despite student pressure to the contrary. It may even be appropriate in the course of certain class discussions where the interchange is particularly lively and engaged to ask my students if they would like to hear how I read the text at hand or if they would prefer to continue puzzling out matters for themselves. Gerald Graff writes compellingly about the importance of student perspectives in his systemic examination of university education *Beyond the Culture Wars: How Teaching the Conflicts Can Revitalize American Education*: "I would not be human if I did not want my students to agree with my interpretations of texts and my views of literature and culture. But I suspect my best courses have been those which helped my students articulately to disagree with me" (44). This comment suggests the importance of steering clear of the coercion students will inevitably feel if the views of the teacher are always the most important in the class. Graff also remarks on the deleterious effect that such coercion may have for education reform: "There are those who justify turning their courses into consciousness-raising sessions on the ground that all teaching is inevitably political anyway. This authoritarian behavior is indeed disturbing, and it has been making enemies out of potential friends of the reform movement" (25).

If tolerance is what we hope to engender by our teaching, coercion is not the way to achieve it. The strategies we employ to teach tolerance must communicate to students that the classroom is indeed a place where their ideas, questions, observations, and objections can be thoughtfully expressed and will be heard by teachers who are learners of tolerance too. Such a dynamic of mutuality will not erase the discomfort that accompanies the exposure to difference or the self-dislodgment necessary for developing more tolerant views and behaviors. But it does communicate, in its most enabling modes, that the work of increasing tolerance and reducing bigotry is largely and rightly a person's own journey. One of Kathleen Norris's stories in *The Cloister Walk* illustrates the importance of presentation that invites an individual's response. She relates the observation of a gay man—who had "been isolated, ostracized in his small hometown in the South, and made to feel unwelcome in the church he was raised in"—about his encounter with Trappist monks:

> He'd written off religion, he told me. Then he met a Catholic priest who'd engaged him in a small group studying the Bible, and one year they went to Spencer for Holy Week. "Boy, did I love that," he said, "just sitting in that church, the way they let you come to church with them. They don't preach at you, they let you experience it for yourself. [. . .] You know, I've never felt so close to God before or since. It blew me the fuck away." (70)

The power in this story, it seems to me, lies in the willingness of the monks to let this visitor experience church along with them in an environment of mutuality and lies in the intensity of the learning the man experienced as a result. This same willingness must characterize my position as a teacher if my students and I are to create a similar environment of mutuality in the classroom. Showing students that I too am a learner of tolerance and inviting them to experience this learning along with me, but in their own ways, can help enable me and my students to address issues of bigotry, diversity, and tolerance in the classroom and consequently in the larger world.

WORKS CITED

Eden, Emily. *Up the Country: Letters Written to Her Sister from the Upper Provinces of India*. London: Virago, 1983.

Graff, Gerald. *Beyond the Culture Wars: How Teaching the Conflicts Can Revitalize American Education*. New York: Norton, 1992.

Norris, Kathleen. *The Cloister Walk*. New York: Riverhead, 1997.

Royster, Jacqueline Jones, et al. "Report of the Task Force against Campus Bigotry." *Profession 2000*. New York: MLA, 2000. 218–38.

LETTERS

TO THE EDITOR:

I appreciate Cary Nelson's exoneration of graduate students from responsibility for "the proliferation and consequent cheapening of all professional activities" and critique of the paternalist response that would cast "the profession in the image of Orson Welles in the Paul Masson television commercial at the end of his career" ("No Wine before Its Time," *Profession 2000* 162, 159). Yet Nelson's preferred solution to this cheapening of our labor, that graduate students and early career faculty refrain from the "unprofessional" publication of "half-baked" essays—in other words, indeed, "Sell no wine before its time"—fails to address the structural causes of the "turboprofessionalization" problem.

The advice would carry more weight if the profession's reward system were as rational as Nelson portrays it: a meritocracy in which "quality not quantity" is the agreed-upon measure. If hiring and promotion and tenure committees valued the quality of publications over quantity, waiting until one's thought had matured would be rational behavior. I'm not sure, however, that our professional institutions (e.g., personnel committees and editorial boards) believe that it is in their best interest to reward only the best that is thought and written.

Instead, the inflated demand for publication seems to drive the reward system and the profession. Most egregiously, the demand is typified by Nelson's provost, who jovially insists that a continual rise in requirements for tenure demonstrates the institution's prestige. The truly prestigious institution, it would seem, is one that can tell its employees to take unpaid leave to complete the scholarship required for tenure. (What other profession says, "This is part of your job, but we won't pay you for doing it"?)

The profession's reward system is also affected by continual growth in venues for scholarship, including conferences and print and electronic journals, which feature the best work they can get. Younger scholars who refrain from publishing in such venues know that someone else will take their place. It takes a great deal of faith in a job market more likely to be characterized as capricious than rational to believe that a candidate with no publications will be as competitive as a candidate with one or more publications.

Further, conferences and journals secure valuable quantifiable faculty achievements for members of organizing committees and editorial boards, providing a further impetus for overproduction. While the production of scholarship that draws "few readers and few if any citations" (159) may indeed be wasteful and irrational behavior at a first-tier institution where citations count, at a great many other institutions any effort at scholarship, any activity that gets the institution mentioned, is viewed favorably. The growing demand for publication is perhaps further evidence of Lindsay Waters's speculation ("A Modest Proposal for Preventing the Books of the Members of the MLA from Being a Burden to Their Authors, Publishers, or Audiences") in *PMLA* (115 [2000]: 315–17) that faculty committees outsource the tenure decision to editors and publishers.

For these structural reasons (as well as the concern that any decrease in the volume of scholarly publication will disproportionately affect non-canonical literature and emergent critical practices), it will be at least as difficult for the profession to counteract rising expectations for publication as it has been for the profession to address the number and size of PhD programs in relation to the demand for new professors. Indeed, that fundamental imbalance supports the spiral of demand. If members of the profession do not address the causes of overproduction, however, the market may act on its own. Outlets for publication may have increased over the last two decades, but for at least ten years library acquisition budgets have been in decline. As a result, publishers no longer can count on library purchases to recover the cost of publishing many titles, as Waters and others have noted, while librarians complain even more loudly about the escalating cost of journals. If provosts and publishers continue to move in opposite directions, perhaps we will wind up with a situation in which tenure becomes nearly impossible to earn.

Whatever the ultimate outcome, it behooves us to take seriously younger scholars' concerns, not because "turboprofessionalization" leads to conferences filled with graduate student presentations or, as Nelson writes, because "proliferation" leads to the "cheapening of all professional activities." Rather, we should recognize that expecting younger scholars will publish their books while "teaching as a postdoc or a part-timer" (Nelson 162) or on wholly unremunerated time, as a condition of gaining a first job, is exploitative behavior on a par with some of the worst labor practices that we rightly decry in other sectors of the economy.

Kevin R. McNamara
University of Houston, Clear Lake

Reply:

I do think a form of rational evaluation does partly shape the profession's reward system. Yet it will surprise no one to say that the profession is, if not quite reckless or impulsive, certainly manic in its pursuit of the most recent news in the ongoing saga of our theoretical agendas. Nonetheless, though there are no guarantees, the people who do the most innovative and influential work in these areas tend to receive the greatest rewards. Less glamorous areas may seem to be left behind, but sometimes those most discontented with their rewards are not merely doing "neglected, traditional scholarship" but actually doing work that is less well written and less challenging intellectually.

Work that is innovative and powerful is more likely to be rewarded than work that is dull. It is true that some teaching colleges will accept a few conference papers and one or two published essays of any quality whatsoever at tenure time. They are simply looking formulaically for minimal evidence of scholarly activity and anything will do. That is a silly, wasteful requirement that should simply be abandoned and that does lead people to publish mediocre work.

The same low-quality work, however, is less likely to benefit job candidates. On the job market I do not believe that any work is better than none. My own experience of mentoring graduate students for three decades suggests that one first-rate essay is better than three second-rate ones. When I hire new PhDs, I focus on the quality of the dissertation and the question of whether it will result in an important book. I do not care whether they have published anything.

Similarly, when faculty members come up for tenure, I am concerned about the quality of the books they have written. We consistently win tenure for people when the internal and external letters combine to persuade the campus that a candidate has written a book that will really matter in his or her field. Beyond that, quantity is largely irrelevant. Of course the reverse is true as well: if the evidence of quality is not there, the new PhD does not get the job and the tenure candidate is fired.

That is potentially frightening news for young scholars, for whom frenetic, low-quality productivity may be not merely easier but nearly irresistible under the pressures they face. It is the job of faculty mentors to get graduate students and young faculty members to breathe deeply, not to panic, and to do the best work of which they are capable. They also need to face an unforgiving time schedule. But an early focus on doing work they care deeply about and that has the potential for wide recognition can pay off throughout this process.

I am not certain that I can agree that expecting a young scholar to complete significant scholarly work while teaching as a postdoc is entirely unreasonable. In truth the possibility of completing a book under poor working conditions depends not only on the amount of free time available but also on the quality of the dissertation. Even with new PhDs I look for dissertations that read largely like finished books. In the current market it behooves people to think of their dissertations as books, write them as books, and bring them as close as possible to publishable quality while in graduate school. This is a brutal system, but people should still be advised how best to succeed in it.

Of course it does not matter how good your book manuscript is if publishers are no longer accepting books in your field. The declining market for literary criticism is threatening the profession's capacity to make fair hiring and tenure decisions. My coauthor Stephen Watt and I rehearse the reasons in our book *Academic Keywords* (1999), where we also offer a partial solution I'll repeat here: every humanities postdoc or assistant professorship should come with a $5,000 book subvention.

That amount represents actual typesetting, printing, and binding costs for a typical scholarly book. It is absurd for a college or university to invest several hundred thousand dollars in salary and benefits for an assistant professor of English and then let a tenure decision rest on whether a publisher thinks it can sell enough copies of a book to recoup an investment of a few thousand dollars. Start-up costs for a science lab for an assistant professor can easily run $500,000. Is 1% of that too much to spend on a scholar of Victorian literature?

There are also overhead costs for publication, so this amount will not encourage publication of inferior books. And the subvention should be conditional on receipt of strong readers' reports. This system would take some of the economic pressure off publishers, especially if humanities faculty encourage libraries to buy books.

Cary Nelson
University of Illinois, Urbana

Successful College and University Foreign Language Programs, 1995–99: Part 1

DAVID GOLDBERG AND ELIZABETH B. WELLES

With funding from the Andrew W. Mellon Foundation, the MLA's Office of Foreign Language Programs conducted a survey in the fall of 1999 to determine what factors contribute to the success of foreign language departments. Because the MLA's enrollment surveys of 1995 and 1998 had revealed a significant decline in student interest in some traditionally taught languages, we defined successful departments as those that had stable or increasing enrollments between 1995 and 1999 in beginning and advanced courses and also those that had steady or growing numbers of majors. We realize that this definition is artificial. Departments may lose enrollments despite excellent teaching and effective practices. For example, a newly introduced credit-transfer arrangement with a local college may draw students away from one institution to another. However, because administrators tend to look at student numbers as a criterion for determining departmental support, we concluded that enrollments do count from an institutional point of view.[1]

The survey collected information about a broad range of features characteristic of language and literature departments; it collected data about undergraduate enrollments, majors, and staffing. This report focuses on three aspects of the study. The first section examines trends in enrollments in introductory and advanced courses and numbers of majors. Section 2 indicates

David Goldberg is Associate Director of MLA Foreign Language Programs and the Association of Departments of Foreign Languages. Elizabeth B. Welles is Director of MLA Foreign Language Programs and the Association of Departments of Foreign Languages.

departmental practices and features, including the distribution of certain teaching approaches, curriculum characteristics, administrative arrangements, and resources for faculty members. Section 3 presents an analysis of the program features associated with growing enrollments in introductory courses. We believe that this information will be useful to departments that wish to compare their situations with those of other departments and that seek ideas for improving their programs and enrollments. Further reports on the relation between program characteristics and growth in enrollments in advanced courses and majors will appear in 2002.

The questionnaire was sent to 2,631 foreign language departments; 1,962, 75%, responded. The distribution of institutional types among the responding departments by control, highest degree granted by the institution, and size is shown in table 1 and indicates that the group of departments

TABLE 1
INSTITUTIONAL CHARACTERISTICS OF DEPARTMENTS CONTACTED AND DEPARTMENTS RESPONDING

TYPE OF INSTITUTION	DEPTS. CONTACTED NUMBER	DEPTS. CONTACTED PERCENTAGE	DEPTS. RESPONDING NUMBER	DEPTS. RESPONDING PERCENTAGE
Control				
Public	1,368	52.0	1,018	51.9
Private	483	18.4	358	18.2
Church-related	645	24.5	492	25.1
Unknown	135	5.1	94	4.8
Highest degree granted				
Doctorate	663	25.2	534	27.2
Master's	666	25.3	506	25.8
Bachelor's	429	16.3	315	16.1
Associate's	738	28.1	513	26.1
Unknown	135	5.1	94	4.8
Size				
Very small (< 1,000)	293	11.1	190	9.7
Small (1,001–2,000)	475	18.1	353	18.0
Medium (2,001–5,000)	641	24.4	491	25.0
Large (5,001–15,000)	664	25.2	498	25.4
Very large (>15,000)	418	15.9	333	17.0
Unknown	140	5.3	97	4.9
Total	2,631	100.0	1,962	100.0

Figures for departments contacted are based on National Center for Education Statistics database.

responding is representative of the departments contacted. Table 2 shows the differences between the highest degree granted by the institution and the highest degree granted by the foreign language department. So that departments can more easily compare their situation with that of similar departments in the study, we present our findings in terms of the highest degree offered by the department and not by the institution.

As might be expected, the number of programs varies considerably by language (table 3). At the introductory level, the number of programs in Spanish is 9.6 times greater than the number in Chinese; at the advanced level, it is 11 times greater. Table 3 shows the percentage of programs that

TABLE 2
HIGHEST DEGREE GRANTED BY INSTITUTION VERSUS HIGHEST DEGREE GRANTED BY DEPARTMENT

	INSTITUTION		DEPARTMENT	
	NUMBER	PERCENTAGE	NUMBER	PERCENTAGE
Doctorate	534	27.2	206	10.5
Master's	506	25.8	166	8.5
Bachelor's	315	16.1	845	43.1
Associate's	513	26.1	389	19.8
No degree	–	–	349	17.8
Unknown	94	4.8	7	0.4
Total	1,962	100.0	1,962	100.0

TABLE 3
PROGRAMS OFFERING INTRODUCTORY AND ADVANCED COURSES, BY LANGUAGE

	NO. OFFERING INTRODUCTORY COURSES	NO. OFFERING ADVANCED COURSES	PERCENTAGE OF PROGRAMS OFFERING BOTH INTRODUCTORY AND ADVANCED COURSES
Chinese	152	96	63.1
French	1,188	825	69.4
German	827	567	68.5
Italian	329	181	55.0
Japanese	319	153	47.9
Russian	221	151	68.3
Spanish	1,568	1,063	67.7

offer both introductory and advanced courses. Overall, 65% of all the programs that offer introductory courses also offer courses at advanced levels.

1: ENROLLMENTS

There has been much concern about declining enrollments in some languages, but this study makes clear that many programs are performing creditably. The survey provides information about fall 1995 and fall 1999 enrollments at introductory and advanced levels for each language program in the responding departments. While we hold that growth in enrollments indicates a strong program, we believe that enrollment stability should also be taken as a sign that a program is doing well. In fact, for all the programs in the study, except for Russian at advanced levels, the combined percentage of stable and growing enrollments is higher than the percentage of decreasing enrollments (tables 4 and 5). This finding, we believe, is a very positive one for language departments.

In introductory courses (table 4), there are more programs with increasing than decreasing enrollments, with the exception of German and Russian. The greatest gains are in PhD-granting departments, except in German. The next largest gains are in BA-granting departments for Chinese, German, Japanese, and Spanish and in AA-granting departments for French, Italian, and Russian. Except for Spanish and Italian, programs in MA-granting departments show declines. Across all languages and institutional types, about two-thirds (67.2%) of all language programs reported stable or increasing enrollments in introductory courses, while one-third reported declining enrollments.

For upper-division courses (table 5), the pattern is essentially the same as for introductory courses. In all languages except Russian, there is a higher percentage of departments with increasing enrollments than with declining enrollments. Across all languages and institutional types, again two-thirds (67.7%) of all language programs reported stable or increasing enrollments in upper-division courses.

This study of enrollment trends based on departmental reports reveals a more positive picture than does the MLA's analysis of student registrations. Readers will recall that enrollment trends tracked in MLA surveys from 1990 to 1995 and from 1995 to 1998 show that Spanish enrollments increased significantly; Chinese, Italian, and Japanese enrollments experienced little variation; and French, German, and Russian enrollments declined, the programs losing more than 25% of their students (see Brod and Welles 26; table 4). But members of the foreign language and literature profession should be encouraged to see that nationwide most programs are stable or growing. It is

TABLE 4
Enrollment Change in the Introductory Sequence between Fall 1995 and Fall 1999 (Percentage)

Enrollment	Overall	Associate's	Bachelor's	Master's	Doctorate
Chinese					
Declining	32.2	33.3	32.4	50.0	20.8
Increasing	54.6	46.7	54.4	38.9	75.0
Stable	13.2	20.0	13.2	11.1	4.2
Increasing and stable combined	67.8	66.7	67.6	50.0	79.2
Number of departments	*152*	*15*	*68*	*18*	*24*
French					
Declining	36.3	27.6	39.8	44.2	44.6
Increasing	43.3	43.1	40.6	41.6	50.8
Stable	20.4	29.3	19.6	14.2	4.6
Increasing and stable combined	63.7	72.4	60.2	55.8	55.4
Number of departments	*1,188*	*225*	*591*	*113*	*65*
German					
Declining	42.7	34.9	41.4	52.9	67.2
Increasing	37.8	36.7	39.7	27.1	29.3
Stable	19.5	28.4	18.9	20.0	3.5
Increasing and stable combined	57.3	65.1	58.6	47.1	32.8
Number of departments	*827*	*109*	*461*	*85*	*58*
Italian					
Declining	19.5	19.2	20.5	19.6	13.3
Increasing	66.6	65.4	61.4	64.7	83.3
Stable	13.9	15.4	18.1	15.7	3.4
Increasing and stable combined	80.5	80.8	79.5	80.4	86.7
Number of departments	*329*	*52*	*132*	*51*	*60*
Japanese					
Declining	32.0	29.2	29.7	45.5	37.5
Increasing	49.5	35.4	53.2	42.4	62.5
Stable	18.5	35.4	17.1	12.1	0.0
Increasing and stable combined	68.0	70.8	70.3	54.5	62.5
Number of departments	*319*	*48*	*158*	*33*	*24*
Russian					
Declining	43.0	30.8	44.4	47.4	48.5
Increasing	41.2	46.2	40.2	36.8	48.5
Stable	15.8	23.0	15.4	15.8	3.0
Increasing and stable combined	57.0	69.2	55.6	52.6	51.5
Number of departments	*221*	*13*	*117*	*38*	*33*
Spanish					
Declining	21.2	20.0	18.7	26.5	33.3
Increasing	61.4	57.5	63.4	62.4	63.6
Stable	17.4	22.5	17.9	11.1	3.1
Increasing and stable combined	78.8	80.0	81.3	73.5	66.7
Number of departments	*1,468*	*355*	*636*	*117*	*66*

TABLE 5
Enrollment Change in the Upper Division between Fall 1995 and Fall 1999 (Percentage)

Enrollment	Overall	Associate's	Bachelor's	Master's	Doctorate
Chinese					
Declining	28.1	0.0	20.0	50.0	27.3
Increasing	55.2	50.0	62.2	50.0	54.5
Stable	16.7	50.0	17.8	0.0	18.2
Increasing and stable combined	71.9	100.0	80.0	50.0	72.7
Number of departments	*96*	*2*	*45*	*14*	*22*
French					
Declining	38.3	22.4	40.1	37.0	45.3
Increasing	43.2	41.1	41.1	49.0	50.0
Stable	18.5	36.5	18.8	14.0	4.7
Increasing and stable combined	61.7	77.6	59.9	63.0	54.7
Number of departments	*825*	*85*	*496*	*100*	*64*
German					
Declining	39.3	20.6	37.9	55.4	39.3
Increasing	43.2	35.3	43.1	33.8	57.1
Stable	17.5	44.1	19.0	10.8	3.6
Increasing and stable combined	60.7	79.4	62.1	44.6	60.7
Number of departments	*567*	*34*	*364*	*74*	*56*
Italian					
Declining	27.6	18.8	27.4	17.1	35.7
Increasing	52.5	31.2	56.5	54.3	51.8
Stable	19.9	50.0	16.1	28.6	12.5
Increasing and stable combined	72.4	81.2	72.6	82.9	64.3
Number of departments	*181*	*16*	*62*	*35*	*56*
Japanese					
Declining	34.6	8.3	36.7	38.1	43.5
Increasing	46.4	41.7	46.8	47.6	47.8
Stable	19.0	50.0	16.5	14.3	8.7
Increasing and stable combined	65.4	91.7	63.3	61.9	56.5
Number of departments	*153*	*12*	*79*	*21*	*23*
Russian					
Declining	53.6	0.0	52.5	45.2	62.5
Increasing	31.8	100.0	32.5	35.4	31.2
Stable	14.6	0.0	15.0	19.4	6.3
Increasing and stable combined	46.4	100.0	47.5	54.8	37.5
Number of departments	*151*	*1*	*80*	*31*	*32*
Spanish					
Declining	21.5	19.4	21.2	25.9	18.5
Increasing	60.3	49.0	61.1	59.8	81.5
Stable	18.2	31.6	17.7	14.3	0.0
Increasing and stable combined	78.5	80.6	78.8	74.1	81.5
Number of departments	*1,063*	*155*	*595*	*112*	*65*

our hope that departments will use the information in this study for justifying ongoing and increased institutional support for language programs.

Majors

While course enrollments are an important measure of a department's strength, they are not the only indicator. The number of majors is also significant because it demonstrates a department's ability to build student commitment. Table 6 shows that more than half the programs in Chinese, Japanese, and Spanish and exactly half in Italian have experienced growth in the number of majors between 1995 and 1999. Of the language programs studied, two-thirds (67.5%) show a stable or growing number of majors.

We also wanted to understand the relation of enrollments in introductory and advanced classes to the number of majors. The ratio of the number of students in introductory courses to the number of majors (table 7) shows that for approximately every four students in introductory courses in the languages with the lowest enrollments (Russian, Japanese, and Chinese) there is one major. We find it remarkable that in the truly foreign languages (i.e., those not cognate with English) a quarter of those who start language study are motivated to become majors. For French, German, and Spanish, the ratio is somewhat higher, and for Italian it is even higher. The ratio of advanced-level enrollments to the number of majors (table 8) is much lower and more consistent across languages; one out of every two or three students in an advanced course is likely to be a major. Spanish programs, which have a much greater number of students than other languages, show about the same ratio as the other languages of advanced-level enrollments to the number of majors.

Minors and Double Majors

We were also interested in the number of minors and double majors, as we have heard these options described as effective methods for attracting students to advanced-level courses. Double majors and minors were quantified in a different way. We asked departments whether the number of students enjoying these options had increased, stayed the same, or decreased from 1995 to 1999. For double majors (table 9), those departments that said they had a gain accounted for 60.3% of the total that responded; 35.3% reported a stable number, 4.5% a decline. For minors (table 10), 69.2% of the programs reported an increase, 25.9% stability, and 4.9% a loss. In other words, the majority of departments offering these options reported that the options are increasingly utilized by students.[2]

We find it noteworthy that departments in MA-granting institutions were less likely to report growth or stability in enrollments and majors in all languages compared with other institutions. As we have seen, there are also

TABLE 6
Change in Number of Majors between Fall 1995 and Fall 1999 (Percentage)

Majors	Overall	Associate's	Bachelor's	Master's	Doctorate
Chinese					
Decreasing	14.0	0.0	12.5	22.2	7.1
Increasing	74.0	0.0	70.8	77.8	78.6
Stable	12.0	0.0	16.7	0.0	14.3
Increasing and stable combined	86.0	0.0	87.5	77.8	92.9
Number of departments	*50*	*0*	*24*	*9*	*14*
French					
Decreasing	36.3	33.3	37.3	36.5	33.3
Increasing	44.5	16.7	43.9	45.9	56.2
Stable	19.2	50.0	18.8	17.6	10.5
Increasing and stable combined	63.7	66.7	62.7	63.5	66.7
Number of departments	*573*	*24*	*394*	*85*	*57*
German					
Decreasing	38.8	33.3	38.2	44.4	40.4
Increasing	40.4	33.4	39.7	37.1	46.8
Stable	20.8	33.3	22.1	18.5	12.8
Increasing and stable combined	61.2	66.7	61.8	55.6	59.6
Number of departments	*376*	*6*	*262*	*54*	*47*
Italian					
Decreasing	33.7	50.0	28.6	33.3	37.2
Increasing	50.0	0.0	53.5	50.0	51.2
Stable	16.3	50.0	17.9	16.7	11.6
Increasing and stable combined	66.3	50.0	71.4	66.7	62.8
Number of departments	*92*	*2*	*28*	*18*	*43*
Japanese					
Decreasing	30.8	33.3	22.6	50.0	37.5
Increasing	52.3	66.7	54.8	50.0	50.0
Stable	16.9	0.0	22.6	0.0	12.5
Increasing and stable combined	69.2	66.7	77.4	50.0	62.5
Number of departments	*65*	*3*	*31*	*12*	*16*
Russian					
Decreasing	53.7	0.0	58.5	28.0	67.9
Increasing	31.5	0.0	24.5	44.0	32.1
Stable	14.8	0.0	17.0	28.0	0.0
Increasing and stable combined	46.3	0.0	41.5	72.0	32.1
Number of departments	*108*	*0*	*53*	*25*	*28*
Spanish					
Decreasing	19.5	25.4	18.5	20.6	22.0
Increasing	63.6	50.9	64.4	63.9	72.9
Stable	16.9	23.7	17.1	15.5	5.1
Increasing and stable combined	80.5	74.6	81.5	79.4	78.0
Number of departments	*737*	*59*	*492*	*97*	*59*

TABLE 7
RATIO OF NUMBER OF STUDENTS IN INTRODUCTORY COURSES TO NUMBER OF MAJORS, BETWEEN FALL 1995 AND FALL 1999

Language	Overall	Associate's	Bachelor's	Master's	Doctorate
Chinese	4.6	0.0	3.7	4.8	5.4
French	7.4	14.8	6.7	8.9	8.9
German	6.9	13.4	6.0	8.1	9.5
Italian	19.6	60.0	14.5	9.6	24.9
Japanese	4.5	7.2	4.0	4.3	6.3
Russian	4.2	0.0	3.7	4.7	4.9
Spanish	9.5	16.0	8.7	8.9	10.2

TABLE 8
RATIO OF ADVANCED-LEVEL ENROLLMENTS TO NUMBER OF MAJORS, BETWEEN FALL 1995 AND FALL 1999

Language	Overall	Associate's	Bachelor's	Master's	Doctorate
Chinese	2.0	0.0	2.0	2.0	2.7
French	2.6	4.0	2.5	2.6	3.7
German	2.7	3.1	2.5	2.4	3.6
Italian	3.7	12.0	2.9	2.5	5.2
Japanese	1.8	1.8	1.8	1.7	2.1
Russian	2.2	0.0	2.3	2.2	2.0
Spanish	2.8	3.6	2.5	2.8	3.7

TABLE 9
Change in Number of Double Majors between Fall 1995 and Fall 1999 (AA-Granting Departments Not Included)

Language	Number	Percentage (Based on Subtotal for Each Language)
Chinese		
Increased	75	55.6
Stayed the same	59	43.7
Decreased	1	0.7
Subtotal	135	100.0
French		
Increased	449	59.3
Stayed the same	267	35.3
Decreased	41	5.4
Subtotal	757	100.0
German		
Increased	378	60.6
Stayed the same	216	34.6
Decreased	30	4.8
Subtotal	624	100.0
Italian		
Increased	173	66.3
Stayed the same	78	29.9
Decreased	10	3.8
Subtotal	261	100.0
Japanese		
Increased	155	61.3
Stayed the same	93	36.8
Decreased	5	2.0
Subtotal	253	100.0
Russian		
Increased	119	59.5
Stayed the same	73	36.5
Decreased	8	4.0
Subtotal	200	100.0
Spanish		
Increased	477	59.7
Stayed the same	282	35.3
Decreased	40	5.0
Subtotal	799	100.0
Total	3,029	

TABLE 10
Change in Number of Minors between Fall 1995 and Fall 1999

Language	Number	Percentage (Based on Subtotal for Each Language)
Chinese		
Increased	92	69.7
Stayed the same	37	28.0
Decreased	3	2.3
Subtotal	132	100.0
French		
Increased	518	68.4
Stayed the same	198	26.2
Decreased	41	5.4
Subtotal	757	100.0
German		
Increased	416	67.9
Stayed the same	168	27.4
Decreased	29	4.7
Subtotal	613	100.0
Italian		
Increased	194	76.1
Stayed the same	50	19.6
Decreased	11	4.3
Subtotal	255	100.0
Japanese		
Increased	180	73.5
Stayed the same	56	22.9
Decreased	9	3.7
Subtotal	245	100.0
Russian		
Increased	119	61.0
Stayed the same	63	32.3
Decreased	13	6.7
Subtotal	195	100.0
Spanish		
Increased	553	69.2
Stayed the same	205	25.7
Decreased	41	5.1
Subtotal	799	100.0
Total	2,996	

many fewer MA-granting departments among our respondents than there are in the national distribution of institutional types (see table 2). The lower rates of growth and stability in MA enrollments may be partly explained by enrollment changes in arts and sciences courses in higher education since the 1960s—especially in comprehensive state institutions, where most MA-granting programs are housed. In an article about trends in undergraduate degrees, Sarah E. Turner and William G. Bowen point out that after 1970, when there were more than enough students to fill college classrooms, institutions were able to improve enrollments in their academic programs. A large part of this increase occurred at the growing state colleges and universities, which previously emphasized preprofessional programs. When the number of students stopped rising and these institutions had to compete for students, the comprehensive institutions returned to career-oriented curricula. This trend may also have affected language enrollments and the kind of language courses these institutions offered. As we see in section 3 ("Practices in Programs Reporting Growth in Introductory Course Enrollments"), language study for special purposes and preprofessional training appears to be particularly strong in MA-granting institutions.

2: Departmental Practices and Features

Survey questions sought to shed light on a department's language requirements, technology, support for faculty members, faculty contribution to departmental directions, curriculum, special opportunities for students to study or practice languages, and connections with high schools and the community. This section of the report is based on the 1,962 responses from departments; results are analyzed in relation to the highest degree offered by the department when this factor suggests significant differences.

Language Requirements

Of great concern to the language field are institutional language requirements: they affect enrollments and staffing and demonstrate an institution's commitment to languages in undergraduate education. We found that 23.7% of the responding institutions had entrance requirements and 60.1% had graduation requirements (table 11).

In comparison with the percentages reported in the MLA's 1995 survey of entrance and degree requirements (Brod and Huber), we see that the entrance requirement in BA-, MA-, and PhD-granting institutions has risen from 21% to 31% and the graduation requirement from 68% to 75.4%. In two-year colleges the entrance requirement rose from 3% to 8.4% and from 23% to 30.9% for graduation. Does the rise in both entrance and graduation requirements suggest that language study is seen more as part of the core curriculum in some institutions? Although the increases are modest, they are encouraging.

Technology

Technological resources are widely available and utilized, as indicated by tables 12A and 12B.

We see from table 12B that over 70% of departments use technology in classroom teaching, make use of a language lab or media center, and expect students to use technology outside class. Technology for distance learning and for testing and placement fell far behind the other uses reported. Looking at distance learning by highest degree granted reveals that it was used by only 24.5% of the BA-, 33.7% of the MA-, and 28.8% of the PhD-

TABLE 11
LANGUAGE REQUIREMENTS (PERCENTAGE)

	AA	BA	MA	PHD	BA, MA, PHD	ALL
Entrance	8.4	26.3	42.1	46.6	31.9	23.7
Graduation	30.9	71.1	86.1	84.5	75.4	60.1

TABLE 12A
TECHNOLOGY AVAILABLE FOR FACULTY MEMBERS AND STUDENTS (PERCENTAGE)

	FACULTY MEMBERS	STUDENTS
E-mail	98.9	86.5
Personal computers	97.1	74.0
World Wide Web	98.3	87.5

TABLE 12B
DEPARTMENTS USING TECHNOLOGY FOR INSTRUCTIONAL PURPOSES (PERCENTAGE)

Classroom teaching	71.2
Student practice outside class	80.4
Media centers	70.4
Testing and placement	30.9
Distance learning	33.4

granting departments. It is striking, in comparison, that 56% of the AA-granting departments reported programs using distance learning. This fact probably reflects response to the needs of the nontraditional students commonly served by two-year institutions.

Faculty Support

Support was also available to most faculty members but varied according to highest degree granted by the department (table 13).

Over 53% of the BA-, MA-, and PhD-granting departments provide support for study abroad; 36% of the two-year colleges do so. Similarly, 78% of the BA-, MA-, and PhD-granting departments provide support for faculty research and scholarship; 32% of the two-year colleges do so.

Mission Statement, Educational Objectives, and Faculty Discussion

We queried not only the prevalence of the mission statement as a formal written document about departmental goals but also the frequency of faculty discussion about the statement. Slightly more than half the departments (50.5%) said that they had a mission statement. Of the departments that had mission statements, 45.9% reported that they reviewed the statement every few years, 26.2% reviewed it annually, 22.2% reviewed it on an ad hoc basis, and 4.8% said that they had not reviewed their statement in the last five years. We also asked how frequently departmental conversations about educational objectives took place. Annual or more frequent meetings for this purpose were characteristic of 65.3% of the departments. Meetings on an ad hoc basis took place in 21.7% of the departments, and meetings were held every few years or had not been held in the last five years in 6% or less of the departments. Only 35% of the departments did not schedule time to discuss their educational aims. It is clear that more often than not faculty members are invited to contribute to a department's sense of direction and that departments set aside time for these discussions.

TABLE 13
DEPARTMENTAL OR INSTITUTIONAL SUPPORT FOR FACULTY ACTIVITIES (PERCENTAGE)

Travel to conferences	91.7
Technology training	75.9
Research and scholarship	63.1
Study abroad	47.9
Course development	41.0

Curriculum

The field has been debating for many decades how best to teach language, literature, and culture. Pedagogical approaches and the place of literature and cultural materials in the curriculum are often key to these debates. Table 14A identifies the relative importance of oral communication, reading, and writing in introductory courses.

The emphasis on oral communication is also shown by the responses to the question about assessment: 46% of respondents said they use some form of an oral proficiency interview, 30% said they use a portfolio, and 28% use other instruments in addition to grades for measuring student progress. Table 14B shows the balance between literature and culture in the introductory language sequence.

It is easy to see that culture, however our respondents construe it, is considered to be more useful and important than literature for teaching language at this level. Notably, however, literature still plays a role in more than a quarter of the courses.

For advanced courses the situation is reversed. Table 15 indicates the relative importance of different kinds of texts and emphases. Respondents were offered eight options: the first three asked about the balance between literary and nonliterary texts; the next five asked about approaches, organizing principles, and types of literature taught. Since most two-year

TABLE 14A
TEACHING EMPHASES IN INTRODUCTORY LANGUAGE COURSES (PERCENTAGE)

More emphasis on reading and writing than on oral communication	5.4
Equal emphasis on reading and writing as on oral communication	38.3
More emphasis on oral communication than on reading and writing	23.1
A balance of reading and writing with oral communication according to the preference of the instructor	32.4

TABLE 14B
LITERATURE AND CULTURE IN INTRODUCTORY LANGUAGE COURSES (PERCENTAGE)

More emphasis on culture than on literature	68.5
Equal emphasis on literature and culture	25.3
More emphasis on literature than on culture	4.9

TABLE 15
Emphases in Advanced Undergraduate Courses Taught in the Target Language in BA-, MA-, and PhD-Granting Departments (Percentage)

Literary and nonliterary texts	
More emphasis on literary than on nonliterary texts	53.4
Equal emphasis on literary and nonliterary texts	35.4
More emphasis on nonliterary than on literary texts	8.5
Types of literature and approaches	
Canonical literature organized by periods, authors, and genres	43.0
Canonical and some noncanonical literature or approaches based on race, class, or gender	49.6
Primarily noncanonical literature	7.4
Primarily surveys of civilization by period	24.1
Nontraditional curriculum emphasizing language for business or other special purposes	27.3

institutions do not have advanced courses, the percentages were calculated only for BA-, MA-, and PhD-granting departments.

Respondents reported that literature is the foundation for slightly more than half their advanced courses; however, the nature of the literature taught and, for nearly half the respondents, the approaches to literature selected have been expanded to include race, class, or gender criticism. The canon remains important: surveys of civilization are not prevalent, and courses based on nonliterary or noncanonical texts are rare. About a quarter of respondents reported that they have a nontraditional language strand for business or other purposes. These data suggest that the curriculum is undergoing gradual change. Innovation has appeared in the kinds of literature being taught, in approaches being used, and in the inclusion of nonliterary materials.

Special Opportunities for Language Learning, Practice, and Use outside Traditional Courses

We were particularly interested in the availability of special student opportunities for language learning outside the regular course schedule or the normal semester- or quarter-length course frame or outside the classroom altogether (table 16). Such opportunities as intensive language study and on- and off-campus practice with native speakers in real-life situations are relatively innovative and have been the topic of much discussion in the field.

Most departments obviously do not offer these extra opportunities; eleven options were present in 30% or less of the departments; six options

TABLE 16
Special Opportunities (Percentage)

Campus- or community-based programs	
Intensive courses	46.8
Service internships in local target community	28.8
Internships in local target community	27.3
Immersion courses	23.7
Language houses	18.4
Winter-break programs	13.4
Weekend programs	11.8
Presemester programs	6.9
Study across institutional units	
Language across the curriculum	20.4
Programs with professional school	19.1
Study abroad	
Exchange programs	51.8
Internships	38.4
Service programs	25.0

were present in less than 20% of the departments. We had been hearing so much about these new opportunities that we were surprised by the small numbers of programs that offer them. But we realize that discussion about them has been generated in part by their novelty. Further, some of the innovations have not been more generally adopted perhaps because they require extra work by faculty members or because they need outside funding at the beginning. Only intensive courses, exchange programs, and internships abroad are widely used. As we see in the third section of this report ("Practices in Programs"), these practices are among the most frequently associated with enrollment gains at the introductory level.

Off-Campus Connections

Activities sponsored by a department outside the college campus demonstrate the department's willingness to look beyond its borders. While such activities may not specifically have to do with teaching students, we believe that strengthening ties with public schools and the community inside or outside the campus opens lines of communication. These lines in turn add to the effectiveness of departmental programs, for example, by facilitating practice teaching in the schools, providing internships in the community, or improving placement of incoming students.

For institutions that draw students from the regional population, connections with high schools are of particular importance in creating the long sequences of learning necessary for language mastery. Table 17 records the percentages of departments that reported articulation activities with local high schools for three different purposes.

While the number of those engaged in articulation activities is not large, we find it encouraging that many departments are making efforts to cross institutional and departmental lines for conversations with their counterparts in secondary schools. Positive responses may have been limited also because many institutions do not draw on local secondary schools for their students.

While the questionnaire did not define "local community," departments were free to interpret this idea of outreach as intended for the campus or off-campus community. Activities sponsored for the local community suggest a dynamic and engaged department, one that is responsive to broad campus and off-campus issues, and conceivably to fund-raising. About half of all departments reported offering programs to the community (table 18). Here it is worthwhile mentioning a few of the prominent variations among departmental types: 79.0% of PhD-granting departments offer lectures to the community, while 69.3% of MA- granting, 57.8% of BA-granting, and 45.5% of AA-granting departments offer a similar service. Two-year colleges, however, are the most likely (69.4%) to offer language courses to the

TABLE 17
REPORTED PURPOSES FOR ARTICULATION WITH HIGH SCHOOLS
(PERCENTAGE)

To facilitate placement of entering students	33.4
To bring faculty members together for exchange of information	42.4
To develop a coherent curriculum	19.5

TABLE 18
PROGRAMS OFFERED BY DEPARTMENTS TO THE COMMUNITY
(PERCENTAGE)

Lectures	55.5
Films	51.4
Language courses	46.9
Other programs	50.9

community (i.e., not to the regular student population); only 39.0% of BA-granting, 47.6% of MA-granting, and 33.5% of PhD-granting departments offer them.

Administrative Arrangements: Language Coordinators, Language Centers, and Teacher Preparation

In recent years, departments and institutions have been working to strengthen language and literature programs, not only through a focus on teaching, pedagogy, and materials but through supervisory and collaborative arrangements as well. Thirty-five percent of the responding departments reported that they have a full-time language coordinator, 20.9% reported that they have a language center, and 39.2% said that they have programs of study for prospective secondary school teachers. Of those that said they have teacher education programs, 11% said the department has primary responsibility for the program, 45% said it shares responsibility with the school of education, and 42% said the school of education has the primary responsibility. The highest degree offered by a department is a determining factor: language coordinators are characteristic of 59.6% of MA-granting and 81.1% of PhD-granting departments but present in only 23.1% of BA- and 32.0% of AA-granting departments. Language centers exist on the campuses of 42.2% of the PhD-granting departments, while less than 20% of institutions with AA-, BA-, and MA-granting departments have them. Ninety percent of the teacher education programs are in BA- and MA-granting departments.

In sum, departments generally have ample access to and use of the Internet and personal computers, offer broad support for faculty members, and sponsor formal conversations about their work on a fairly regular basis. Most have study-abroad programs for students, and almost half offer intensive courses. The introductory curriculum is likely to be based on culture and oral communication, while advanced courses tend to be based on literature both traditional and nontraditional. Many departments also offer films, lectures, and language courses for the local community and promote discussion with faculty members in local high schools. Less common are departments with special opportunities for student language practice and study outside the normal course framework, teacher education programs, language coordinators, or language centers. While the picture is shifting slightly according to the highest degree granted by a department, the shift occurs only in regard to a few features. The question that remains for this report to address is which of these factors are associated with successful departments.

3: Practices in Programs Reporting Growth in Introductory Course Enrollments

We have seen that between 1995 and 1999 a majority of programs had either stable or rising enrollments in the introductory sequence of language courses. If we compare the percentage of programs that gained enrollments and reported having a particular feature with the percentage of programs that gained enrollments and reported not having that feature, we can calculate the likelihood and strength of the co-occurrence or association between enrollment growth and a given practice.[3] Of the practices described in the previous section, this section highlights those that are consistently or frequently associated with programs reporting enrollment growth in the introductory language sequence.

Reporting the association of enrollment growth with a particular feature in percentages allows us to compare the likelihood of growth in two comparable groups—one having a particular attribute and one lacking that attribute—without concern that the two groups might contain considerably different numbers of programs. For example, a group of programs (e.g., a subset of all Chinese programs in BA-granting departments) with attribute x might contain twenty instances, while a group without attribute x (also a subset of all Chinese programs in BA-granting departments) might contain forty instances. If we simply compared counts of programs reporting growth, we might find that the number was the same (e.g., four) in both the group that has attribute x and the group that does not. But reporting only the numbers of programs that have attribute x would mask the significant finding that the likelihood of growth (the association between growth and attribute x) is actually higher in the group with attribute x (four of twenty = 20%) than in the group without it (four of forty = 10%). The use of percentages thus allows us to discuss the relative frequency of growth. In the discussion that follows, we use the term *relative growth* to express, as a percentage, the increase in likelihood that programs with certain characteristics will have growth in introductory course enrollments compared with similar programs that do not have these characteristics.[4]

We are cautious about drawing conclusions on the basis of an association or co-occurrence: there are too many possible combinations of practices to say that a co-occurrence of any single feature and rising enrollments definitively isolates a cause. The size of the percentage of relative growth must also be interpreted carefully.[5] Because enrollments in different languages differ enormously, it is probably not useful to look for meaning in small differences between percentage values. Instead, we think it is useful to distinguish between weak and strong relative growth. Although an association of any magnitude suggests a positive relation between growth and a given practice, a relative growth rate of less than 10% has been taken in this study to be comparatively weak, a relative growth rate of greater than 10% to be comparatively strong.

Special Opportunities on Campus and off Campus

A number of special opportunities for campus- or community-based language study or practice outside normal semester-length classroom programs are frequently associated with growth in enrollments in the introductory language sequence. For example, in table 19 consider French programs in departments that offer immersion programs. Within the group of French programs in departments that grant BA degrees, those that offered immersion programs were 16.8% more likely than those that did not to have experienced growth in introductory-level French courses. Similarly, among French programs in departments that grant MA degrees, those that offered immersion programs were 10.8% more likely to report growth in introductory courses. And French programs in PhD-granting departments that reported offering immersion programs were an extraordinary 56.5% more likely to have experienced growth in their introductory course enrollments.

We asked departments whether they offered campus-based intensive courses, immersion programs, presemester programs, winter-break programs, weekend programs, language houses, and stateside internships or service programs in a target-language community. Many of these special opportunities are more than 10% likely to be associated with growth in introductory enrollments.

- BA-granting departments offering language houses (in all languages),[6] weekend programs (in all but Chinese), and immersion programs (in all but Chinese and Spanish) show a stronger than 10% likelihood, in comparison with departments not offering such programs, of also having rising introductory enrollments.
- MA-granting departments offering intensive programs (except in Chinese and Italian), immersion programs (in French and German), presemester programs (in German, Japanese, and Spanish), winter-break programs (in Italian), weekend programs (in French, Italian, and Spanish), language houses (in French, Italian, and Spanish), internships (in Italian and Japanese), and service programs in the community (in Spanish) are more than 10% likely to have rising introductory enrollments.
- PhD-granting departments offering intensive programs (in German, Italian, and Russian), immersion programs (in French, German, and Spanish), presemester programs (in all reported languages), winter-break programs (in Spanish), weekend programs (except in Spanish), language houses (in Italian and Japanese), internships (in Chinese, Italian, Japanese, and Russian), and service programs (in Chinese, Japanese, Russian, and Spanish) show a stronger than 10% likelihood of also having rising introductory enrollments.

TABLE 19
Relative Growth in Introductory Course Enrollments in Programs Reporting Campus and Off-Campus Special Opportunities for Language Study (Percentage)

Special Opportunities	All[6]	Chinese	French	German	Italian	Japanese	Russian	Spanish
Intensive courses								
BA-granting		34.7		32.7			4.0	
MA-granting	28.2		38.9	113.2		20.0	22.2	37.1
PhD-granting	2.2		19.2	67.3			33.3	
Immersion programs								
BA-granting	9.5	1.3	16.8	24.7	36.2	40.6	47.0	
MA-granting	4.4		10.8	59.3				
PhD-granting	14.5		56.5	56.3	8.3			13.5
Presemester programs								
BA-granting	10.2	21.0	26.2				79.0	16.2
MA-granting	14.0			68.6	5.0	66.7		35.7
PhD-granting	43.9	50.0	21.1	22.2	11.7	111.1	114.3	68.0
Winter-break programs								
BA-granting	4.1		13.4	31.9			10.0	
MA-granting					37.8			
PhD-granting			2.0		0.5			17.1
Weekend programs								
BA-granting	19.3		28.5	21.4	26.5	19.7	35.3	13.8
MA-granting	16.4		47.7		21.6			28.1
PhD-granting	13.2	50.0	63.6	63.6	27.5	33.3	75.0	
Language houses								
BA-granting	19.2	27.9	16.0	25.5	49.5	20.7	52.3	12.6
MA-granting	22.5		32.9		58.7	2.0		65.5
PhD-granting			8.3		15.2	53.1		
Internships in the community								
BA-granting	9.6		5.7	7.5	13.1	15.7	22.4	17.1
MA-granting	0.5		1.6		22.0	20.0		8.6
PhD-granting	9.5	25.0			12.2	25.0	29.9	5.2
Service programs in the community								
BA-granting	11.9	1.3	32.3		7.4	29.2	11.6	12.2
MA-granting								10.7
PhD-granting	12.3	29.6		6.5		35.4	24.7	46.2

Positive relative growth percentages (see note 4) express the increase in likelihood that programs with certain characteristics will have growth in introductory course enrollments compared with similar programs that do not have those characteristics.

Variables such as language, highest degree granted by the department, and interaction with numerous other program features make it difficult to explain with certainty why one special opportunity is associated with growth in a particular program and another is not. The data taken together, however, demonstrate that classroom-based and off-campus special opportunities outside the normal three- or four-times-a-week class frame are frequently associated with rising enrollments. While it is the usual semester-length, classroom-based introductory courses that see growth in enrollments, the availability of learning experiences outside the traditionally scheduled format seems to attract students to the department and to traditional classes.

Most of these special opportunities are not widespread, though some are more common than others (see table 16). Intensive courses, the most frequently occurring of the special opportunities, are found in 33.3% of the programs in BA-granting, 49.2% of the programs in MA-granting, and 75.9% of the programs in PhD-granting departments. Presemester programs, one of the least frequently reported of the special opportunities for stateside language study, occur in only 4.9% of the programs in BA-granting departments, 5.5% of the programs in MA-granting departments, and 8.2% of the programs in PhD-granting departments.

That a practice is unusual does not negate the statistical evidence of a strong association with rising enrollments, although a limited number of cases means that a few errors in reporting might noticeably alter the resulting percentages. This risk is unavoidable in a study of innovative practices: only a limited number of departments experiment with these special opportunities. Presemester programs, for instance, are found in only 32 of 636 Spanish programs in BA-granting departments. Despite the small number of departments offering such innovations, however, the association of these innovations with rising enrollments is notable. Spanish programs offering presemester study are 16% more likely to report gains in enrollments in the introductory sequence than programs that do not offer this feature (see table 19).

Language Study across Institutional Units

Programs offering students opportunities to study languages across institutional units—for example, through language-across-the-curriculum programs or through associations with professional schools—frequently report rising enrollments. These data support the general finding that special opportunities outside the traditional class- and department-based frame are associated with growth in enrollments in the introductory sequence. Here the data suggest not only that special scheduling and opportunities for practice in real situations co-occur with growth but also that opportunities to use language for intellectual purposes and professional preparation are associated with growth as well. Table 20 describes the relative growth rate in introductory course enrollments in programs offering opportunities for language learning across the curriculum and special arrangements with professional schools. Notably, most co-occurrences of enrollment growth and such opportunities are in programs in MA-granting departments. That MA-granting departments are strong in programs emphasizing applied language use was corroborated by the response to a separate question we asked about languages for special purposes: here too programs in MA-granting departments showed the strongest and most frequent association with rising enrollments (table 25, sec. 8). These findings are consistent with the findings of Turner and Bowen.

Uses of Technology

As we have seen above (table 12B), the most frequent use of technology is for student practice outside the classroom. In decreasing order of frequency follow use of technology in the classroom, use of technology for testing and placement, and use of technology for distance learning. While 80.4% of all departments report using technology for practice outside the classroom, only 30.9% report using it for distance learning.

This picture takes on a very different aspect when we examine the association between various uses of technology and growth in enrollments in

TABLE 20
RELATIVE GROWTH IN INTRODUCTORY COURSE ENROLLMENTS IN PROGRAMS REPORTING SPECIAL OPPORTUNITIES FOR LANGUAGE STUDY ACROSS INSTITUTIONAL UNITS (PERCENTAGE)

SPECIAL OPPORTUNITIES	ALL	CHINESE	FRENCH	GERMAN	ITALIAN	JAPANESE	RUSSIAN	SPANISH
Language across the curriculum								
BA-granting	2.4		7.2		32.8		24.0	
MA-granting	14.4		42.9	15.4	26.3	1.8		16.1
PhD-granting			15.4					
Programs with professional schools								
BA-granting	6.7	50.5		19.8	21.7		13.4	0.7
MA-granting	24.7		29.0	7.4	13.0	352.4	2.9	31.6
PhD-granting	1.4	80.0		46.3				

Positive relative growth percentages (see note 4) express the increase in likelihood that programs with certain characteristics will have growth in introductory course enrollments compared with similar programs that do not have those characteristics.

the introductory sequence (table 21). The use of technology that is most consistently associated with enrollment growth is testing and placement. In table 21, across the entire field of 21 program types described (i.e., programs in the 7 languages in each of the 3 department types: BA-, MA-, and PhD-granting), 17 (81%) of those using technology for testing and placement reported growth in introductory enrollments.[7] Programs that used technology for distance learning reported growth in enrollments in 12 of the 21 (57%) program types questioned. Programs using technology for practice outside class reported growth in enrollments in only 8 of the 21 (38%) program types questioned.

The range of relative growth rates across languages in the area of testing and placement is wide. Language programs in BA-granting departments that use technology for testing and placement (with the exception of Japanese) are between 6.0% (Spanish) and 53.0% (Chinese) more likely to

TABLE 21
RELATIVE GROWTH IN INTRODUCTORY COURSE ENROLLMENTS IN PROGRAMS REPORTING USES OF TECHNOLOGY (PERCENTAGE)

USES OF TECHNOLOGY	ALL	CHINESE	FRENCH	GERMAN	ITALIAN	JAPANESE	RUSSIAN	SPANISH
Teaching in class								
BA-granting	0.4			1.5	26.5		3.0	
MA-granting				33.3				
PhD-granting				124.0	6.4			26.7
Practice outside class								
BA-granting				0.1		21.7		
MA-granting	7.0				20.5	88.2		16.3
PhD-granting		215.8			92.2	64.3		
Testing and placement								
BA-granting	10.7	53.0	15.6	8.1	34.1		16.8	6.0
MA-granting	23.3		29.5	36.1	42.9			9.7
PhD-granting		28.6	4.6	112.5	8.0	14.3		0.7
Distance learning								
BA-granting	3.6	9.1	20.9	8.4	7.7	6.0	8.0	
MA-granting			38.8	54.5				
PhD-granting	1.3	13.8			15.4	82.0	55.6	

Positive relative growth percentages (see note 4) express the increase in likelihood that programs with certain characteristics will have growth in introductory course enrollments compared with similar programs that do not have those characteristics.

report rising enrollments than programs that do not. Programs in MA-granting departments (with the exception of Chinese, Japanese, and Russian) are between 9.7% (Spanish) and 42.9% (Italian) more likely to report rising enrollments if they use technology for testing and placement. Programs in PhD-granting departments (with the exception of Russian) are between 0.7% (Spanish) and 112.5% (German) more likely to report rising enrollments if they use technology for testing and placement. French, German, Italian, and Spanish programs in all department types are more likely to report enrollment growth if they use technology for testing and placement.

Full-Time Introductory and Intermediate Course Coordinator

Two hundred eighty-three programs in BA-granting departments whose enrollments have grown report that they use a full-time coordinator; 831 programs in BA-granting departments whose enrollments have grown report not having a coordinator. The 283 programs with an introductory sequence coordinator are overall 16.6% more likely to experience growth in enrollments than are the 831 programs without a coordinator. French, Italian, Japanese, and Russian programs in BA-granting departments having a coordinator show notably strong relative growth rates (table 22). It is perhaps surprising that this association with growth occurs only very occasionally in programs in MA- and PhD-granting departments, which are the types more likely to have full-time coordinators. We can only hypothesize that BA programs that have made the less usual (for their type of department) and probably more recent effort to provide this additional layer of administrative attention are more rewarded than programs in MA- and PhD-granting departments, which have commonly used coordinators for a long time.

TABLE 22
Relative Growth in Introductory Course Enrollments in Programs Reporting Presence of a Full-Time Coordinator or Supervisor of Introductory and Intermediate Courses (Percentage)

Full-Time Coordinator	All	Chinese	French	German	Italian	Japanese	Russian	Spanish
BA-granting	16.6	9.1	18.4	9.8	21.9	19.4	16.7	5.2
MA-granting			7.5				55.6	
PhD-granting			4.6	35.4				

Positive relative growth percentages (see note 4) express the increase in likelihood that programs with certain characteristics will have growth in introductory course enrollments compared with similar programs that do not have those characteristics.

Language Centers and Language Resource Centers

Having an entity that is separate from language departments and to some degree responsible for language teaching—for example, a language center or a language resource center—is strongly associated with enrollment growth in almost all languages in MA- and PhD-granting departments (table 23).[8] Across all languages, programs in PhD-granting departments in institutions with a language center were 30.4% more likely to have experienced growth in introductory course enrollments than similar programs in institutions without a language center. Programs in MA-granting departments in institutions with a language center were 18% more likely to have seen growth in introductory course enrollments. Notably, German programs in MA-granting departments in institutions with a language center were 79.5% more likely to report rising enrollments in introductory courses than comparable programs in institutions without a language center. Only Chinese and Japanese programs in MA-granting departments and German programs in PhD-granting departments do not demonstrate a strong association. In BA-granting departments, by contrast, Chinese programs alone show evidence of a strong association between enrollment growth and language centers.

Emphasis on Reading and Writing versus Oral Communication in the Introductory Language Sequence and on Curricular Approaches in Advanced Courses

Emphasis in the introductory language sequence

Respondents were asked to describe the actual practice in their introductory language sequence, with reference to the degree of emphasis placed on

TABLE 23
RELATIVE GROWTH IN INTRODUCTORY COURSE ENROLLMENTS WITH EXISTENCE OF ON-CAMPUS LANGUAGE CENTER OR LANGUAGE RESOURCE CENTER (PERCENTAGE)

LANGUAGE CENTER	ALL	CHINESE	FRENCH	GERMAN	ITALIAN	JAPANESE	RUSSIAN	SPANISH
BA-granting		39.7	7.1		0.3			
MA-granting	18.0		24.8	79.5	23.5		66.1	11.0
PhD-granting	30.4	55.6	70.4		18.5	25.0	38.9	24.6

Positive relative growth percentages (see note 4) express the increase in likelihood that programs with certain characteristics will have growth in introductory course enrollments compared with similar programs that do not have those characteristics.

reading, writing, and oral communication (table 24). Programs that emphasized oral communication in introductory-level classes were twice as likely to report growth as those that emphasized either reading and writing or reading and writing balanced with oral communication. The association of an emphasis on oral communication with growth in enrollments occurs in 17 of the 21 (81%) program types analyzed. By contrast, only 9 of the 21 (43%) program types show a positive association between an emphasis on reading and writing and rising enrollments; of programs reporting a balance in emphasis, again 9 of the 21 (43%) program types show a positive association with rising enrollments. Twenty-nine percent or 6 of the 21 program types show an association between leaving curricular emphasis in the introductory sequence up to the instructor's discretion and enrollment growth in those courses.

Advanced curricular emphasis

The impact of curricular emphasis in advanced undergraduate courses on growth in introductory enrollments varies widely across program types

TABLE 24
RELATIVE GROWTH IN INTRODUCTORY COURSE ENROLLMENTS AND CURRICULAR EMPHASIS IN INTRODUCTORY COURSES (PERCENTAGE)

Curricular Emphasis	All	Chinese	French	German	Italian	Japanese	Russian	Spanish
Reading and writing								
BA-granting	3.5		9.1		35.5	34.2	68.9	2.5
MA-granting				58.8				
PhD-granting	23.7		125.9				114.3	79.4
Balance between reading and writing and oral communication								
BA-granting	2.3	14.3	14.7	12.7	5.9	14.7	6.8	
MA-granting							41.2	
PhD-granting				65.0	7.8			
Oral communication								
BA-granting	2.8	0.3	0.5			3.4	14.3	10.1
MA-granting	17.3		6.5	34.3	39.9	97.1		7.1
PhD-granting	9.0	20.0	54.6	9.1	11.4	42.9	19.0	1.9
Instructor's discretion								
BA-granting								0.7
MA-granting								6.4
PhD-granting		57.1				91.7	38.1	45.0

Positive relative growth percentages (see note 4) express the increase in likelihood that programs with certain characteristics will have growth in introductory course enrollments compared with similar programs that do not have those characteristics.

(table 25). Both traditional and less traditional approaches show occasional association with enrollment growth. If we look at the first three numbered categories of table 25, it appears that growth in introductory enrollments is most frequently associated with a balanced emphasis between literary and nonliterary texts. But if we look only at the strong rates of relative growth reported, those over 10%, a more diffuse distribution emerges. The data suggest three instances of strong association between an emphasis on literary texts at the advanced level and growth in enrollments at the introductory level, five instances of strong association between a balanced emphasis and growth, and five instances of strong association between an emphasis on nonliterary texts and growth.

Similarly, the data in categories 4 through 7 suggest that many different approaches are associated with enrollment growth. In BA-granting departments, emphasis on "canonical literature by period, author, or genre" and emphasis on "the canon with a recent addition of some noncanonical literature or approaches based on race, class, or gender" both show a strong association with rising enrollments in four instances: both approaches show this association in Chinese and French; Italian and Spanish programs associate growth with the period, author, or genre approach to canonical literature; and German and Russian programs associate growth with an approach emphasizing the canon but containing some noncanonical literature. In other words, neither emphasis stands out as the preferred option in BA-granting departments.

German and Russian programs in BA-, MA-, and PhD-granting departments reporting an emphasis on noncanonical literature all demonstrate a strong likelihood of showing gains in enrollments when compared with departments not reporting this emphasis. Italian programs in BA-granting departments and Chinese and Japanese programs in PhD-granting departments also reported this association. It must be stressed that very few programs described their curricula in these terms, but the data still demonstrate that these programs are notably successful in attracting students to their elementary-level language sequences.

While these instances seem to suggest evidence of the benefits of a revamped, nontraditional curriculum, data gathered in response to the next question offer strong and possibly surprising evidence that a highly traditional curricular approach can also draw students. Programs were asked if their upper-level curriculum could be described as "based primarily on surveys of civilization by period." Though the group responding in the affirmative was again small, these programs also demonstrated a strong likelihood of enrollment growth in their introductory sequence. Chinese, Japanese, and Russian programs in BA-granting departments; German and

TABLE 25
Relative Growth in Introductory Course Enrollments and Emphasis in the Advanced Undergraduate Curriculum (Percentage)

Emphasis in Curriculum	All	Chinese	French	German	Italian	Japanese	Russian	Spanish
1. On literary texts								
BA-granting		8.4						3.1
MA-granting						28.6		
PhD-granting	16.3	96.4				1.3		21.1
2. On literary and nonliterary texts equally								
BA-granting	4.0			3.0	18.9	13.8	16.8	0.8
MA-granting					6.7	2.2	60.3	
PhD-granting		20.0			7.9	4.2	5.0	
3. On nonliterary texts								
BA-granting		0.3	17.5	10.2				7.1
MA-granting								
PhD-granting		26.7					122.9	36.8
4. On canon by period								
BA-granting	1.7	21.2	10.5		13.5			14.2
MA-granting				11.1		58.3		
PhD-granting	3.0	8.9		128.3		1.3		8.4
5. On canon, with some noncanonical literature								
BA-granting	12.5	16.7	16.7	21.8			25.5	7.3
MA-granting					21.4			
PhD-granting								
6. On noncanonical literature								
BA-granting				10.5	12.0		46.2	
MA-granting				114.3			80.0	
PhD-granting		53.3		63.1		91.7	104.5	
7. On surveys of civilization								
BA-granting	4.6	44.0				16.2	31.9	3.5
MA-granting				92.0		97.1		
PhD-granting	15.9	20.0	38.8	235.4	2.8	25.0		9.3
8. On language for special purposes								
BA-granting	10.4	2.9	18.8	13.1	15.2			5.7
MA-granting	15.4			24.0	44.4	104.2		12.5
PhD-granting		15.4		1.4			20.0	

Positive relative growth percentages (see note 4) express the increase in likelihood that programs with certain characteristics will have growth in introductory couse enrollments compared with similar programs that do not have those characteristics.

Japanese programs in MA-granting departments; and Chinese, French, German, and Japanese programs in PhD-granting departments all showed an association between a survey of civilization curriculum and enrollment growth at the elementary level. Again, the conclusion indicated is that no single curricular approach at the advanced undergraduate level is exclusively associated with rising enrollments in the introductory sequence.

We cannot see in these data any clear pattern of association across all languages and program types between enrollment growth and curricular emphasis. Specialists in specific languages may recognize trends, but what emerges finally is evidence that curricular emphasis in upper-level classes is not a uniformly strong predictor of elementary-level enrollment growth, that students at the elementary level are not consistently drawn to departments by any one curricular approach in advanced courses. Both traditional and less traditional approaches show occasional association with enrollment growth.

Formal Faculty Discussion

Formal faculty discussion around a variety of professional issues is often associated with rising enrollments across all levels and languages. As discussed above, we asked respondents about the frequency of formal faculty interaction concerning a departmental mission statement and broad educational objectives. We also asked if issues in language education had been discussed in faculty-wide conversations about methodology or objectives that included reference to content-based teaching, teaching for oral proficiency, or the Standards for Foreign Language Learning. Overall, formal faculty discussion is associated just over 50% of the time with enrollment growth. Most notable is the frequent association of growth in enrollments in the introductory sequence with discussions of content-based teaching and oral proficiency (table 28). With the exception of the consistently strong association of discussions in these two areas with growth, there is no uniform pattern in the distribution of strong associations between formal faculty discussion and enrollment growth. (A few specific languages and department types provide exceptions.) Despite the apparent absence of a clear pattern, the relative frequency of the association of enrollment growth with formal faculty discussions of method and content seems significant to us.

Table 26 describes programs that reported a positive association between rising introductory enrollments and faculty discussion of a departmental mission statement. We have seen that only about half of all responding departments have a mission statement. While programs that show the most frequent strong associations between growth and statement

TABLE 26
RELATIVE GROWTH IN INTRODUCTORY COURSE ENROLLMENTS IN PROGRAMS REPORTING FACULTY DISCUSSION OF MISSION STATEMENT (PERCENTAGE)

DISCUSSION OF MISSION STATEMENT	ALL	CHINESE	FRENCH	GERMAN	ITALIAN	JAPANESE	RUSSIAN	SPANISH
Annually or more often								
BA-granting	0.4	3.3			14.5		3.3	9.3
MA-granting						212.5		
PhD-granting	6.1		40.0		22.7	50.0		
Every few years								
BA-granting		54.4		5.7		2.1		
MA-granting					1.6			11.6
PhD-granting		8.9					12.5	30.4
On an ad hoc basis								
BA-granting	3.5		16.2		8.4	19.5	18.4	
MA-granting	5.7		20.4	31.6	22.2	13.3		
PhD-granting	4.1	40.0	36.4		26.3		43.2	51.0

Positive relative growth percentages (see note 4) express the increase in likelihood that programs with certain characteristics will have growth in introductory course enrollments compared with similar programs that do not have those characteristics.

review are those that report discussions on an ad hoc basis (rather than annually or "every few years"), the data also suggest that, overall, regular review of the departmental mission statement (be it annual, every few years, or ad hoc) is frequently associated with enrollment growth. Table 27 describes the association between rising enrollments and faculty discussion of broad educational objectives, although here strong rates of relative growth are more evenly distributed, regardless of whether discussions took place annually, every few years, or on an ad hoc basis.

Enrollment growth is associated most frequently with discussions that dealt with content-based teaching (62%, or 13 of the 21 program types), teaching for oral proficiency (52%, or 11 of the 21 program types), and the Standards for Foreign Language Learning (38%, or 8 of the 21 program types). Table 28 gives these relative growth rates. Here the data suggest even more than in the previous two tables that a program in which faculty members engage in formal discussions about teaching and department-wide practices is inclined to be an effective program, attracting increasing numbers of students to its introductory courses. There are a few exemplary languages: Italian records seven instances of strong relative growth, and

TABLE 27
RELATIVE GROWTH IN INTRODUCTORY COURSE ENROLLMENTS IN PROGRAMS REPORTING FACULTY DISCUSSION OF BROAD EDUCATIONAL OBJECTIVES (PERCENTAGE)

DISCUSSION OF BROAD EDUCATIONAL OBJECTIVES	ALL	CHINESE	FRENCH	GERMAN	ITALIAN	JAPANESE	RUSSIAN	SPANISH
Annually or more often								
BA-granting	2.5	37.0	3.8			59.6	28.1	1.0
MA-granting				9.5				
PhD-granting	0.7			57.1	11.1			2.6
Every few years								
BA-granting	0.5		20.0	18.0				13.3
MA-granting	16.9		17.3	108.0	20.0	1.8		11.5
PhD-granting	17.5	26.7	13.5		5.7	68.9	48.7	
On an ad hoc basis								
BA-granting				3.2	13.3			
MA-granting	5.1				7.7	43.8	286.7	5.0
PhD-granting			18.4			27.3		24.2

Positive relative growth percentages (see note 4) express the increase in likelihood that programs with certain characteristics will have growth in introductory course enrollments compared with similar programs that do not have those characteristics.

German and Spanish each record five instances of strong relative growth. The German and Spanish instances are particularly interesting because, as reported in the MLA's 1998 survey, enrollments in these two languages over the period reported have been notably divergent, Spanish enrollments growing dramatically and German enrollments falling (Brod and Welles). The current data indicate that departments, by effective faculty practices, may distinguish themselves in enrollment growth despite overall trends.

Department-Sponsored Activities for the Local Community

Programs were asked if they sponsored activities such as lectures, films, or language courses for the local community, whether these activities were offered on campus or in the community beyond the campus. Programs that sponsored such activities were more likely to report growth in introductory sequence enrollments than those that did not. Table 29 records the association between sponsoring activities and enrollment growth. Russian and Italian programs in particular reflect a strong association between outreach through cultural programs and rising enrollments at the introductory level. This finding is particularly interesting because Russian and Italian

TABLE 28
RELATIVE GROWTH IN INTRODUCTORY COURSE ENROLLMENTS IN
PROGRAMS REPORTING FACULTY DISCUSSION OF METHODOLOGICAL
PRACTICES (PERCENTAGE)

Subject of Discussion	All	Chinese	French	German	Italian	Japanese	Russian	Spanish
Content-based teaching								
BA-granting	2.2	11.5	9.8	0.1	16.7			
MA-granting	17.9		13.0	272.4	12.5		28.6	12.0
PhD-granting	6.9	14.0	18.4		12.7			15.0
Teaching for oral proficiency								
BA-granting				25.2	4.7			
MA-granting	32.9		30.4		15.2		40.6	10.5
PhD-granting	3.7	114.3	50.0	80.0	40.6			14.0
Standards for Foreign Language Learning								
BA-granting				3.8			13.7	3.5
MA-granting	3.1			65.8	41.7			10.7
PhD-granting				31.2	14.0			

Positive relative growth percentages (see note 4) express the increase in likelihood that programs with certain characteristics will have growth in introductory course enrollments compared with similar programs that do not have those characteristics.

programs have experienced very different overall enrollment patterns during the period in question, Italian rising dramatically and Russian suffering considerable losses. The data here suggest that programs in both languages benefit from strong outreach components. French, Japanese, and Spanish programs also show the benefits of outreach through cultural programs.

Study Abroad

Increasing participation in study-abroad programs is clearly associated with rising enrollments in the introductory sequence in BA- and MA-granting departments (table 30). In all 2,391 reporting BA-granting programs, we find that departments with increasing enrollments in programs abroad are 20.1% more likely to have also gained enrollments in the introductory sequence than departments whose study-abroad enrollments did not increase. Increasing participation in programs abroad is also associated with rising enrollments in the introductory sequence in all reporting programs in MA-granting departments, with the exception of Chinese: those programs with increasing enrollments in study abroad are 35.6% more likely to have gained in introductory enrollments between 1995 and 1999.[9] In programs in PhD-granting departments, with the exception of German,

TABLE 29
RELATIVE GROWTH IN INTRODUCTORY COURSE ENROLLMENTS IN DEPARTMENTS SPONSORING ACTIVITIES FOR THE LOCAL COMMUNITY (PERCENTAGE)

ACTIVITY FOR THE COMMUNITY	ALL	CHINESE	FRENCH	GERMAN	ITALIAN	JAPANESE	RUSSIAN	SPANISH
Lectures								
BA-granting	5.2	12.5	5.7		6.6		42.1	9.1
MA-granting	3.3		20.0		48.1			37.4
PhD-granting	10.2		44.0		25.0		106.9	1.9
Films								
BA-granting	5.7			1.2	13.7	5.3	87.4	9.1
MA-granting	0.2			17.2	20.0	25.0		2.6
PhD-granting	4.3		29.8	18.2	10.0			15.2
Language courses								
BA-granting		17.3	7.0				66.6	
MA-granting	16.3		16.8	87.9	42.6	2.9	11.8	
PhD-granting	14.8	63.6			15.9	175.0	35.7	23.2
Other (unspecified)								
BA-granting	2.3	0.7	4.6		9.8	9.6	62.8	
MA-granting	18.1		2.1			111.8		41.4
PhD-granting	2.4	50.0	3.7			44.7	12.5	

Positive relative growth percentages (see note 4) express the increase in likelihood that programs with certain characteristics will have growth in introductory course enrollments compared with similar programs that do not have those characteristics.

TABLE 30
RELATIVE GROWTH IN INTRODUCTORY COURSE ENROLLMENTS AND ENROLLMENT TRENDS IN STUDY-ABROAD PROGRAMS (PERCENTAGE)

STUDY-ABROAD PROGRAMS	ALL	CHINESE	FRENCH	GERMAN	ITALIAN	JAPANESE	RUSSIAN	SPANISH
BA-granting	20.1		21.4	20.6	25.2	23.7	47.9	29.2
MA-granting	35.6	12.0	77.8	7.1	125.0	65.0	42.2	
PhD-granting				50.9				

Positive relative growth percentages (see note 4) express the increase in likelihood that programs with certain characteristics will have growth in introductory course enrollments compared with similar programs that do not have those characteristics.

the picture is different: programs reporting greater participation in study-abroad programs are 2.3% less likely to report rising enrollments in the introductory sequence.

While the percentages vary, this pattern is by and large sustained across individual languages. Programs in BA-granting departments reporting increased study-abroad enrollments are between 20.6% (German) and 47.9% (Russian) more likely to have increased enrollments in the introductory sequence between 1995 and 1999 than departments whose study-abroad enrollments have not increased. Only in Chinese language programs in BA-granting departments are study-abroad enrollments not tied positively to enrollments in the introductory sequence. In MA-granting departments the relative growth ranges from a low of 7.1% in Italian programs to 125% in Japanese programs.

In PhD-granting departments, the picture in individual languages is much the same as in all PhD-granting departments taken together: departments with rising enrollments in study-abroad programs are less likely to have an enrollment gain in the introductory language sequence. This finding is surprising, given the relative strength of study-abroad programs in PhD-granting departments (not shown in table): departments whose study-abroad enrollments are rising outnumber those whose study-abroad programs are not, in Chinese, 13 to 11; in French, 41 to 23; in Italian, 43 to 16; in Japanese, 13 to 11; and in Spanish, 43 to 22.

Minors and Double Majors

Programs in which the numbers of minors and double majors increased between 1995 and 1999 frequently reported enrollment growth in introductory language courses (tables 31 and 32). When we look at the data in terms of languages, the association between enrollment growth and number of minors is found in programs in French, German, Japanese, and Spanish across all department types; with double majors it is found in all programs except French in MA-granting departments and Japanese in PhD-granting departments. Apparently a department that includes advanced foreign language and literature courses in students' programs without demanding the commitment that a major requires presents the kind of dynamic and engaging image that attracts undergraduates to the earlier levels of language study.

Looking at the data in terms of department types, we find that an increase in the number of minors is associated with growth in introductory courses in all language programs in BA-granting departments and selected languages in MA- and PhD-granting departments. Increases in BA-granting departments in the number of double majors was associated with

TABLE 31
Relative Growth in Introductory Course Enrollments and Number of Minors in a Department (Percentage)

Number of Minors	All	Chinese	French	German	Italian	Japanese	Russian	Spanish
Increased								
BA-granting	22.2	6.5	14.2	18.5	8.7	21.2	17.9	42.7
MA-granting	17.5		18.3	54.2		87.5		33.6
PhD-granting			20.4	50.0		14.3		7.9
Stable								
BA-granting		13.6						
MA-granting			2.8		29.9		84.1	
PhD-granting		26.7				51.8		8.4

Positive relative growth percentages (see note 4) express the increase in likelihood that programs with certain characteristics will have growth in introductory course enrollments compared with similar programs that do not have those characteristics.

TABLE 32
Relative Growth in Introductory Course Enrollments and Number of Double Majors in a Department (Percentage)

Number of Double Majors	All	Chinese	French	German	Italian	Japanese	Russian	Spanish
Increased								
BA-granting	21.3	10.0	32.0	39.6		2.6	17.9	28.8
MA-granting	2.1			52.2		66.7		24.5
PhD-granting	6.7		139.4	110.5				28.0
Stable								
BA-granting		2.5				5.6		
MA-granting	10.6		44.8				23.8	10.3
PhD-granting		40.0			9.5	20.0		

Positive relative growth percentages (see note 4) express the increase in likelihood that programs with certain characteristics will have growth in introductory course enrollments compared with similar programs that do not have those characteristics.

growth in introductory courses for all languages except Italian. This association is found in MA-granting departments offering double majors in programs in German, Japanese, and Spanish and in PhD-granting departments in programs in French, German, and Spanish. Perhaps as significant as programs reporting an increase of double majors and minors between 1995 and 1999 are programs in which the number of students selecting either option has remained stable. If we include the programs with stable numbers of double majors and minors, the picture is even more striking. Growth or stability in the number of double majors and in the number of minors correlates with increasing enrollments in elementary-level courses in 17 of the 21 (81%) program types.

The results of this study are preliminary rather than definitive, but they tell us a great deal about practices that contribute to effective teaching, administration, and design of foreign language programs. Some of the programmatic features and pedagogical practices that we have found to be associated with enrollment growth may not in and of themselves attract students to departments or programs. For example, a student would not be likely to say, "I am going to take Chinese because the modern language department uses technology for testing and placement." But the student may hear of a lively department in which incoming students are placed at appropriate levels and are enthusiastic about their progress. The student may never recognize that appropriate placement and a careful monitoring of student accomplishments are among the reasons for the positive buzz about the department on campus. Behind the buzz that attracts students are an engaged faculty and lively, varied programs that offer the maximum number of opportunities to learn effectively, to practice and apply the language beyond the traditional classroom format, and to be exposed to cultural difference in a variety of contexts.

Much about the survey has yet to be analyzed. Future reports will interpret the relation of departmental practices to enrollment growth in advanced courses and to number of majors. We will also report on fluctuation in faculty size by department and the relation of number of full-time faculty members to enrollment patterns. Phase 2 of the project will be a more detailed study of a limited number of programs; we hope it will provide information and perspectives on nonquantifiable factors of departmental success.

NOTES

The authors wish to thank Calvin Jones, who served as a consultant to this project, and Lee Robeson, our contact at Roper Starch, who oversaw the collection of data and building the database. We also thank our colleagues on the MLA staff: Natalia Lusin, for her advice and help in preparing tables in this report, and Beverly Celusak, for her part in preparing data for presentation.

[1] There are, of course, programs that measure success by decreasing rather than increasing enrollments in the introductory sequence. Such programs encourage better preparation at the high school level and provide noncredit support to help false beginners jump over the introductory sequence and enter more advanced courses. We assume, however, that there are too few such programs to outweigh the general concept of more is better that we have applied here. Readers may suggest that other measures of success, particularly student achievement, need to be considered for a complete picture. The absence of uniformly applied assessments of achieved levels of language proficiency (oral proficiency interviewing, for instance, or some modified version of it, is used in fewer than half the responding departments) precludes this study's looking at that crucial measure of effective language programs.

[2] The analysis of minors and double majors in tables 9 and 10 is based on the pool of 6,022 programs in the 1,962 departmental respondents minus those that did not indicate whether the number of student minors or double major programs were up or down, minus those in languages other than the seven included for analysis, and minus those in degree categories other than the BA, MA, and PhD.

[3] The data in this section of the report, unless otherwise indicated, refer to language programs rather than to departments. Since many departments contain any number of distinct language programs, when we analyze the data by individual languages, we deal with a pool much larger than the 1,962 departments discussed above. Departments were asked to report on their five biggest programs. The entire pool of language programs reported on in the survey, including those in AA-, BA-, MA-, and PhD-granting departments, totals 6,022. For the purpose of this section of the report, the 1,084 programs in AA-granting departments were removed from the pool to be dealt with in a later study. In addition, since only data from BA-, MA-, and PhD-granting departments were analyzed, 983 programs in departments granting no degree and 29 departments that simply did not respond to the question of what degree they granted were also removed from the pool. Thus the pool discussed here totals 3,926 programs in BA-, MA-, and PhD-granting departments. The number is even smaller—3,469 programs—when we discuss only those programs with falling, stable, and rising enrollments, since not every program provided enrollment figures that allowed us to place it in one of these categories (e.g., a program that reported data only for 1999).

[4] The formula for calculating positive relative growth percentages is as follows: the percentage of programs reporting feature x that gained in enrollments between 1995 and 1999 (gain-yes programs) minus the percentage of programs that reported not having feature x but that nonetheless gained in enrollments between 1995 and 1999 (gain-no programs) yields the percentage-point difference. This difference divided by the percentage of gain-no programs yields the percentage of relative growth. The calculation allows us to make the statement that departments that have feature x are y% more likely to have experienced enrollment gains between 1995 and 1999 than departments that do not. Negative growth percentages (i.e., where the feature is associated with shrinking introductory-level enrollments) are not shown in tables 19–32.

[5] Very small actual program numbers tend to produce dramatic percentage changes. We have corrected for this to some degree by not reporting cases in which the number

of departments with the feature that gained enrollments and the number of departments without the feature that gained enrollments together total fewer than ten.

[6] The data reported in the "All" column in tables 19 through 32 are an aggregate of the data for all reported languages, Arabic to Zulu, and not a total of the numbers given for the seven languages listed in the other columns in the table.

[7] Figures for the numbers of program types exhibiting an association between growing enrollments and a particular feature (always expressed as "X of the 21 program types") are not explicitly reported in the tables. We have rounded off these percentages to the nearest whole number. Percentages of relative growth are rounded off to the nearest tenth.

[8] Because the terms used by different institutions for such an entity designated a range of administrative structures, it is difficult to know exactly what respondents had in mind when they answered that their institution had "an entity separate from language departments that is to some degree responsible for language teaching." We asked respondents to specify whether the center provides all or some language teaching on campus; evaluates, supervises, and supports all language teaching; evaluates, supervises, and supports language teaching at the request of the department; or functions as a media center.

[9] The percentage differences for Italian language programs in MA-granting departments are 7%, quite smaller than for all other languages, but Italian programs in MA-granting departments reporting stable rather than rising study-abroad enrollments were 48% more likely than departments without stable study-abroad enrollments to have rising enrollments in the introductory sequence. In other languages, stable study-abroad enrollments generally did not correlate positively with enrollment growth.

WORKS CITED

Brod, Richard, and Bettina Huber. "The MLA Survey of Foreign Language Entrance and Degree Requirements, 1994–95." *ADFL Bulletin* 28.1 (1996): 35–43.

Brod, Richard, and Elizabeth B. Welles. "Foreign Language Enrollments in United States Institutions of Higher Education, Fall 1998." *ADFL Bulletin* 31.2 (2000): 22–29.

Turner, Sarah E., and William G. Bowen. "The Flight from the Arts and Sciences: Trends in Degrees Conferred." *Science* 16 Oct. 1990: 517–21.

The 1999 MLA Survey of Staffing in English and Foreign Language Departments

DAVID LAURENCE

In 1999, the Modern Language Association conducted a survey of English and foreign language departments' use of tenured and tenure-track, full-time non-tenure-track, and part-time faculty members and graduate teaching assistants in colleges and universities in the United States and Canada. The survey asked for information about who taught what in the fall semester of that year, including the number of instructors in each employment category and the number of undergraduate course sections that instructors in each category taught. The survey also asked about the professional support, benefits, and compensation for full-time non-tenure-track faculty members, part-time faculty members paid on a per-course basis, and part-time faculty members paid a fractional full-time salary.

The survey was designed as a census of all modern language departments in the United States and Canada. Accordingly, in November 1999 the MLA contacted 5,245 departments in two- and four-year institutions identified from its database of departmental administrators. Data collection was completed in April 2000. Overall, 2,182 of the departments returned questionnaires, a 42% response rate. United States institutions accounted for 4,969 departments that received a questionnaire (94.7% of the total) and 2,081 that responded (95.4% of the total). Canadian institutions accounted for 276 departments that received a questionnaire (5.3%) and 101 that responded (4.6%). Departments in institutions that grant the doctorate had the highest

The author is Director of MLA English Programs and the Association of Departments of English.

response rate (51%), those in institutions granting associate's degrees the lowest (33%). Departments in four-year institutions (including doctoral departments) had a 46% response rate. The findings presented here summarize information for 1,991 departments—673 English departments, 889 foreign language departments, 187 combined English and foreign language departments, and 242 humanities divisions. (Excluded were responding departments of linguistics, comparative literature, English as a second language, and general education that had been part of the original mailing.)

Nine of the disciplinary societies that participate with the MLA in the Coalition on the Academic Workforce (CAW) did surveys parallel to the MLA's. Comparative data for all ten surveys can be accessed at www.theaha.org/caw/cawreport.htm, a section of the Web site of the American Historical Association. Included in the CAW report are results from societies representing anthropology, art history, cinema studies, independent composition programs, English and foreign languages, history, linguistics, classics, and philosophy.

The MLA survey's design as a census of all English and foreign language departments in the United States and Canada originated in a motion that the MLA Delegate Assembly approved at its meeting in December 1998. The motion also provided for the MLA to make results available in a report that identifies departments by name together with the information those departments provided. Information for individual departments can be accessed at www.mla.org. Because the survey was designed as a census, collective findings should be regarded as indicating conditions in responding departments rather than as a statistically verified sample for generalization.

PERCENTAGES OF INSTRUCTORS IN DIFFERENT EMPLOYMENT CATEGORIES

Table 1 reports head count, summarizing the percentage of instructors in different employment categories who taught undergraduate courses in responding departments in fall 1999. The percentages are broken down by the department type (English, foreign language, combined English and foreign language, humanities division) and by the highest degree a department grants.

Ninety-eight percent of the responding English and foreign language departments in four-year institutions reported employing tenured or tenure-track faculty members in fall 1999. The percentages are lower for two-year associate's-granting departments: 79% for English and 84% for foreign languages. Part-time non-tenure-track faculty members were employed by 91% of the responding English departments and 83% of the

TABLE 1
Percentage of Instructors in Different Employment Categories by Head Count, Fall 1999

	English	Foreign Language	Combined	Humanities Division	All
All departments					
Full-time tenured or tenure-track	36.3	35.5	34.4	29.4	35.3
Full-time non-tenure-track	9.5	12.4	10.6	12.9	10.8
Part-time	31.9	28.9	52.6	57.0	35.0
Graduate student TA	22.2	23.3	2.5	0.7	18.9
Number of departments	*670*	*888*	*187*	*242*	*1,987*
Doctoral departments					
Full-time tenured or tenure-track	30.5	28.4	–	–	29.9
Full-time non-tenure-track	8.1	11.7	–	–	9.4
Part-time	16.9	12.1	–	–	15.1
Graduate student TA	44.6	47.9	–	–	45.6
Number of departments	*106*	*161*	*3*	*1*	*271*
MA-granting departments					
Full-time tenured or tenure-track	39.9	38.5	46.4	30.9	39.6
Full-time non-tenure-track	10.9	11.6	16.7	16.1	11.5
Part-time	33.9	27.2	29.0	49.5	32.1
Graduate student TA	15.3	22.8	7.9	3.5	16.8
Number of departments	*155*	*112*	*20*	*11*	*298*
BA-granting departments					
Full-time tenured or tenure-track	53.6	46.3	45.9	37.0	47.5
Full-time non-tenure-track	10.5	14.8	12.4	16.3	13.3
Part-time	35.8	35.4	41.7	45.9	37.5
Graduate student TA	0.2	3.5	0.0	0.8	1.7
Number of departments	*260*	*468*	*67*	*84*	*879*
AA-granting departments					
Full-time tenured or tenure-track	31.8	26.2	24.2	23.4	27.0
Full-time non-tenure-track	6.3	4.9	8.5	11.3	8.1
Part-time	61.8	68.8	67.2	65.2	64.8
Graduate student TA	0.1	0.0	0.1	0.0	0.1
Number of departments	*76*	*51*	*68*	*93*	*288*
Departments granting no degree					
Full-time tenured or tenure-track	28.0	24.4	30.5	30.4	27.7
Full-time non-tenure-track	14.7	12.6	8.6	10.3	12.6
Part-time	49.6	61.0	60.9	59.0	55.7
Graduate student TA	7.7	2.0	0.0	0.3	3.9
Number of departments	*73*	*96*	*29*	*53*	*251*

Note: Percentages are not calculated for data representing fewer than ten respondents, except in the tables giving ranges of salary and per-course compensation.

responding foreign language departments, overall. The employment of full-time non-tenure-track faculty members varied according to the highest degree granted by the responding English or foreign language department. Eighty-six percent of the responding doctorate-granting and 81% of the master's-granting departments reported employing full-time non-tenure-track faculty members in fall 1999, in comparison with 59% of the bachelor's-granting and only 34% of the associate's-granting departments.

Across responding departments, tenured and tenure-track faculty members made up only 35% of the total number of instructors teaching undergraduate courses in fall 1999 and less than half the faculty (i.e., after graduate TAs were excluded). Faculty members holding part-time appointments accounted for 32% of all instructors in the English departments and 29% of all instructors in the foreign language departments.

Two-year-college departments reported the highest percentage of part-time instructors teaching in fall 1999: 62% in English and 69% in foreign language departments. In associate's-granting departments, only 32% of instructors in English and 26% of instructors in foreign language held tenured or tenure-track appointments.

Graduate student TAs made up a plurality of the instructors in the responding doctorate-granting departments: 45% in English and 48% in foreign language departments. Faculty members holding tenured or tenure-track appointments made up the next largest category: 31% in English and 28% in foreign language departments. But if graduate student TAs are combined with part-time faculty members as an overall category of part-time instructors, this category in doctorate-granting departments (61% in English and 60% in foreign language) resembles the part-time instructor head count percentage for two-year colleges.

Departments granting the bachelor's degree had the highest percentages of tenured and tenure-track faculty members in responding departments: 54% of instructors in English and 46% of instructors in foreign language. Part-time faculty members made up the next largest category in these departments: 36% in English and 35% in foreign language.

Percentages of Undergraduate Course Sections Taught by Instructors in Different Employment Categories

Table 2 shows the percentage of undergraduate course sections that teachers in each of the four employment categories taught in fall 1999, by the highest degree a department grants. Findings are shown in greater detail in table 3A (English departments) and table 3B (foreign language departments), which include percentages for first-year writing or first-year language sections, other

TABLE 2
Percentage of Undergraduate Course Sections Taught by Instructors in Different Employment Categories, Fall 1999

	English	Foreign Language	Combined	Humanities Division	All
All departments					
Full-time tenured or tenure-track	42.2	41.4	44.2	41.6	42.1
Full-time non-tenure-track	15.4	18.0	16.6	15.2	16.2
Part-time	28.6	25.5	38.2	42.7	29.9
Graduate student TA	13.9	15.1	1.0	0.5	11.7
Number of departments	*673*	*889*	*187*	*242*	*1,991*
Doctoral departments					
Full-time tenured or tenure-track	30.7	25.7	–	–	29.3
Full-time non-tenure-track	15.1	19.2	–	–	16.4
Part-time	19.1	14.4	–	–	17.5
Graduate student TA	35.1	40.7	–	–	36.8
Number of departments	*106*	*161*	*3*	*1*	*271*
MA-granting departments					
Full-time tenured or tenure-track	43.2	43.6	54.0	33.0	43.7
Full-time non-tenure-track	18.1	17.6	23.7	21.1	18.4
Part-time	28.6	24.8	19.2	44.5	27.5
Graduate student TA	10.1	14.0	3.1	1.4	10.4
Number of departments	*155*	*112*	*20*	*11*	*298*
BA-granting departments					
Full-time tenured or tenure-track	58.7	54.2	55.0	43.7	54.5
Full-time non-tenure-track	14.2	18.7	16.6	19.5	17.1
Part-time	27.1	25.2	28.4	36.5	27.6
Graduate student TA	0.0	1.8	0.0	0.3	0.8
Number of departments	*260*	*468*	*67*	*84*	*879*
AA-granting departments					
Full-time tenured or tenure-track	47.3	41.3	34.3	38.4	41.6
Full-time non-tenure-track	7.1	9.6	16.4	14.0	11.1
Part-time	45.4	49.1	49.3	47.6	47.2
Graduate student TA	0.1	0.0	0.0	0.0	0.1
Number of departments	*76*	*51*	*68*	*93*	*288*
Departments granting no degree					
Full-time tenured or tenure-track	38.2	33.9	40.8	48.1	39.0
Full-time non-tenure-track	22.3	16.6	11.0	8.5	17.1
Part-time	36.2	48.0	48.2	43.2	42.0
Graduate student TA	3.3	1.4	0.0	0.2	1.9
Number of departments	*76*	*97*	*29*	*53*	*255*

TABLES 3A AND 3B
PERCENTAGE OF FIRST-YEAR WRITING OR FIRST-YEAR LANGUAGE AND OTHER UNDERGRADUATE COURSE SECTIONS TAUGHT BY TEACHERS IN DIFFERENT EMPLOYMENT CATEGORIES, FALL 1999

3A. ENGLISH
(NUMBER OF DEPARTMENTS)

SECTIONS	DOCTORAL DEPTS. (106)			MA-GRANTING DEPTS. (155)			BA-GRANTING DEPTS. (260)			AA-GRANTING DEPTS. (76)		
	FIRST-YEAR WRITING	OTHER UNDER-GRADUATE	ALL UNDER-GRADUATE	FIRST-YEAR WRITING	OTHER UNDER-GRADUATE	ALL UNDER-GRADUATE	FIRST-YEAR WRITING	OTHER UNDER-GRADUATE	ALL UNDER-GRADUATE	FIRST-YEAR WRITING	OTHER UNDER-GRADUATE	ALL UNDER-GRADUATE
Full-time tenured or tenure-track	5.9	52.9	30.7	20.0	68.6	43.2	42.2	73.2	58.7	44.8	51.3	47.3
Full-time non-tenure-track	17.5	12.9	15.1	22.0	13.9	18.1	17.0	11.8	14.2	7.2	6.9	7.1
Part-time	24.3	14.5	19.1	40.3	15.8	28.6	40.7	15.0	27.1	47.8	41.8	45.4
Graduate student TA	52.2	19.7	35.1	17.6	1.7	10.1	0.1	0.0	0.0	0.2	0.0	0.1
All undergraduate course sections that were sections of first-year writing	47.2			52.3			46.9			60.6		

3B. FOREIGN LANGUAGES
(NUMBER OF DEPARTMENTS)

SECTIONS	DOCTORAL DEPTS. (161)			MA-GRANTING DEPTS. (112)			BA-GRANTING DEPTS. (468)			AA-GRANTING DEPTS. (51)		
	FIRST-YEAR LANG.	OTHER UNDER-GRADUATE	ALL UNDER-GRADUATE	FIRST-YEAR LANG.	OTHER UNDER-GRADUATE	ALL UNDER-GRADUATE	FIRST-YEAR LANG.	OTHER UNDER-GRADUATE	ALL UNDER-GRADUATE	FIRST-YEAR LANG.	OTHER UNDER-GRADUATE	ALL UNDER-GRADUATE
Full-time tenured or tenure-track	7.4	40.3	25.7	23.2	60.4	43.6	41.8	65.8	54.2	40.5	44.1	41.3
Full-time non-tenure-track	19.6	19.0	19.2	17.5	17.6	17.6	21.1	16.5	18.7	6.9	19.1	9.6
Part-time	15.7	13.3	14.4	33.4	17.8	24.8	34.7	16.4	25.2	52.5	36.7	49.1
Graduate student TA	57.4	27.5	40.7	25.9	4.2	14.0	2.4	1.3	1.8	0.0	0.0	0.0
All undergraduate course sections that were sections of first-year language	44.3			45.1			48.5			78.1		

types of undergraduate sections, and all undergraduate sections. To provide some context for the percentages of course sections taught, the percentage is also given of all undergraduate course sections that were first-year writing or first-year language. Table 4 shows the percentage, by instructor category, of undergraduate teaching that was made up of first-year writing or first-year language sections, broken down by the highest degree a department grants.

Tenured and tenure-track faculty members taught a plurality of undergraduate course sections in responding departments: 42.2% in English, 41.4% in foreign language. Part-time faculty members taught the next highest percentage: 28.6% in English, 25.5% in foreign language. But percentages are more revealing when broken down by the departmental degree granted and course type.

In English departments, undergraduate sections that tenured and tenure-track faculty members taught ranged from a high of 59% in bachelor's-granting to a low of 31% in doctorate-granting departments. The corresponding figures for foreign language departments are a high of 54% in bachelor's-granting and a low of 26% in doctorate-granting departments.

In doctoral departments, graduate student TAs taught a plurality of the undergraduate sections: 35% in English, 41% in foreign language. Part-time faculty members taught an additional 19% of undergraduate sections in English and 14% in foreign language.

First-year writing and first-year language accounted for almost half the undergraduate course sections the departments taught in fall 1999. At the associate's-degree level, first-year writing accounted for more than 60% of all sections, first-year language for more than 78%.

The survey findings reflect that, while undergraduate enrollments have grown, the size of the professorial faculty has not grown proportionately. Consequently, institutions, particularly institutions with doctoral programs, assign tenured and tenure-track faculty members to the advanced undergraduate and graduate courses for which those faculty members are most qualified and rely on part- or full-time adjunct faculty members (or, where they are available, graduate student teaching assistants) to handle the many sections of introductory writing and language courses. In the doctoral English departments, tenured and tenure-track faculty members taught 6% of the first-year writing sections, which represented 9% of the undergraduate sections such faculty members taught. In the doctoral foreign language departments, tenured and tenure-track faculty members taught 7% of the first-year language sections, 13% of the undergraduate sections they taught. By contrast, in departments that grant the bachelor's as their highest degree, tenured and tenure-track faculty members taught 42.2% of first-year writing sections and 41.8% of first-year language sections, representing 34%

TABLE 4
Percentage of the Undergraduate Teaching Assignment of Instructors for First-Year Writing or First-Year Language in Different Employment Categories, Fall 1999

	English	Foreign Language	Combined	Humanities Division	All
All responding departments					
Full-time tenured or tenure-track	31.1	34.5	48.8	50.7	35.7
Full-time non-tenure-track	59.3	51.7	64.5	63.4	57.7
Part-time	67.2	66.0	67.4	67.8	67.0
Graduate student TA	74.3	66.3	87.7	82.1	71.4
Number of departments	*673*	*889*	*187*	*242*	*1,991*
Doctoral departments					
Full-time tenured or tenure-track	9.1	12.8	–	–	10.5
Full-time non-tenure-track	54.8	45.1	–	–	50.7
Part-time	60.0	48.4	–	–	56.2
Graduate student TA	70.4	62.4	–	–	67.5
Number of departments	*106*	*161*	*3*	*1*	*271*
MA-granting departments					
Full-time tenured or tenure-track	24.2	24.0	31.7	18.1	24.6
Full-time non-tenure-track	63.5	44.9	65.2	46.6	58.8
Part-time	73.7	60.5	67.9	67.7	70.3
Graduate student TA	91.7	83.6	86.0	–	89.0
Number of departments	*155*	*112*	*20*	*11*	*298*
BA-granting departments					
Full-time tenured or tenure-track	33.7	37.4	40.7	40.8	36.7
Full-time non-tenure-track	56.1	54.6	58.5	61.1	56.3
Part-time	70.5	66.6	71.6	65.3	68.2
Graduate student TA	–	63.6	–	–	65.2
Number of departments	*260*	*468*	*67*	*84*	*879*
AA-granting departments					
Full-time tenured or tenure-track	57.4	76.6	63.6	66.6	62.3
Full-time non-tenure-track	61.7	56.4	65.3	71.3	65.3
Part-time	63.7	83.6	64.3	71.5	67.6
Graduate student TA	–	–	–	–	–
Number of departments	*76*	*51*	*68*	*93*	*288*
Departments granting no degree					
Full-time tenured or tenure-track	56.7	64.5	62.6	49.1	57.7
Full-time non-tenure-track	60.9	74.2	79.0	65.5	66.2
Part-time	65.0	76.1	74.7	64.7	69.7
Graduate student TA	–	58.3	–	–	40.7
Number of departments	*76*	*97*	*29*	*53*	*255*

Note: Not all departments reported having instructors in each category.

and 37%, respectively, of the undergraduate sections taught by that group. Tenured and tenure-track faculty members in two-year colleges taught the highest percentage of the first-year writing and first-year language sections in their departments, 44.8% in English and 40.5% in foreign languages, representing 57% and 77%, respectively, of the teaching they did.

The teaching duties of part-time faculty members and graduate student TAs were concentrated in first-year writing and first-year language courses. Graduate student TAs in doctoral English departments taught 52% of the first-year writing sections (70% of all sections those TAs taught); in doctoral foreign language departments, TAs taught 57% of the first-year language sections (62% of all sections they taught). Part-time faculty members taught an additional 24% of the first-year writing sections and 16% of the first-year language sections in doctoral departments. In the bachelor's-granting departments, where graduate students are not available as teaching assistants, part-time faculty members taught 41% of the first-year writing sections and 35% of the first-year language sections. Across all responding departments, two-thirds of the undergraduate sections taught by part-time faculty members were first-year writing or first-year language.

SALARIES, BENEFITS, AND PROFESSIONAL SUPPORT

Table 5 shows average pay in fall 1999 reported for part-time faculty members who are paid by the course. Table 6 shows 1999–2000 average annual salaries reported for full-time non-tenure-track faculty members, and table 7 shows average annual salaries for part-time faculty members who are paid on a fractional basis.

Per-course pay for part-time faculty members was highest in doctoral departments, lowest in associate's-granting departments. Departments reported that, on average, part-time faculty members paid by the course taught two courses in their departments in fall 1999. The two-course average held across all degree-granting types, regardless of the varying teaching loads that tenured and tenure-track faculty members assume.

The average annual salary for full-time non-tenure-track faculty members was $33,559 in English departments, and $33,912 in foreign language departments. The national salary survey conducted annually by the College and University Personnel Association (CUPA) provides a useful comparison. The CUPA survey for 1999–2000 reports that on average faculty members in English holding the rank of instructor earned $28,027 in public institutions and $31,405 in private institutions. In foreign languages those holding the rank of instructor earned $28,983 in public institutions and $32,294 in private institutions. That same academic year, salaries for new assistant

TABLE 5
COMPENSATION FOR PART-TIME FACULTY MEMBERS, BY COURSE, FALL 1999

	ENGLISH	FOREIGN LANGUAGE	COMBINED	HUMANITIES DIVISION	ALL
Departments with part-time faculty members paid by course	86.9% (585)	77.2% (686)	93.0% (174)	91.7% (222)	83.7% (1,667)
All departments	673	889	187	242	1,991
United States departments Average per-course compensation	$2,293 (544)	$2,788 (607)	$1,736 (163)	$1,783 (214)	$2,358 (1,528)
Canadian departments Average per-course compensation (Canadian dollars)	$5,058 (28)	$5,420 (40)	– (1)	– (4)	$5,247 (73)
Ranges of per-course compensation in United States departments					
Under $1,200	5.5% (30)	4.6% (28)	12.3% (20)	12.6% (27)	6.9% (105)
$1,200–$1,500	19.3% (105)	10.0% (61)	37.4% (61)	34.6% (74)	19.7% (301)
$1,501–$2,000	25.2% (137)	22.2% (135)	30.7% (50)	26.6% (57)	24.8% (379)
$2,001–$2,500	20.4% (111)	18.3% (111)	7.4% (12)	15.9% (34)	17.5% (268)
$2,501–$3,000	12.5% (68)	16.5% (100)	8.0% (13)	3.7% (8)	12.4% (189)
Over $3,000	17.1% (93)	28.3% (172)	4.3% (7)	6.5% (14)	18.7% (286)
Number of departments	544	607	163	214	1,528
Average per-course compensation for United States departments, by departmental degree granted					
Doctorate	$3,210 (77)	$4,495 (79)	– (2)	– (1)	$3,848 (159)
MA	$2,231 (131)	$2,603 (84)	$1,932 (19)	$2,425 (10)	$2,344 (244)
BA	$2,283 (204)	$2,660 (328)	$1,805 (61)	$1,826 (70)	$2,377 (663)
AA	$1,715 (73)	$1,953 (42)	$1,596 (56)	$1,590 (87)	$1,686 (258)
No degree	$1,978 (59)	$2,215 (74)	$1,580 (25)	$1,931 (46)	$2,005 (204)

Note: Figures in parentheses indicate number of departments.

professors in English, CUPA reports, were $38,300 and $36,619 in public and private institutions, respectively. In foreign languages, salaries for new assistant professors were $38,593 and $36,736 in public and private institutions, respectively. The average annual salary for part-time faculty members paid by the fraction was $21,951 in English, $21,213 in foreign language.

For non-tenure-track faculty members, there were significant differences in benefits offered between those who worked full-time and those who worked part-time. Table 8B shows that no more than 20% of departments reported health benefits for part-time faculty members who were paid by the course, while 70% of English departments and 65% of foreign language departments reported that these faculty members were offered no health, retirement, or life insurance benefits at all. By contrast, three-quarters or more of departments reported offering health, retirement, and life insurance benefits to full-time non-tenure-track faculty members, and fewer than 2% of departments reported that these faculty members were offered no benefits (table 8A). Availability of benefits for part-time faculty members paid by fraction falls between benefits for full-time non-tenure-track faculty members and benefits for part-time faculty members paid by course (table 8C).

Instructors of all categories and across all degree-granting department types generally receive basic professional support such as office space; access to a computer, telephone, mailbox, and photocopying; and library privileges. The quality of the support, however, differs markedly with the category of instructor. More than three-quarters of full-time non-tenure-track faculty members in responding departments enjoy a private office and private computer access, whereas more than three-quarters of part-time faculty members who are paid per course must share office space, and two-thirds share computer access (tables 9A and 9B).

TABLE 6
ANNUAL SALARIES FOR FULL-TIME NON-TENURE-TRACK FACULTY MEMBERS, FALL 1999

	ENGLISH	FOREIGN LANGUAGE	COMBINED	HUMANITIES DIVISION	ALL
Departments with full-time non-tenure-track faculty members	66.0% (444)	63.8% (567)	59.4% (111)	57.4% (139)	63.3% (1,261)
All departments	673	889	187	242	1,991
United States departments Average	$33,559 (413)	$33,912 (497)	$34,029 (106)	$34,701 (124)	$33,881 (1,140)
Canadian departments Average (Canadian dollars)	$40,888 (16)	$42,395 (24)	– (1)	– (4)	$41,803 (45)
Ranges in United States departments					
$25,000 or less	14.0% (58)	9.5% (47)	14.2% (15)	12.1% (15)	11.8% (135)
$25,001–$30,000	26.6% (110)	25.6% (127)	23.6% (25)	21.8% (27)	25.4% (289)
$30,001–$35,000	26.4% (109)	25.4% (126)	22.6% (24)	27.4% (34)	25.7% (293)
$35,001–$40,000	16.9% (70)	24.7% (123)	20.8% (22)	17.7% (22)	20.8% (237)
Over $40,000	16.0% (66)	14.9% (74)	18.9% (20)	21.0% (26)	16.3% (186)
Number of departments	413	497	106	124	1,140
Average in United States departments, by departmental degree granted					
Doctorate	$32,491 (82)	$34,577 (121)	$36,667 (3)	$35,000 (1)	$33,783 (207)
MA	$31,708 (126)	$32,177 (77)	$32,220 (19)	$31,278 (6)	$31,898 (228)
BA	$35,167 (133)	$33,608 (252)	$31,305 (45)	$33,467 (53)	$33,807 (483)
AA	$34,562 (25)	$35,092 (14)	$39,500 (28)	$35,760 (42)	$36,360 (109)
No degree	$35,299 (47)	$37,342 (33)	$33,654 (11)	$36,573 (22)	$35,984 (113)

Note: Figures in parentheses indicate number of departments.

TABLE 7
ANNUAL SALARIES FOR PART-TIME FACULTY MEMBERS PAID BY FRACTION, FALL 1999

	ENGLISH	FOREIGN LANGUAGE	COMBINED	HUMANITIES DIVISION	ALL
Departments with part-time faculty members paid by fraction	18.6% (125)	17.0% (151)	11.8% (22)	8.3% (20)	16.0% (318)
All departments	673	889	187	242	1,991
United States departments Average	$21,951 (105)	$21,213 (108)	$18,319 (14)	$16,798 (16)	$21,074 (243)
Canadian departments Average (Canadian dollars)	– (7)	– (6)	– (1)	– (1)	$26,274 (15)
Ranges in United States departments					
Under $10,000	14.3% (15)	10.2% (11)	28.6% (4)	12.5% (2)	13.2% (32)
$10,000–$20,000	37.1% (39)	38.9% (42)	21.4% (3)	50.0% (8)	37.9% (92)
$20,001–$30,000	26.7% (28)	35.2% (38)	35.7% (5)	31.3% (5)	31.3% (76)
Over $30,000	21.9% (23)	15.7% (17)	14.3% (2)	6.3% (1)	17.7% (43)
Number of departments	105	108	14	16	243
Average in United States departments, by departmental degree granted					
Doctorate	$22,114 (27)	$23,796 (33)	– (–)	– (–)	$23,039 (60)
MA	$19,208 (33)	$19,857 (15)	– (3)	– (2)	$19,359 (53)
BA	$24,776 (39)	$19,589 (51)	– (6)	$14,395 (10)	$20,703 (106)
AA	– (1)	– (1)	– (3)	– (4)	$21,851 (9)
No degree	– (5)	– (8)	– (2)	– (–)	$21,429 (15)

Note: Figures in parentheses indicate number of departments.

TABLES 8A, 8B, AND 8C
PERCENTAGE OF DEPARTMENTS REPORTING BENEFITS FOR NON-TENURE-TRACK FACULTY MEMBERS

	ENGLISH	FOREIGN LANGUAGE	COMBINED	HUMANITIES DIVISION	ALL
8A. FULL-TIME NON-TENURE-TRACK FACULTY MEMBERS					
Health plan paid by both	75.5	77.3	73.0	70.3	75.5
Health plan paid by school	29.3	28.2	38.7	34.1	30.2
Health plan paid by staff	3.6	4.3	0.9	6.5	4.0
Retirement plan	81.1	82.7	89.2	92.0	83.7
Life insurance	75.7	78.9	82.9	84.8	78.8
No benefits offered	1.8	1.1	0.9	1.4	1.4
Minimum requirement*	37.3	37.9	33.3	42.0	37.7
Number of departments	440	560	111	138	1,249

*The minimum might depend on class load, length of service, or percentage of a full-time salary.

	ENGLISH	FOREIGN LANGUAGE	COMBINED	HUMANITIES DIVISION	ALL

8B. PART-TIME FACULTY MEMBERS PAID BY COURSE

Health plan paid by both	17.1	20.1	9.3	13.8	17.0
Health plan paid by school	4.7	6.4	0.6	3.2	4.7
Health plan paid by staff	5.9	7.3	9.3	6.9	7.0
Retirement plan	15.9	16.6	15.7	16.6	16.2
Life insurance	9.5	13.2	4.1	5.5	9.9
No benefits offered	70.1	64.8	73.8	68.7	68.2
Minimum requirement*	20.2	24.4	14.5	16.6	20.8
Number of departments	*579*	*657*	*172*	*217*	*1,625*

8C. PART-TIME FACULTY MEMBERS PAID BY FRACTION

Health plan paid by both	58.3	65.2	47.6	50.0	60.2
Health plan paid by school	20.8	22.2	9.5	22.2	20.7
Health plan paid by staff	3.3	6.7	14.3	5.6	5.8
Retirement plan	62.5	51.9	57.1	55.6	56.8
Life insurance	54.2	46.7	42.9	50.0	49.7
No benefits offered	20.0	18.5	23.8	22.2	19.7
Minimum requirement*	55.0	62.2	33.3	50.0	56.5
Number of departments	*120*	*135*	*21*	*18*	*294*

*The minimum might depend on class load, length of service, or percentage of a full-time salary.

TABLES 9A, 9B, AND 9C
PERCENTAGE OF DEPARTMENTS OFFERING FORMS OF PROFESSIONAL SUPPORT TO NON-TENURE-TRACK FACULTY MEMBERS

	ENGLISH	FOREIGN LANGUAGE	COMBINED	HUMANITIES DIVISION	ALL

9A. FULL-TIME NON-TENURE-TRACK FACULTY MEMBERS

Private office space	75.3	81.3	89.9	77.5	79.5
Shared office space	28.6	23.9	12.8	27.5	25.0
Private computer access	76.7	84.0	85.3	75.4	80.6
Shared computer access	18.5	20.1	13.8	18.8	18.9
Mailboxes	98.9	98.4	100.0	99.3	98.8
Parking	80.8	77.7	84.4	85.5	80.2
Telephone in office	98.2	98.7	99.1	98.6	98.5
Photocopying	98.4	98.7	96.3	99.3	98.5
Library privileges	99.5	99.3	100.0	100.0	99.5
Secretarial help	84.7	88.1	85.3	80.4	85.8
Six weeks' advance notice of teaching assignments	91.8	88.5	89.9	87.0	89.6
Invitation to participate in department meetings	92.9	90.1	98.2	94.9	92.3
Travel to professional meetings	84.9	77.5	89.0	83.3	81.8
Departmental workshops for teacher development	61.6	59.0	59.6	57.2	59.8
Regular salary increases	78.3	81.3	77.1	77.5	79.4
Access to institutional research grants	57.0	62.9	62.4	53.6	59.8
Number of departments	*437*	*556*	*109*	*138*	*1,240*

Percentage of Departments Offering Forms of Professional Support to Non-Tenure-Track Faculty Members (Cont.)

	English	Foreign Language	Combined	Humanities Division	All
9B. Part-Time Faculty Members Paid by Course					
Private office space	17.2	21.7	15.2	13.8	18.3
Shared office space	77.8	78.3	70.8	77.5	77.2
Private computer access	17.2	20.5	11.1	9.2	16.8
Shared computer access	66.1	65.4	61.4	62.8	64.9
Mailboxes	97.6	94.3	93.0	97.2	95.7
Parking	80.4	75.0	80.7	79.8	78.2
Telephone in office	88.0	88.4	76.0	80.7	85.9
Photocopying	98.5	96.7	97.1	99.1	97.7
Library privileges	99.3	96.1	95.3	98.6	97.5
Secretarial help	80.0	82.7	75.4	79.4	80.6
Six weeks' advance notice of teaching assignments	64.9	66.9	60.2	58.3	64.3
Invitation to participate in department meetings	62.7	64.5	63.2	74.8	65.1
Travel to professional meetings	25.1	24.2	25.7	27.1	25.1
Departmental workshops for teacher development	58.0	47.1	53.8	50.0	52.0
Regular salary increases	38.4	40.8	33.3	37.6	38.7
Access to institutional research grants	15.1	18.2	14.6	17.0	16.6
Number of departments	*581*	*665*	*171*	*218*	*1,635*
9C. Part-Time Faculty Members Paid by Fraction					
Private office space	46.2	43.1	60.0	44.4	45.5
Shared office space	53.0	56.9	35.0	50.0	53.4
Private computer access	51.3	47.4	50.0	33.3	48.3
Shared computer access	39.3	43.1	45.0	50.0	42.1
Mailboxes	99.1	98.5	95.0	100.0	98.6
Parking	79.5	73.0	85.0	77.8	76.7
Telephone in office	98.3	95.6	90.0	88.9	95.9
Photocopying	96.6	98.5	90.0	100.0	97.3
Library privileges	98.3	99.3	90.0	100.0	98.6
Secretarial help	82.9	85.4	95.0	83.3	84.6
Six weeks' advance notice of teaching assignments	82.1	82.5	90.0	66.7	81.5
Invitation to participate in department meetings	81.2	76.6	80.0	94.4	79.8
Travel to professional meetings	65.8	43.8	55.0	66.7	54.8
Departmental workshops for teacher development	56.4	56.2	65.0	50.0	56.5
Regular salary increases	74.4	62.8	70.0	50.0	67.1
Access to institutional research grants	46.2	32.1	35.0	44.4	38.7
Number of departments	*117*	*137*	*20*	*18*	*292*

Final Report

MLA AD HOC COMMITTEE ON TEACHING

Teaching matters. It matters especially at this moment, when higher education is under pressure to document departments' work with students in terms of educational outcomes. It matters when a new emphasis on immediate vocational utility puts in question the central place of the humanities and the value of liberal education. It matters when the concept of the teacher-scholar is undermined by budgetary constraints that restrict the number of full-time tenure-track faculty members in modern languages. Teaching has always mattered to the MLA and its constituency. However, as we confront the future, we must strengthen that commitment.

The conditions for teaching are felt differently at different institutions, whether in a two-year college, a baccalaureate college, a comprehensive university, or a doctorate-granting research university. Thus, the term *teaching* itself is regarded differently by different members of our community. As delineated in the context framing this report, we propose an overarching view of and reflective stance toward the teaching of language, literature, and culture, one that includes:

curriculum
classroom practices
research on teaching
theories of teaching
relations between teaching and scholarship

The MLA Executive Council appointed the Ad Hoc Committee on Teaching in 1998. We were charged with making recommendations about the ways the MLA can provide additional support for the improvement of teaching in a variety of institutional settings and contribute to what is known about effective teaching in the field. The committee had its first meeting in September 1998 and met again in February and November 1999 and September 2000. It held open hearings at the MLA conventions in San Francisco in 1998 and Chicago in 1999, where members were invited to contribute to the committee's discussions and share their views about the MLA's relation to teaching.

The MLA Executive Council was prompted to form this ad hoc committee by a strongly felt need for a wider concern with teaching. The committee has worked to represent this concern, to urge that the MLA take a much more active role in promoting excellent teaching at all levels and in all the media it has at its disposal. This report is presented in the hope that it will stir public and private discussions based on the recommendations articulated here.

The Context

The climate of higher education in the United States has changed. Pressures for public accountability have led to an emphasis on superior teaching, an emphasis reflected in the relatively recent importance of documentation on teaching in tenure files and the increasing recognition and number of substantial awards for teaching excellence. These forces have led to a rethinking of working relations with high schools, consortium institutions, and across colleges and departments within institutions. Of necessity, the same technologies that have contributed to the changed climate of learning and afforded new options for the pragmatic learning that society demands (e.g., distance learning) may well provide the means for this cooperative curriculum planning.

In a society that has moved from an industrial and agricultural base to an economy relying heavily on the international marketplace and a commodity-driven service industry, the ability to respond quickly and imaginatively to changing business and social needs has placed language and literature teaching in a new position. That the likelihood of a single lifetime job has been replaced by the likelihood of two or even three different careers in a lifetime necessitates the retraining of returning students whose needs can be met only by programs that address the changing marketplace of academia. Combined, these developments have led to new goals for the teaching of English and foreign languages based on a revised concept of literacy—the literacy of critical thinking combined with discourse skills that result in effective communication in multiple social and technological contexts.

Teaching and the Reward System

With increasing urgency, the need to secure a more prominent place for teaching in the profession's systems of reward has been the subject of national attention. Given this public focus, if teaching is to matter in our profession, it must figure substantively and visibly in those systems. For the purposes of this report, the committee understands a reward system to mean the structures undergirding job security (tenure or long-term contracts vital for continuity of and commitment to program development and promotion) as well as other sorts of systemic rewards, such as book prizes, publishing contracts, sabbaticals, and grants.

The problem of making teaching matter is inextricably linked to what our committee has identified as the need to foreground teaching in our profession. That need stems from institutional and cultural practices and holds significant, public ramifications for the profession. To matter, teaching must be concretely, emphatically valued by tenure and promotion committees; by those who make part-time and adjunct appointments; and by those who award prizes, publishing contracts, sabbaticals, and grants.

Teaching and Scholarship

A major lacuna in professional discussions about teaching is the absence of direct links to the scholarly communities to which all of us as teachers belong. Committed as this committee is to the improvement of teaching, we affirm the relation between scholarship and teaching at all levels of higher education. We view scholarship as a prerequisite and a corequisite for good teaching, because teachers' scholarship legitimizes their expertise, informs their classroom practice, and provides their students with models for intellectual inquiry. Consequently, this committee's report concurs with the "ADE Statement of Good Practice: Teaching, Evaluation, and Scholarship" that "teaching and scholarly activity are mutually reinforcing, [and] departments and institutions should create conditions that encourage all faculty members to engage in intellectual inquiry." While recognizing the range and different missions of institutions, from two-year college to research university, we agree that all

> faculty members need to engage in scholarly projects that sustain and renew their intellectual lives. Especially in institutions like two-year colleges, where teaching has long dominated the mission and the reward system, faculty members need support that affirms the ways in which scholarship vitalizes teaching. [. . .] Scholarship, broadly defined, is essential to effective teaching and to a satisfying professional life in the humanities. (41)

The committee understands scholarly renewal as a continuing dialogue. The scholarship-teaching connection we envision benefits not only the scholar but also that scholar's students, institution, and professional associations.

REFLECTIVE PRACTICE

To create meaningful discourse between scholarship and the classroom, the committee believes *reflective practice* is the operative term that best describes the attitude and activities that make teaching matter. As defined by Donald Schon, a reflective practitioner "turns thought back on action and on the knowing which is implicit in action." While trying to make sense of an action, a reflective practitioner "reflects on the understandings which have been explicit in his action, understandings which he surfaces, criticizes, restructures, and embodies in further action" (50). If teaching matters, then reflection about the practice of teaching is crucial, not only as represented by the formal research of the scholarship of teaching but also in every faculty member's classroom, in every graduate program, and in the relations that exist among subject matter disciplines, teacher education programs, and future teachers.

The Scholarship of Teaching

Historically, *PMLA* has privileged literary scholarship both in English and foreign languages. Research, by and large, has focused on textual study from various theoretical perspectives. With few exceptions, neither the MLA nor individual scholars have concerned themselves with how such knowledge reaches students.

In part, any delay between the discovery and the communication of scholarly knowledge is related to the inevitable delay in the way ideas circulate in communities. But with respect to teaching as a topic of professional discussion, the MLA Ad Hoc Committee on Teaching posits a more fundamental cause: we find that the MLA as an organization has not granted scholarship on teaching the same status it has granted textual scholarship.

We urge, then, that scholarship applied in the classroom needs to be afforded pride of place in our professional organizations and our scholarly journals. This plea for integration of teaching and scholarship extends beyond a token representation on convention programs and special journal sections. We urge that teaching in all its problematics (from classroom ethnographics to the sociolinguistics of textbook selection to the politics of teacher preparation at the graduate school level) be an intrinsic part of dialogues at the national convention and in scholarly publications.

To point to some options for introducing such dialogues, we offer, first, the following orienting set of questions: What is teaching? How do we understand what we do in our classrooms? What can we learn from making our acts of teaching more visible to ourselves, one another, and the profession at large? How is such an effort a scholarly activity? In what ways can the MLA foster activities to support such inquiry? What might be the potential benefits? What, if any, are the drawbacks? To what extent can administrators be profitably involved in these discussions?

A major step has already been taken by the MLA in integrating the teaching of literature, language, and rhetoric into the MLA bibliography. That step recognizes that professional disciplines about the teaching of language and rhetoric have grown and diversified significantly in recent years. Their innovative classroom research, using methods such as ethnographies and case studies of classroom life, speak to modern language teachers of all kinds. Their special contribution deserves attention in deliberating about standards, common goals, and the relation between teaching and scholarship.

Graduate Education

The committee in the strongest possible terms points to the urgent need to develop graduate programs whose scholarly emphases are explicitly linked to teaching concerns in a range of instructional settings as well as in applications outside academia. Increased attention to pedagogy in higher education has tended to focus on the undergraduate level. We urge greater attention to exploring how graduate courses can be designed to include professional and pedagogical issues as well as subject matter. The MLA can and should articulate the case for systematic, progressive faculty development in language and literature departments.[1]

Effective pedagogy at the graduate level must include mentoring students at every stage of their graduate careers. This mentoring should involve career consultation, experience with and feedback on course development by graduate students that is linked to their graduate work, support through the examination and dissertation process, and assistance with the job-search process.

The committee recognizes that the dynamics of many graduate programs is shifting under a number of external institutional pressures. Traditionally at the bottom of the academic ladder, graduate students often begin their careers as teachers under taxing and demanding conditions, hampered by low wages, lack of benefits, and the heavy classroom duties common in introductory classes. Many graduate student teachers live in a state of unremitting ambivalence about whether to shortchange their students, their class work, or their dissertation. As undergraduate ranks swell and budgets for hiring new full-time professors shrink, graduate students are taking on a substantial share of undergraduate teaching,[2] and many are likely to be teaching throughout their years completing course, exam, and dissertation requirements.

Playing the double role of student and teacher at the same time presents many challenges. Learning to be both student and teacher is crucial to professional success, but this process can be destructive when the teacher role threatens to overwhelm the student role. Graduate students may lack power and authority in their graduate classes but be invested with great power and authority in the classes they teach, often without sufficient training and support during those important first years of teaching. In addition, reliance on graduate students to staff burgeoning service courses for low wages and few or no benefits puts inordinate stress on these students and must be considered in any examination of graduate education. The committee affirms support for graduate students in their dual role as teacher-scholars.

The paucity of jobs forces a good number of graduate students to remain for many years at their graduate institutions, teaching part-time while pursuing full-time employment. Thus, the traditional view of the graduate student as apprentice teacher, learning the craft of teaching under the tutelage of seasoned pedagogues, can be inaccurate and patronizing when applied to many who are often as energetic, dedicated, and in touch with undergraduates as are our profession's best graduate faculty members.

Teacher Education

In conjunction with its recommendation that explicit teaching components be built into graduate programs, the committee urges that all programs in English and foreign languages identify and encourage students who may be potential teachers for elementary and secondary schools. Increasingly, teacher-scholars are beginning to recognize, in James Marshall's words, that "all teaching is about teaching—just as all writing is about writing—and [. . .] every class that enrolls prospective teachers is a class in teacher preparation" (380–81). This recognition forms an important part of this committee's charge and holds significant implications for the role of the MLA's constituent disciplines in the preparation of secondary school teachers. To increase the visibility of teaching in our fields, we must also increase the visibility of a section of our student population too often allowed to slip through the cracks—students who are planning a teaching career at the elementary or secondary level.[3]

The committee feels that the preparation of future teachers is central to the work that we do in our disciplines and of crucial importance for the future of our fields.[4] Award systems, particularly those sponsored by the MLA, will articulate and enhance the role of teaching both inside and outside the academic community.

Working Conditions

The committee cautions that our profession must assume more responsibility for assessing the quality of teaching or be forfeit to outside forces that will set teaching standards for us. More and more, decisions about higher education are being made by legislators who do not understand the contexts in which we work. "Institutions are expected to perform, to document performance, and to be accountable for producing returns on taxpayer and student investment" (Boggs 4). Not being fully aware of what actually takes place in the halls of the academy, legislators often believe that colleges and universities spend too much money on research and not enough on teaching. They act on their beliefs most often by applying quantifiable measures to assess teaching and learning. These measures include statewide testing, which in some instances may even determine what institutions of higher education are allowed to offer entering students. For example, in Wisconsin "the goals of the State Faculty Education Workload Policy include seeing that the regents are provided with 'regular managerial information regarding educational workload'" ("Politics" 48). In Tennessee, some funding for education is controlled by a performance-based formula that ties the money received by an institution to the test scores earned by students and to other quantitative measures.

The AAUP recognizes there is a need for reform in higher education ("Work" 35). Likewise, administrators and faculty members generally agree that reform is necessary, but they cannot condone reform instituted by those government agencies that use quantity rather than quality as a criterion. To curtail outside intervention in how the teaching environment is managed and to enable teachers to teach well, those in the academy must come together and redefine faculty workload. This new definition must include research, instruction, testing, and environment. The definition of faculty workload presented by the AAUP in its 1994 report addresses a broader view of teaching:

> Since teaching—in its full meaning, going beyond classroom lecturing and discussion—is based on and strengthened by scholarship [in the sense expressed earlier in this report], a course load that makes scholarship possible is essential to teaching of high quality. Conversely, scholarship and research are often enhanced when tested in the classroom [...], by implication or demonstration before students.   ("Work" 44)

For these reasons, the committee report endorses the guidelines issued by the ADE ("ADE Guidelines") and the ADFL ("ADFL Guidelines") for teaching loads and class size and believes that only by adherence to these guidelines will the type of teacher-scholar we envision be possible.

A Call to Action:
The Committee's Recommendations

We urge a renewed commitment by the MLA to excellence in teaching. It is a commitment worth making, one that will speak for our association to our many academic constituencies and to the larger public, which places a high premium on the instruction of our students.

Because the MLA believes teaching matters, it must expand the ways in which scholars can explore pedagogies, examine classroom practice, and find support for their efforts to develop programs in modern languages that are appropriate to the twenty-first century. By providing occasions for members to discuss their teaching outside their departments, the MLA fosters communication and community building, both inside and beyond the academy.

As the largest national organization devoted to teaching and scholarship in higher education for all the modern languages, the MLA can also foster the type of dialogue so needed today, a dialogue involving faculty members and students at all levels in modern language departments and between those departments and their wider constituencies in their institutions and in their communities. This committee affirms the MLA's mission to support and to influence the ways in which teaching is understood, valued, and rewarded.

Recommendations to the MLA

A Standing Committee on Teaching

Our strongest recommendation is for the establishment of a standing committee on teaching so that the MLA can better address the issues that we believe to be most critical at this time in our profession, regardless of institutional setting. By establishing a standing committee on teaching, the MLA will demonstrate that teaching as a scholarly and professional endeavor remains a central concern of our organization. Further we believe that the issues identified below constitute a rationale for the establishment of a standing committee and may serve as a guide for the development of an agenda for action. We suggest that this agenda be developed in consultation with the divisional committees on teaching, with the various publication committees, and with the membership as a whole.

> *Accordingly, we recommend*
> that the MLA establish a standing committee on teaching to provide a place for ongoing attention to questions related to teaching

The issues we identified as important for this standing committee to address follow. We formulate them as guidelines for the committee to conduct its work and as questions that the broader MLA membership may take back to their home institutions for further discussion.

Publications

Debates about the state of the canon and definitions of cultural literacy occur in popular media and conference presentations and are addressed in important policy journals such as the *ADFL Bulletin* and *ADE Bulletin*. However, no broader-based, prestigious publication exists in the MLA for constructive dialogue about teaching.

Accordingly, we recommend
- that the MLA publication program continue to seek out new and varied examinations of teaching, including new understandings of classroom practice and classroom life
- that the MLA publish a second issue annually of *Profession* that focuses on teaching issues
- that at regular intervals *PMLA* devote a special section to teaching
- that the MLA sponsor a member-moderated electronic discussion list in which MLA members explore the values and assumptions they bring to the act of teaching

Collaboration between the MLA and Other Organizations

The committee recognizes the need for information sharing among all members of the profession. We assert the value of collaborative activities devoted to the teaching of and research on culture, language, literature, and writing. To that end, the committee supports the MLA's initiative in sharing sponsorship of and collaborating on proposals for funding to support internships, institutes, publications, and other activities.

Accordingly, we recommend
- that the MLA actively explore means of facilitating collaboration on teaching with other organizations in the field of modern languages

RECOMMENDATIONS TO THE PROFESSION AT LARGE

The Reward System

If teaching matters, it must figure substantively and visibly in our profession's reward system: job security (tenure or long-term contracts), promotion, and other sorts of systemic rewards, such as book prizes, publishing contracts, sabbaticals, and grants.

Aware of teaching's complex implications in local politics, state budget crunches, individual institutions' ambitions, and the politics of the diverse fields the MLA represents, the committee nevertheless tenders the following recommendations as steps both flexible enough to be adapted to local situations and concrete enough to feature teaching more prominently in the reward systems of our profession and of the MLA itself.

Accordingly, we recommend
> that institutions and departments develop clear statements about the place of teaching in tenure and promotion
> that institutions and departments design mechanisms to evaluate teaching
> that institutions and departments design mechanisms and provide necessary support for continuing education and materials to improve teaching

The Scholarship of Teaching

This committee strongly supports the idea that research on classroom practice is a valid and important aspect of our professional lives. Paying attention to and documenting what happens in college classrooms brings visibility to teaching and learning. It focuses on how students learn and the methods by which we teach them. It asks questions about processes as well as products. And it takes the life of the classroom as its central focus.

A commitment to documenting and studying classroom life will require many changes both inside and outside the academy. In institutions of higher learning, it will mean substantial changes in curricula, graduate programs, teacher training, and tenure decisions. Outside our institutions, such scholarship will enlarge public understanding of what is entailed in educating students.

Accordingly, we recommend
> that institutions and departments value the scholarship of teaching—of the methods, assessment procedures, and ways to improve teaching—as equivalent to traditional forms of scholarship, when it is subjected to equivalent scrutiny by the rest of the profession
> that institutions and departments create interdisciplinary seminars and hold colloquia regarding language development and literacy issues
> that English and foreign language departments build bridges to scholars in education schools and departments
> that English and foreign language departments develop seminars on qualitative and quantitative research methods
> that institutions and departments encourage collaboration among and within departments

Teacher Education

The committee believes that the preparation of future teachers is central to the work that we do in our disciplines and of crucial importance for the future of our fields. Research on the contributions of content-area course work to teacher performance and future development has many potential benefits. Further, there is great potential for collaboration in research between collegiate and precollegiate teachers. Solid work on the contributions of our disciplines to teacher preparation could address public misconceptions and doubts about the commitment of higher education to teacher reform. The matter of teacher education speaks profoundly to making the value of our disciplines—of our scholarship and our teaching—known.

> *Accordingly, we recommend*
> that faculty members make the rationales behind their pedagogical choices visible in their classrooms
> that faculty members clarify to students why our fields matter in the academy and in society at large
> that institutions and departments keep track of majors throughout their careers
> that institutions and departments provide formal structures for liaisons between academic disciplines and secondary school teachers
> that institutions and departments support and reward those faculty members involved in the training of teaching assistants and teacher education
> that institutions and departments encourage research contributing to learning and curriculum

Graduate Education

Graduate education provides the institutional setting for the development of the teacher-scholar. As such, the committee believes that graduate education should demonstrate that teaching matters by offering courses in pedagogy, preparing students for a range of teaching situations, mentoring students, providing models of reflective practice, and helping students with the job-search process.

> *Accordingly, we recommend*
> that graduate programs give higher priority to and strengthen programs in the teaching of language, literature, linguistics, writing, and culture that will orient and train new faculty members in the art and science of teaching and learning

that graduate programs follow the recommendations of the Committee on Professional Employment (*Final Report*) relating to the expansion of the graduate curriculum to include courses in pedagogy that will prepare students for a range of teaching situations and familiarize them with the complex system of postsecondary education in the United States and Canada

that graduate programs provide students with mentoring and collaborative activities for professional development at every stage of their graduate careers

that graduate programs provide consultation and supervisory support through every stage of the program, from candidacy exam through dissertation

that graduate programs provide early discussion of career options as well as direct assistance with the job-search process

Working Conditions

While recognizing the differences in institutional conditions that exist in higher education, the committee strongly believes that teaching—in its full meaning, going beyond classroom lecturing and discussion—is based on and strengthened by the scholarship of both subject-matter content and pedagogy. Thus, a course load and class sizes that make scholarship possible are as essential to teaching of high quality as fair labor and contract practices.

Accordingly, we recommend

that institutions and departments, by assigning reasonable teaching loads and limiting class sizes, create conditions conducive to enabling the effective teacher-scholar we envision

that institutions and departments provide professional recognition, appropriate contractual arrangements, and pro rata compensation for part-time faculty members

that institutions and departments provide professional recognition, appropriate contractual arrangements, and appropriate compensation for non-tenure-track faculty members

Our committee completes its report to the association with a sense of gratitude to the Executive Council for being chosen for such a formidable task and an equally strong sense of satisfaction and pride that we have worked hard in our research, in our many discussions, and in the formulation of our final recommendations.

We are a varied group of MLA colleagues, older and younger, from different kinds of institutions of higher learning, and with both research and teaching interests. We have often disagreed on priorities, strategies, and the most effective ways of articulating our recommendations, but out of strong dialogue a consensus has emerged.

What has made us a confident and collegial committee is our deep commitment to the centrality of excellence in teaching—whether done by a tenure-track, adjunct, or graduate student instructor—in the life of college and university. At a time of uncertainty and challenge in our culture, such teaching, properly attended to and strongly supported, will shape the good student and the good citizen. The Modern Language Association should be in the forefront of this venture, lending its prestige, its strong voice, and its active support.

Submitted by
Helen R. Houston, language, literature, and philosophy, Tennessee State University
Elizabeth L. Keller, comparative literature, Rutgers University, New Brunswick
Lawrence D. Kritzman, French, Dartmouth College
Frank Madden, English, Westchester Community College, State University of New York, chair
John L. Mahoney, English, Boston College
Scott McGinnis, National Foreign Language Center
Susannah Brietz Monta, English, Louisiana State University, Baton Rouge
Sondra Perl, English, Graduate Center, City University of New York
Janet Swaffar, Germanic Studies, University of Texas, Austin

NOTES

[1]This comment is not unique to this ad hoc committee. The American Association of State Colleges and Universities recently stated in its report *Facing Change: Building the Faculty of the Future*, "Higher education has failed to effectively articulate the case for systematic, progressive faculty development" (20). The report goes on to assert, "Higher education faculty are not regularly trained in teaching, learning, advising, or the overall teaching and learning enterprise. New priority must be given to strengthening training programs for the next generation of teachers and to developing programs that will orient and train new faculty in the art and science of teaching and learning" (21).

[2]The ADE Ad Hoc Committee on Staffing did a sample survey in 1996–97 of staffing in representative departments. In PhD departments responding, TAs taught 61% of the first-year writing sections, 30% of the lower-division literature courses, and 3% of the upper-division literature sections ("Report").

[3]Donald Gray has argued that our profession has tended historically to believe that teacher education is the responsibility of a select few, people in other departments (4). The potential benefits of taking the responsibility of teacher preparation as an integral

part of our work are, however, enormous. As Kathryn T. Flannery et al. note, "Perhaps more than any other group of students in English, not excluding PhDs, preservice English teachers are a continuing responsibility, to the university, to their teachers, and to themselves. No other group has a greater impact on the hardest question of all: How will the knowledge, abilities, and canons of judgment that make up what we call English exist and do their work in the culture and politics of our country?" (61).

[4] Phyllis Franklin recently argued that teacher preparation is one of the most publicly influential things we do: "For almost a decade MLA members have insisted on the need for the field to reach an audience outside the academy in order to promote a better public understanding of how the humanities and especially the study of language and literature contribute to society, prepare students for careers, and enrich people's lives. I cannot imagine a more effective way of reaching this audience than to participate in the effort to strengthen the quality of schooling in the United States. Each knowledgeable, intellectually lively teacher we educate will affect the lives of thousands of young people and affirm the value of the subjects we teach" (5).

WORKS CITED

"ADE Guidelines for Class Size and Workload for College and University Teachers of English: A Statement of Policy." Mar. 1992. *ADE Policy Statements*. 28 Oct. 1998. 5 June 2001 <http://www.ade.org/policy/index.htm>.

"ADE Statement of Good Practice: Teaching, Evaluation, and Scholarship." Mar. 1993. *ADE Policy Statements*. 28 Oct. 1998. 5 June 2001 <http://www.ade.org/policy/index.htm>.

"ADFL Guidelines on the Administration of Foreign Language Departments." 1993. *Projects and Reports*. 30 Nov. 2000. 5 June 2001 <http://www.adfl.org/projects/index.htm>.

American Association of State Colleges and Universities. *Facing Change: Building the Faculty of the Future*. Washington: Amer. Assn. of State Colls. and Univs., 1999.

Boggs, George R. "What the Learning Paradigm Means for Faculty." *AAHE Bulletin* 51.5 (1999): 3–5.

Final Report of the MLA Committee on Professional Employment. New York: MLA, 1997.

Flannery, Kathryn T., et al. "Watch This Space; or, Why We Have Not Revised the Teacher Education Program—Yet." Franklin, Laurence, and Welles 49–64.

Franklin, Phyllis. "An Urgent Request to Rethink Teacher Preparation." *MLA Newsletter* 31.2 (1999): 4–5.

Franklin, Phyllis, David Laurence, and Elizabeth B. Welles, eds. *Preparing a Nation's Teachers: Models for English and Foreign Language Programs*. New York: MLA, 1998.

Gray, Donald. "Introduction: What Happens Next? And How? And Why?" Franklin, Laurence, and Welles 1–16.

Marshall, James. "Closely Reading Ourselves: Teaching English and the Education of Teachers." Franklin, Laurence, and Welles 380–89.

"The Politics of Intervention: External Regulation of Academic Activities and Workloads in Public Higher Education." *Academe* Jan.-Feb. 1996: 46–52.

"Report of the ADE Ad Hoc Committee on Staffing." *ADE Bulletin* 122 (1999): 7–26.

Schon, Donald. *The Reflective Practitioner*. New York: Harper, 1983.

"The Work of Faculty: Expectations, Priorities, and Rewards." *Academe* Jan.-Feb. 1994: 35–48.